Navigating Network Complexity

Navigating Network Complexity

Next-generation Routing with SDN, Service Virtualization, and Service Chaining

Russ White

Jeff Tantsura

Addison-Wesley
800 East 96th Street
Indianapolis, Indiana 46240 USA

Navigating Network Complexity

Next-generation Routing with SDN, Service Virtualization, and Service Chaining

Copyright © 2016 Pearson Education, Inc.

Published by: Addison Wesley

All rights reserved. Printed in the United States of America. This publication is protected by copyright, and permission must be obtained from the publisher prior to any prohibited reproduction, storage in a retrieval system, or transmission in any form or by any means, electronic, mechanical, photocopying, recording, or likewise. To obtain permission to use material from this work, please submit a written request to Pearson Education, Inc., Permissions Department, 200 Old Tappan Road, Old Tappan, New Jersey 07675, or you may fax your request to (201) 236-3290.

Text printed in the United States on recycled paper at RR Donnelley, Crawfordsville, IN

First Printing November 2015

Library of Congress Cataloging-in-Publication Number: 2015950654

ISBN-13: 978-0-13-398935-9
ISBN-10: 0-13-398935-6

Trademarks

Many of the designations used by manufacturers and sellers to distinguish their products are claimed as trademarks. Where those designations appear in this book, and the publisher was aware of a trademark claim, the designations have been printed with initial capital letters or in all capitals.

Warning and Disclaimer

The author and publisher have taken care in the preparation of this book, but make no expressed or implied warranty of any kind and assume no responsibility for errors or omissions. No liability is assumed for incidental or consequential damages in connection with or arising out of the use of the information or programs contained herein.

Special Sales

For information about buying this title in bulk quantities, or for special sales opportunities (which may include electronic versions; custom cover designs; and content particular to your business, training goals, marketing focus, or branding interests), please contact our corporate sales department at corpsales@pearsoned.com or (800) 382-3419.

For government sales inquiries, please contact governmentsales@pearsoned.com.

For questions about sales outside the U.S., please contact international@pearsoned.com.

Visit us on the Web: informit.com/aw

Publisher
Paul Boger

Associate Publisher
David Dusthimer

Executive Editor
Brett Bartow

Senior Development Editor
Christopher Cleveland

Managing Editor
Sandra Schroeder

Project Editor
Mandie Frank

Copy Editor
Cenveo® Publisher Services

Technical Editors
Ignas Bagdonas
Jon Mitchell

Editorial Assistant
Vanessa Evans

Cover Designer
Alan Clements

Composition
Cenveo® Publisher Services

Indexer
Cenveo® Publisher Services

About the Authors

Russ White began his network engineering career installing terminal emulation cards and inverse multiplexers in the United States Air Force. In 1996, he moved to Raleigh, N.C., to join Cisco Systems in the Technical Assistance Center (TAC) routing protocols team. From TAC, Russ moved to the global escalation team, and then into engineering, and finally into sales as a Distinguished Architect. He is currently a network architect working in the area of network complexity and large scale design, a member of the IETF Routing Area Directorate, an active speaker and writer, and active in the Internet Society. He holds CCIE #2637, CCDE 2007:001, the CCAr, a Masters in Information Technology from Capella University, and a Masters in Christian Ministry from Shepherds Theological Seminary. He lives in Oak Island, N.C., with his wife and two children, and is currently a P.h.D student at Southeastern Baptist Theological Seminary.

Jeff Tantsura started his network engineering career in early 1990s at a small ISP as system/network administrator, later working for bigger ISPs where he was responsible for network design and architecture, vendor selection.

Currently Jeff is heading Technology Strategy Routing at Ericsson as well as chairing IETF Routing Working Group.

Jeff holds MSc in Computer Science and Systems Analysis from University of Georgia and Executive Certificate of Business Excellence from Haas School of Business, Berkeley.

He also holds CCIE R&S #11416 and Ericsson Certified Expert IP Networking #8

Jeff lives in Palo Alto, CA, with his wife and youngest child.

About the Technical Reviewers

Ignas Bagdonas

Ignas Bagdonas has been involved in the network engineering field for last two decades, covering operations, deployment, design, architecture, development, and standardization aspects. He has worked on multiple large SP and enterprise networks worldwide, participated in many of the world's first technology deployments, and has been involved with building community awareness via conferences, seminars, and workshops. His current focus covers end-to-end network architecture evolution and new emerging technologies. Ignas holds Cisco CCDE and CCIE certifications.

Jon Mitchell

Jon Mitchell, CCIE No. 15953, is a network engineer in Google's Technical Infrastructure organization where he works on their global backbone. Prior to Google, Jon has worked in roles of network architecture at Microsoft, systems engineering at Cisco Systems, network architecture and engineering at AOL, and network engineering at Loudcloud for the last 15 years that he has been in the networking industry. He is also an active IETF participant in various routing area working groups. Through all of these roles, Jon has always had a passion for working on large-scale problems and solving them through simplification and automation. When Jon is not thinking about networking, he enjoys many other passions such as hiking, running, supporting clean water, microbreweries, and spending time with his wife and four children.

Dedications

Russ White: This book is dedicated to Bekah and Hannah. Thank you for sticking with your grumpy old dad through thick and thin.

Jeff Tantsura: This book is dedicated to my family: Marina, Ilia, Miriam, and Davy—thank you for your support!

Acknowledgments

Russ White:

I would like to thank the many people who have taught me networking through the years, including Denise Fishburne, Don Slice, Alvaro Retana, Robert Raszuk, and a host of others—too many to name. I would also like to thank Dr. Doug Bookman for driving me to be a better thinker, Dr. Will Coberly for driving me to be a better writer, and Dr. Larry Pettegrew for driving me just to be a better person. Finally, I'd like to thank Greg Ferro and Ethan Banks for inspiring me to start writing again.

Jeff Tantsura:

I would like to thank the people who taught and helped me through the years to understand networking better: Acee Lindem, Tony Przygienda, Tony Li, Jakob Heitz and many others, too many to help.

Special thanks to my co-author Russ for inspiring me!

Contents at a Glance

Contents

Introduction

Every engineer, no matter what type of engineering they do, face complexity almost constantly. The faster, cheaper, higher quality triad are the constant companion of everything the engineer does. Sometimes, though, the complexity isn't so obvious. For instance, how long will the software project take? Two hours, two weeks, or too long is the common reply—another encounter with complexity.

While research into complexity theory has proceeded apace in the scientific and mathematical worlds, the application of the theories and ideas to more practical engineering problems, particularly in a way that the "average engineer" can read and understand, simply hasn't kept pace. This book aims to fill that gap for network engineering.

In a move that will probably be disappointing to readers with a math degree, this book is devoid of the elegant mathematical models complexity theorists are working with. Rather, the focus is on the practical application of the theoretical constructs of complexity. Instead of being focused on the "pure theory" and math, this book is focused on the practical application of the ideas being investigated by complexity theorists.

This book, then, is targeted at the "average" network engineer who wants to gain an understanding of why particular common constructs work the way they do, such as hierarchical design, aggregation, and protocol layering. By getting behind these widely accepted ways of designing a network, exposing the reasons for the tradeoffs designed into the system in each case, the authors hope the reader learns to take lessons learned in one area and apply them to other areas. After reading this book, network engineers should begin to understand why hierarchical design and layering, for instance, work, and how to see and change the tradeoffs in more specific situations.

How This Book Is Organized

This book begins, in the first chapter, with a high level view of complexity theory. This is not deep theory, but it is rather designed to provide a hands-on view of complexity without diving into heavy math (or any math at all). The second chapter provides an overview of various attempts at measuring complexity in a network, including some of the problems plauging each attempt. The third chapter proposes a model of complexity that will be used throughout the rest of the book.

Chapter 4 through 7 consider examples of complexity in network and protocol design. The point these chapters attempt to drive home is how the models and concepts in the first three chapters. Chapter 8 is something of an important detour into the world of complex system failure in network engineering terms. The rest of the book is dedicated to first providing an overview of three new technologies network engineers face at the time of writing, and then an analysis of each one in terms of complexity tradeoffs.

Note, Documents referenced with the form draft-xxx are IETF works in progress, and therefore do not have stable document names or uniform resource locators (URLs). Because of these limitations, explicit references have not been given, but rather just the title of the document and the document name. To find these documents , please perform a document search at the IETF website (ietf.org).

Chapter 1

Defining Complexity

Computer networks are complex.

But what does "computer networks are complex" mean? Can you put a network on a scale and have the needle point to "complex"? Is there a mathematical model into which you can plug the configurations and topology of a set of network devices that will, in turn, produce a "complexity index"? How do the concepts of scale, resilience, brittleness, and elegance, relate to complexity? The answers to these questions are—unfortunately—complex. In fact, the most difficult issue involved in answering these questions is deciding where to begin.

The best place to begin is at the beginning—in this case a few definitions of complexity, from "everything I don't understand," to "that which involves a lot of unintentional consequences." There is at least some truth in each of these answers; some part of each of these answers is helpful in building a picture of complexity in general, and complexity in network design and architecture.

Once the meaning of complexity has been examined, this book will turn to asking why computer networks must be complex in the first place. Wouldn't things be a lot simpler if engineers just avoided all complexity from protocol design to network management? Can't complexity be "managed out" in some way? The second section of this chapter provides an overview of research in the field of complexity. As it turns out, complexity is a necessary tradeoff in the real world. Getting there will require winding through some rather—pardon the pun—complex material. It's going to be necessary to look at the components of complexity and to dissect a broad idea into a set of components that can actually be understood in a useful way.

Chapter 2, "Components of Complexity," will begin investigating the intersection between complexity and network engineering, considering various reactions to complexity. Network engineers tend to have one of five reactions to complexity, three of which can be shaped into positive responses and two are generally destructive. The three positive responses are as follows:

1. Abstract the complexity away, to build a black box around each part of the system, so each piece and the interactions between these pieces are more immediately understandable.

2. Toss the complexity over the cubicle wall—to move the problem out of the networking realm into the realm of applications, or coding, or a protocol. As RFC1925 says, "It is easier to move a problem around (e.g., by moving the problem to a different part of the overall network architecture) than it is to solve it."[1]

3. Add another layer on top, to treat all the complexity as a black box by putting another protocol or tunnel on top of what's already there. Returning to RFC1925, "It is always possible to add another level of indirection."[2]

The two generally negative responses are as follows:

1. Become overwhelmed with the complexity, label what exists as "legacy," and chase some new shiny thing that will solve all the problems in what is perceived as a much less complex way.

2. Ignoring the problem and hoping it will go away. Arguing for an exception "just this once," so a particular business goal can be met, or some problem fixed, within a very tight schedule, with the promise that the complexity issue will be dealt with "later," is a good example.

These reactions show up as solutions to complexity in many different realms of network design, including operational complexity, design complexity, and protocol complexity; each of these areas will be examined in more detail in individual chapters to gain a better understanding of the costs and benefits of adding complexity in each one.

Once all this background material is covered, it will be time to turn to some more practical examples. The basic operation and/or concepts behind different technologies that promise to help tame the complexity monster in our networks

---

1. Ross Callon, ed., "The Twelve Networking Truths" (IETF, April 1996), https://www.rfc-editor .org/rfc/rfc1925.txt.

2. Ibid.

will be considered, including an examination of where each one reduces and increases complexity.

The final chapter will bring it all together. The final goal is to build a generalized view of complexity in network systems that can be applied to making real decisions about operations, design, and protocols. While it will take some theory to get from here to there, the final goal is imminently practical: to learn how to recognize and mange complexity in the real world of computer networks.

What Is Complexity?

When confronted with the question, "what is complexity," you might reply, "Complexity—like beauty—is in the eye of the beholder." It's harder to live with this definition, however, because it internalizes complexity. Making complexity into an internal state of mind, or an impression, leaves complexity with no corresponding reality, and hence leaves engineers with no tools or models with which to understand, control, or manage complexity. On the other hand, there is real value in confronting the *perception* of complexity, as the perception can help you see, and understand, the *reality* of complexity in networks.

A useful place to begin is defining complexity with two broad perceptions: complexity is anything I don't understand, and complexity is anything with a lot of (moving) parts. Moving beyond these, it's important to consider complexity as state versus intent, and then, finally, complexity and the law of unintended consequences.

Anything I Don't Understand

What is complex for one person might be simple for another. Or, as Clarke's third law says, "Any sufficiently advanced technology is indistinguishable from magic."[3] From these observations, you could conclude that *complexity is anything you don't understand*. A few definitions from a coder's point of view illustrate this state of mind:

- A clean solution is a solution that works, and that I understand.

- A complex solution is a solution that works, and that I don't understand.

- Obscure code is code that I don't understand, and isn't commented.

---

3. Arthur C. Clarke, *Profiles of the Future: An Inquiry into the Limits of the Possible* (London: Phoenix, 2000), n.p.

- Self-documenting code is code that I wrote, and therefore I can understand without comments.

- A hack is a piece of code that doesn't work, I didn't write, and I don't understand.

- A temporary workaround is a piece of code that I did write and I do understand.

But is "anything I don't understand" a workable definition in the real world? Several points should illustrate the fallacy of settling on this as a final definition of complexity:

- There are a number of complex systems in the real world that no one understands in their entirety. In fact, there are a number of networks in the real world that no one understands in their entirety. It might, for instance, be possible for a network operator to understand one specific piece of the Internet, or a general outline of how the Internet really works, but for someone to claim that they know how every part and piece of the Internet works would be absurd.

- Increased understanding necessarily means reduced complexity if this definition is true. For any given phenomenon, once it is "understood" in purely materialistic terms, it can be declared "not complex." For instance, no one in the early 1900s understood the complex operation of a biological system such as the eye. Since that time, the operation of the eye has been researched and documented (at least to some degree). Does this mean the eye is now less complex than it once was?

- In the same way, understanding the intent of a designer might make a design appear less complex without actually changing the design itself. For instance, using Type-Length-Value (TLV) constructions in a protocol might seem to increase the overall complexity for very little gain—but when future proofing a protocol against new functionality is taken into account, using more complex structures might make perfect sense.

In short, the connection between complexity and understanding is tenuous at best—gaining a better understanding of any given system doesn't really make it less complex, it just makes it more understandable. Don't underestimate the underlying premise of this definition, though. Why does gaining a better understanding of a system make it appear less complex? Several points can be mentioned here, each of which will be developed more fully through the rest of this book:

- Understanding how a system works allows you to comprehend and account for the interactions between the various parts. One of the steps you can use to manage complexity, then, is to discover the interactions between the parts of the system.

- Understanding how a system works allows you to predict the output based on a set of given inputs, or rather to construct a mental model of the system's output based on inputs. Another step you can use to manage complexity is to abstract any given system into a set of inputs and outputs that can be used as a proxy for that system within a larger context (or system).

- A mental model of the system also allows you to recognize when the system isn't operating correctly, and to work around these unplanned outputs, discover why the system is acting the way it is and repair the fault, or determine why the inputs don't match your expectations (and correct them).

While defining complexity as "anything I don't understand" isn't a full definition, it does help scope the definition in some very important ways. Exploring things perceived as being "hard to understand" can lead to a fuller definition—a definition that will be more useful in the real world.

Anything with a Lot of Parts

In designing large-scale solutions, one recurring refrain is to "use the minimum possible number of moving parts." In general, anything with a lot of parts or lots of different parts is seen as complex, from large-scale networks to complex crystal structures. But is the number of parts, or the number of moving parts, or even the number of different parts, really a proxy for complexity? Not necessarily. Two specific examples provide counters to the idea that the number of moving parts is a good determinate of complexity.

The first of these is illustrated in Figure 1.1—a three-dimensional Mandelbulb fractal taken at a high resolution.[4]

While there is a lot of apparent complexity in the illustration, it is all actually created by iteratively running the same algorithm—so, in reality, there is

---

4. "File:Mandelbulb140a.JPG—Wikimedia Commons," n.p., accessed July 8, 2014, https://commons.wikimedia.org/wiki/File:Mandelbulb140a.JPG.

Figure 1.1 *A Three-Dimensional Mandelbulb*

only one "moving piece." A second example, from the networking world, is the interaction of two routing protocols, such as Open Shortest Path First (OSPF) and the Border Gateway Protocol (BGP). While both of these protocols are fairly simple in their design and construction, deploying either one in a large-scale network actually involves a good deal of complexity. Layering BGP on top of OSPF adds a much larger amount of complexity than someone unfamiliar with network design might expect. There are a number of unexpected interactions between these two protocols, from calculating the best path to determining the next hop to use toward a specific destination. Their interaction while converging (in reaction to a change in the network topology) can be especially entertaining.

That complex patterns can result from simple rule sets should remind you not to confuse the appearance of complexity with complexity itself. Simply because something *looks* complex does not mean it actually *is* complex; instead you must reach beyond appearances to get a true understanding of complexity. Something with a lot of moving parts isn't necessarily complex, any more than something with just a few moving parts is necessarily simple. What really matters is the interaction between the moving parts.

- The more often each piece of a system interacts with others, and the more pieces any given piece of a system interacts with, the more complex the system itself will be. The number of interactions between the various parts of a system can be called the interaction plane; the larger the plane of interaction, the more the parts of the system interact with one another. Likewise, the smaller the plane of interaction, the less the parts of the system interact with one another.

- The deeper the relationship between the various parts of a system, the more complex the system will be.

Figure 1.2 illustrates these concepts in a more visual way.

To give a more concrete example, consider an application designed to run across a network. Four possibilities are provided in order of increasing complexity, parallel to the illustration in Figure 1.2:

- One instance of the application transmits blocks of information using the Transmission Control Protocol (TCP), while a second instance receives this information. The application relies on TCP and the underlying network to

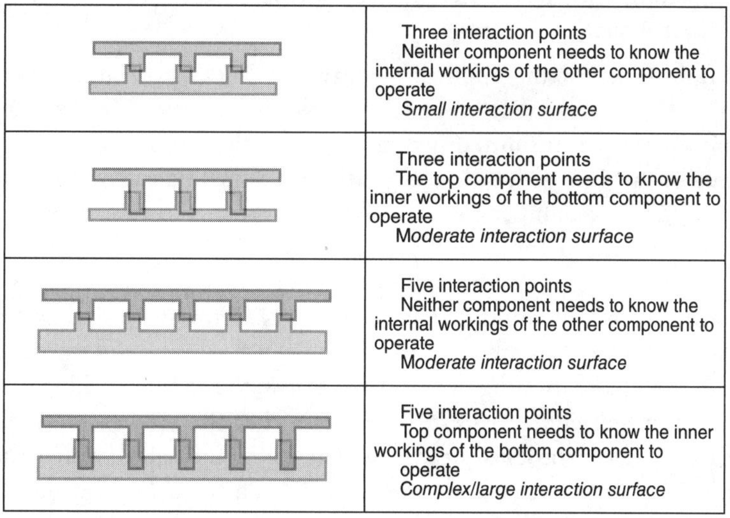

	Three interaction points Neither component needs to know the internal workings of the other component to operate *Small interaction surface*
	Three interaction points The top component needs to know the inner workings of the bottom component to operate *Moderate interaction surface*
	Five interaction points Neither component needs to know the internal workings of the other component to operate *Moderate interaction surface*
	Five interaction points Top component needs to know the inner workings of the bottom component to operate *Complex/large interaction surface*

Figure 1.2 *Illustration of Interaction Surface and Depth*

deliver these blocks of information without error, but doesn't possess any information about the TCP process' current state or implementation. This would be a shallow, narrow interaction surface; the application interacts with TCP in multiple places, but knows little about TCP's internal state.

- One instance of the application transmits blocks of information using TCP, while a second instance receives this information. Because the information being transmitted can sometimes be time sensitive, the application examines the state of the TCP queue from time to time, adjusting the rate at which it is sending blocks, and can request the TCP process to push a block, rather than waiting for the TCP buffer to fill up. This is a deeper interaction surface because the application must now understand something about the way TCP works, and interact with how TCP works intelligently. The interaction surface is still narrow, however, as it is only between TCP and the application at multiple points.

- One instance of the application transmits blocks of information using TCP, while a second instance receives this information. As in the first example, the application doesn't interact with TCP's state in any way; it simply places blocks of data into TCP's buffer and assumes TCP will deliver it correctly across the network. The application is, however, time sensitive, and therefore also reads the clock, which is dependent on Network Time Protocol (NTP) for accuracy, on a regular basis. This interaction surface can be considered a bit broader, as the application is now interacting with two different network protocols, but both interactions are rather shallow.

- One instance of the application transmits blocks of information using TCP, while a second instance receives this information. Because the information being transmitted is time sensitive, the application examines the state of the TCP queue from time to time, adjusting the rate at which it is sending blocks, and can request the TCP process to push a block, rather than waiting for the TCP buffer to fill up. To time these push requests, the application monitors the local time, which it assumes is kept synchronized among multiple devices using NTP (or some similar solution). The interaction surface in this example is both broader and deeper, in that the application again needs to know the inner workings of TCP's data transmission. It is also broader, in that the application is interacting with two protocols (or systems, in the larger sense), rather than one. In fact, in this example, the state of NTP is now tied to the internal state of TCP through the application—and neither protocol knows about this connection.

The interaction surface, then, is simply the number of places where two systems interact and the depth of those interactions; each additional Application Programming Interface (API), socket, or other point of contact increases the interaction surface. It's clear that as the amount and level of interaction between two subsystems within a system increases, the complexity level is driven up.

These concepts will be related to network design and architecture more fully as this book works through various examples, but consider this: OSPF and Intermediate System-to-Intermediate System (IS-IS), for instance, run as "ships in the night" routing protocols. They both rely on the same information about IP addresses, link states, metrics, and other information drawn directly from the network topology. OSPF and IS-IS, even if they're running on the same network, don't interact unless they are configured to interact (through redistribution, for instance). Do OSPF and BGP interact in the same way? No, because BGP relies on the underlying IGP to provide IP reachability for building peering relationships and next hop information. Using the model described here, the interaction surface is larger between OSPF and BGP than it is between OSPF and IS-IS, and the APIs are fairly opaque.

Anything for Which There Is More State Than Required to Achieve a Goal

Virtually anyone in the engineering world has seen a cartoon of a Rube Goldberg Machine, such as the one in Figure 1.3.[5]

Figure 1.3 *A Rube Goldberg Machine*

---

5. Public domain; taken from: "Professor_Lucifer_Butts.gif (428 × 302)," n.p., accessed July 7, 2014, https://upload.wikimedia.org/wikipedia/commons/a/a6/Professor_Lucifer_Butts.gif.

Quite often these contraptions were labeled as a simple way to solve some problem, from using a napkin during a meal (as in Figure 1.3) to jacking a car up to replace the tire (an elephant atop the car is induced to move onto a platform that levers one end of the car up into the air). *Simple* is the key word, because these machines were obviously anything other than simple. But why are such machines considered complex—even to the point of being humorously complex? Because they illustrate two specific points about the nature of complexity.

Rube Goldberg's contraptions are always multistep solutions for a simple problem. The automatic napkin machine shown in Figure 1.3, for instance, replaces the simple action of picking the napkin up and wiping your mouth with it. It's absurd to use such a machine when you obviously have one hand free that could be used for the same task—and even if your other hand isn't free, it's simpler to put a fork down on the table and pick up a napkin than to build this crazy machine to do the same thing. Your perception of complexity, then, is related to the relationship between the problem being solved and the solution offered. Any system that adds unnecessary steps, interactions, or parts to solve a specific problem is seen as complex, no matter how simple the problem or the solution when viewed objectively.

Rube Goldberg's contraptions always focus on the problem at hand to the exclusion of the side effects of the solution proposed. The automatic napkin requires a rocket that must be replaced each time it is used, a bird that must be fed, a clock that must be wound and maintained, and a biscuit that must be replaced after each use. Is the solution really simpler than picking a napkin up? The elephant used to lever the car up so the tire can be replaced must be carried and fed. What should the owner of the car do when the elephant is asleep and the tire needs to be replaced?

The comic genius of Rube Goldberg and his fabulous machines teaches us:

- The complexity of the solution must be directly related to the problem being solved. If there is a simpler solution available, engineers will (and should) gravitate to that solution. Call this the "Occam's Razor" of complexity in engineering: if two solutions have been proposed to resolve a problem, the simpler solution should always be preferred, given both solutions solve the problem equally well.

- It is easy to create unnecessary complexity by narrowing the focus too far. A simpler solution might actually seem simpler until it meets the test of the future, or engages with reality. It might seem easier to design a protocol with just the encodings needed, and without messy constructions like TLVs—at least until you need to modify the protocol to address some problem you didn't think of when doing the initial design work. To put this another way, there is often an unexpected brittleness to the (apparently) cleanest and simplest design available. In the same way, not all the problems with a particular solution are obvious until the solution is actually deployed.

Examples of these two principles will crop up on a regular basis as you consider specific instances of complexity in the real worlds of network architecture and network protocol design.

Unintended Consequences

In 1996, websites discussing the Super Bowl, the most famous football game in the world, were being blocked by various search engines. Why would any search engine on the Internet block sites related to football? Because each Super Bowl is numbered sequentially starting in 1967 with the first game, Super Bowl I. The numbers in the name have always been in roman numerals. The 1996 Super Bowl was game number 30, so it was appropriately called Super Bowl XXX. But XXX also represents a particular type of material widely available on the Internet that many people don't want to see in their search results. Hence, Super Bowl XXX, because of the "XXX," was blocked from many search engines.[6]

This (perhaps amusing) story is one of a long chain of such incidents in the history of attempting to censor content on the Internet—but it makes a larger point about the power of unintended consequences. In 1996, Robert K. Merton listed five sources of unintended consequences.[7] Three of these directly apply to large computer network systems:

- Ignorance, making it impossible to anticipate everything, thereby leading to incomplete analysis

- Errors in analysis of the problem or following habits that worked in the past but may not apply to the current situation

- Immediate interests overriding long-term interests

---

6. "E-Rate and Filtering: A Review of the Children's Internet Protection Act" (General. Energy and Commerce, Subcommittee on Telecommunications and the Internet, April 4, 2001), n.p., accessed July 8, 2014, http://www.gpo.gov/fdsys/pkg/CHRG-107hhrg72836/pdf/CHRG-107hhrg72836.pdf.

7. Robert K. Merton, "The Unanticipated Consequences of Purposive Social Action," *American Sociological Review* 1, no. 6 (December 1, 1936): 894–904, accessed September 15, 2015, http://www.jstor.org/stable/2084615.

How does the concept of unintended consequences apply to the complexity of a network? As a system becomes more complex, it becomes more difficult to predict the output based on any given input. As an example, a lot of research is done into the real results of various inputs into the Internet routing system—how long does it take for an update in topology or reachability to propagate throughout the Internet as a whole, how does one provider changing or implementing a specific policy impact other providers, and how do seemingly straightforward ideas, such as route flap dampening work in the real world? That research must be undertaken to discover the answers to these questions implies that the Internet, at large, is a complex system. Given a specific input, you can guess at a likely outcome, but there's no assurance that the outcome will be what you expect.

Large complex systems with a lot of interconnected parts are difficult to analyze, leading to incomplete analysis, and hence unintended consequences through ignorance. In a large enough system, with enough components that have transparent interactions and large interaction surfaces, it's almost impossible to know all the ways in which a single change will affect the system.

In the same way, large complex systems tend to be managed more by experience (seat of the pants flying) and rule of thumb—the cost to do a full analysis is often perceived to be much higher than the cost of a failure if the rule of thumb is wrong. This again relates to the problem of complexity through the scale and subsystem interaction. The more complex a system, the more likely errors in analysis are to creep into everyday operational models.

> **Note**
>
> Before pilots had instruments that could tell them the angle of the airplane (called yaw, pitch, and roll), they would "fly by the seat of their pants." This literally means that they would judge the speed of the plane in relation to the sharpness of a turn by whether or not they slid in their seat when making the turn. If you were sliding in your seat, you weren't flying fast enough for the turn—the centrifugal force of the speed of the plane in the turn should keep the pilot in place in the seat.

The final problem is one every network engineer knows well—it's the two-in-the-morning phone call, the application that's down and will cost the company millions if it's not "up—right now," and the shortcut taken to get things back working. We always tell ourselves we'll look at it in the morning, or we'll put it on the to-do list to fix sometime later, but the tyranny of the immediate takes over soon enough, and the hack stays in as part of the normal operational profile of the network. A single hack in a network of a thousand routers might not seem like it will have many negative consequences. In reality, however, a single hack can quickly bring down a thousand-router network, and a thousand hacks in a network of ten thousand routers, however, are a disaster just waiting to happen.

> **Note**
>
> Another term for the concept of building in complexity simply to address a problem at hand, without considering the future impact, is *technical debt.*[8]

The power of unintended consequences teaches that to better understand, and manage, network complexity, engineers need to focus on the ability to analyze and understand the various states and interactions between the various components used to build a functioning network. The more tools and concepts you can apply to understanding the various states into which a network can fall—such as models and measurement tools—the better you will be able to deal with complexity in the real world. At the same time, there is a limit to human understanding, and therefore a limit to the number of side effects anyone can foresee.

Why So Much Complexity?

If complexity is so—complex—then why not just design networks and protocols that are simpler? To put the question another way, why does every attempt to make anything simpler in the networking world end up apparently making things more complex in the long run? For instance, by tunneling on top of (or through) IP, the control plane's complexity is reduced, and the network is made simpler overall. Why is it, then, that tunneled overlays end up containing so much complexity?

There are two answers to this question. The first is that human nature being what it is, engineers will always invent ten different ways to solve the same problem. This is especially true in the virtual world, where new solutions are (relatively) easy to deploy, it's (relatively) easy to find a problem with the last set of proposed solutions, and it's (relatively) easy to move some bits around to create a new solution that is "better than the old one." The virtual space, in other words, is partially so messy because it's so easy to build something new there.

---

8. "Technical Debt," *Wikipedia, the Free Encyclopedia*, September 2, 2015, accessed September 15, 2015, https://en.wikipedia.org/w/index.php?title=Technical_debt&oldid=679133748.

The second answer, however, lies in a more fundamental problem: complexity is necessary to deal with the uncertainty involved in difficult to solve problems. Alderson and Doyle state:

In our view, however, complexity is most succinctly discussed in terms of functionality and its robustness. Specifically, we argue that complexity in highly organized systems arises primarily from design strategies intended to create robustness to uncertainty in their environments and component parts.[9]

This statement can be expressed in a chart as shown in Figure 1.4.

This is counterintuitive—in fact, it's almost the opposite of most discussions around network engineering. Engineers often assume that increasing simplicity leads to increasing robustness—but this is not true. Instead, increasing complexity increases robustness until the solution moves beyond the peak on the robustness curve. Why should this be? Because of uncertainty. As a simple example, let's return to TLV encodings often used in network protocols. Which is better?

- Designing a protocol that can handle a large number of situations in its original format, and also support many different extensions that hadn't been thought of when the protocol was designed.

- Designing a protocol that will support, using the minimal set of information possible, the requirements laid out at the very beginning of the design phase.

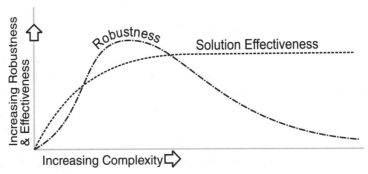

Figure 1.4 *Complexity, Robustness, and Solution Effectiveness*

9. David L. Alderson and John C. Doyle, "Contrasting Views of Complexity and Their Implications for Network-Centric Infrastructures," *IEEE Transactions on Systems, Man, and Cybernetics* 40, no. 4 (July 2010): 840.

There is a strong argument to be made, in the single protocol case, for the second option—designing the protocol to support the requirements presented at the beginning of the design phase with the minimal amount of information required. There are two specific reasons; the second might appear to be the most optimal.

The on-the-wire profile of an optimally designed protocol will always be smaller than one designed with flexible additions. For any TLV, there must be a TLV header—something must describe the type and length of the value. On the other hand, any protocol that is designed to optimally carry just a specific set of information doesn't need to carry any information about what the carried information is. To put this in other terms, the metadata, or data description, must be carried with the data if the protocol is to be flexible enough to add new data types in the future. If the protocol is "closed," however, the metadata is part of the protocol description, and need not be carried on the wire with the data. The metadata in a flexible protocol is internalized, or carried in line with the data itself to create flexibility; it is externalized, or located in the protocol implementation, to create optimal use of bits on the wire.

The processing profile of an optimally designed protocol will always be better than one designed with flexible additions. In the same way, a protocol designed around TLVs, or any other format that allows more types of information to be carried in the future, will require more complex processing. Offsets into the packet cannot be used to find any piece of information contained anywhere in the packet—instead, the data stream must be "walked," to find the next TLV header, and the TLV must be processed according to a set of per TLV rules. See Figure 1.5 for an illustration of this concept.

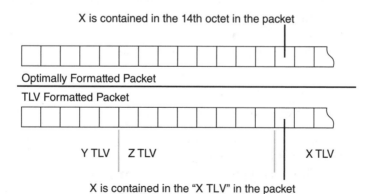

Figure 1.5 *TLV versus Optimally Structured Packet Formats*

Compare the processing required to find the octet containing the value of X in both cases. For the optimally formatted packet:

- Count off 14 octets.
- Read the value of X from the contents of the 14th octet.

For the TLV formatted packet:

- Read the first TLV header.
- This is a Y TLV; find the length and skip to the end of the TLV in the packet.
- Read the second TLV header.
- This is a Z TLV, find the length and skip to the end of the TLV in the packet.
- Read the third TLV header.
- This is an X TLV.
- Jump into the X TLV, based on the format of this particular TLV, and read the value of X.

The processing for the optimally formatted packet is much simpler; processing TLVs requires more bits to be moved into and out of memory, examined, etc. Protocols optimized to carry very specific pieces of data can have that data organized to make processing easier, and hence to reduce processor utilization. This is particularly important in the area of packet switching, where customized hardware is used to switch packets at a very high rate, and other places where hardware is used to process packets in near real time.

On the other side of this equation, however, there is the unexpected (or unpredicted). Using the TLV example allows you to see this in two ways: future extensions and error handling.

Future Extensions versus New Protocols

Assume you've designed some new protocol that is perfectly optimized both on the wire and in terms of processing requirements to transport information about the number of widgets being produced on a daily basis in each factory at a large company. Soon enough, the company sees an opportunity in offering loans for anyone who wants to buy one of these widgets, and a new requirement arises:

the ability to transport information about loans for widgets across the network. In the spirit of perfectly optimized network performance, you design a new protocol to transport loan information across the network—again, the protocol is designed to minimize bandwidth utilization and processing requirements throughout the network. As the loan business expands, the company decides high finance is a good business to be in, so they decide to expand their outlets to sell not just widgets, but five or six other items, and to provide financing for each of those items as well. The question quickly becomes—should you continue designing and deploying individual protocols to manage each new requirement separately, or should you have designed a single, flexible protocol that could manage a wider range of requirements in the first place?

In the TLV format example discussed previously, TLV formatted packets require more on-the-wire bandwidth, and more power to process, but they also allow for a single protocol to be used for counting widgets, loans for widgets, loans in general, and other products in general. If a protocol is designed to manage a broad range of data types within a single set of goals, then the system actually ends up being simpler than one in which each goal is met with a separate protocol.

This example might be a little stretched, but as you get into the more practical sections of this book it will become ever more apparent just how it is a real question designers and architects face on a regular basis. There is always a temptation to extend the network by simply putting a new protocol "over the top," but without some solid ideas about goals, functional separation, and domain separation, "over the top," quickly becomes a euphemism for "spaghetti on top of the plate." Another example of this phenomenon is putting a protocol designed for one purpose into a completely different role. For instance, the Resource Reservation Protocol (RSVP) was originally designed to reserve queue and processing space along a path for a particular flow of packets. The most common use for RSVP today is the signaling of traffic engineering paths through a network—a purpose far outside the original design of the protocol.

Unexpected Errors

Another source of uncertainty in the real world is errors; for whatever reason, things don't always go as planned. How a protocol or network reacts to these unexpected events is a crucial consideration, especially as networks become a "normal" part of life, relied on for everything from gaming to financial transactions to medical procedures.

An example of added complexity for added robustness in the area of handling network errors is the error detection or correction code found in many protocols. Figure 1.6 illustrates a simple parity-based scheme.

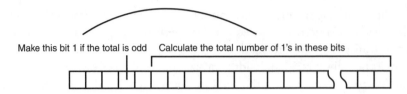

Figure 1.6 *The Parity Bit and Error Detection*

The parity bit is a simple example of an error detection code. When the packet is built, the total number of binary 1s is counted to determine if there is an even or odd number of 1s. If the number of 1s is odd, then the parity bit is set to 1 to make the number of 1s even. If a packet is received where the total number of 1s, including the parity bit, is odd, the receiver knows that the packet must have been corrupted during transmission in some way. This doesn't tell the receiver what the correct information is, but it does let the receiver know it needs to ask for another copy of the data.

Adding a parity bit increases the complexity of packet processing. Each packet must be stored in a buffer someplace while the number of 1s in the packet are counted, ignoring the parity bit itself. If the number of 1s is odd, then the parity bit must be set before the packet is transmitted. The receiver must likewise take the extra step of counting the number of 1s in the packet before accepting the data, and the protocol must have some mechanism built in for the receiver to ask for another copy of the information. Is this added complexity worth it? It all depends on how often failures that can be detected through such a system happen in normal operation, or how catastrophic a single failure would be. As the complexity of the error detection or correction mechanism ramps up, the ability of the application to recover from malformed transmissions is also increased. The cost is additional packet processing, along with the errors potentially introduced through the addition of the error correction code itself.

Why Not Build Infinitely Complex Systems?

Adding complexity, then, allows a network to handle future requirements and unexpected events more easily, as well as provides more services over a smaller set of base functions. If this is the case, why not simply build a single protocol running on a single network that can handle all the requirements potentially thrown at it, and can handle any sequence of events you can imagine? A single network running a single protocol would certainly reduce the number of moving parts network engineers need to deal with, making all our lives simpler, right?

Maybe not. At some point, any complex system becomes brittle—*robust yet fragile* is one phrase you can use to describe this condition. A system is robust yet fragile when it is able to react resiliently to an expected set of circumstances, but an unexpected set of circumstances will cause it to fail. To give an example from the real world—knife blades are required to have a somewhat unique combination of characteristics. They must be hard enough to hold an edge and cut, and yet flexible enough to bend slightly in use, returning to their original shape without any evidence of damage, and they must not shatter when dropped. It has taken years of research and experience to find the right metal to make a knife blade from, and there are still long and deeply technical discussions about which material is right for specific properties, under what conditions, etc.

There is one specific stage of making a knife blade of particular interest in the quest to understand complexity: the tempering process. To temper a knife blade, the blade is first heated to a very high temperature, and then allowed to cool. Repeating this process several times aligns the molecules of the steel so it forms a grain within the steel, as shown in Figure 1.7.[10]

This graining acts just like the grain in wood, creating dimensional strength, thus making the resulting piece of steel very hard—in fact, steel can become so hard through this process that it can shatter if dropped on a hard surface, such as a concrete or tile floor. The blade, at this point, is robust yet fragile; it is able

High-carbon AISI/SAE 1095 Steel

Figure 1.7 *Grain in Hardened Steel*

---

10. Image taken from http://practicalmaintenance.net/wp-content/uploads/High-carbon-AISI-1095-Steel.jpg.

to achieve its primary design (cutting material) very well, but it doesn't react well to unexpected events (being dropped on a hard surface, or having torsion applied). To make the knife useable, the blade must be "detempered," before it is actually used. To do this, the steel is heated (normally to a slightly lower temperature than used in hardening the steel), and then quenched in a bath of oil. This process destabilizes the graining the hardening process has created, making the steel slightly softer—but in the process, the steel also becomes much more flexible. The end result of the process is a blade that holds an edge, is hard enough to cut, and yet is flexible enough for everyday use.

The grain created through the hardening process represents the complexity put into networks and protocols in various ways, such as adding metadata into the packet format by adding TLVs, or adding more paths between the source and destination, or even automating a process that is normally handled by humans to reduce the number of mistakes made in handling changes to the network. The distempering process is also needed, as well, in the form of layering protocols, setting general (and often narrow) goals for different parts of the network, breaking up failure domains, etc.

Complexity, then, can be seen as a tradeoff. If you go too far down the scale in one direction, you wind up with a network that isn't resilient because there is no redundancy, or there is a single failure domain, etc. If you go down the scale in the other direction, you wind up with a network that isn't resilient because the protocols and systems cannot cope with a rapid change. There is no "perfect point" on this scale—just as with steel, it all depends on the goals the network engineer sets out to meet. Two more illustrations, taken from the technical world, will help to cement this concept.

Quick, Cheap, and High Quality: Choose Two

Just about everyone knows this, but it bears repeating on a regular basis. Faced with just about any decision, you will have three goals: *quick, cheap,* and *high quality.* Of those three, you can choose any two—but never all three. If you choose a solution that is cheap and quick, you will almost certainly not end up with a quality solution. If you choose a solution that is high quality and cheap, it will take a long time to implement. You can visualize this three-way tradeoff in a somewhat unusual way, as shown in Figure 1.8.

In Figure 1.8, the darker shaded area is what might be called "the realm of reality." The larger, more lightly shaded triangle is what might be called "the realm of goals." While the goals contain all three possibilities, reality is structured so you can only fill some part of the goals given. You can choose, as on the far left, to balance all three goals equally. In the next illustration, the focus

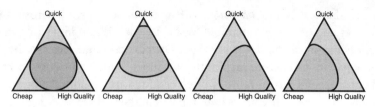

Figure 1.8 *The Quick, Cheap, Quality Conundrum*

has been moved to *quick,* with a resulting movement away from *cheap* and *high quality.*

Consistency, Availability, and Partition Tolerance: Choose Two

At the Association for Computing Machinery's Symposium on the Principles of Distributed Computing in 2000, Eric Brewer presented a paper titled "Towards Robust Distributed Systems."[11] In this paper, Brewer noted that distributed systems don't work well because applications demand that the information be consistent among all copies of a distributed database. Brewer argued that to get to true distributed computing, application designers must give up consistency. In 2002, Brewer's theorem was proven correct, and it is now known as the *CAP theorem.* The CAP theorem briefly states that you cannot have a database that is consistent, available, and exhibits partition tolerance—you can only choose two of the three properties. To better understand the CAP theorem in its native environment, let's look at the three terms involved in a little more detail.

- A database is *consistent* when any user of a database will read the same information no matter when and where the read takes place. For instance, if you put an item in your shopping cart at an online retailer, every other user on that same site should see the inventory reduced by the item in your cart. If the database is not consistent, then two people can order the same item while only one shows as being in inventory. Consistency is often called *atomicity*; atomic operations always leave a database in a state where all users have the same view of the data after every operation.

- A database is *accessible* when no user is refused access to the database for read (or often write) operations. While the definition of accessibility is often variable, in general, it means that the database is never inaccessible for longer than an outside process or user that relies on the database can tolerate.

---

11. Eric Brewer, "Towards Robust Distributed Systems," July 19, 2000, n.p., accessed July 11, 2014, http://wisecracked/~brewer/cs262b-2004/PODC-keynote.pdf.

- A database *tolerates partitions* when it can be spread across multiple devices and processes separated by a network without impacting the overall operation of the database itself. Distributed databases are, by definition, partitioned across each of the machines that contain some part of the database—and partitioning is often required to support the performance and resilience requirements of databases in the real world.

The diagram shown in Figure 1.8, by simply replacing the labels with *consistent, accessible,* and *partitionable,* can be used to illustrate the CAP theorem.

> **Note**
>
> One direct application of the CAP theorem to network engineering lies in the observation that routing protocols are simply distributed real-time database systems.

Journey into the Center of Complexity

What we've learned about complexity to this point can be summarized in a few statements:

- Complexity has a range of definitions centering around the concept of comprehensibility (including unintended consequences), surface interactions, and the relationship of the problem to the system being used to solve the problem.
- Complexity is a reaction to the twin uncertainties of the future and the real world.
- Complexity is required to build systems supporting a lot of capabilities and functions within a restricted physical or virtual space.
- Complexity is a set of impossibly opposed tradeoffs, rather than a single "thing."

To carry this last point further, the quality/speed/cost conundrum and the CAP theorem can be looked at in pairs rather than threes, as well. In any pair of related items, there is a curve between the two items that can be described using the formula $C \leq 1/R$, illustrated in Figure 1.9, as a tradeoff between cost and fragility. This curve is often referred to as the Turing curve.

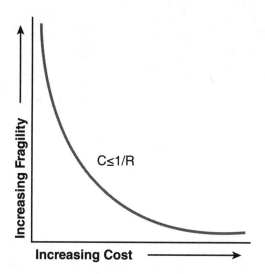

Figure 1.9 $C \le 1/R$ *Shown as a Tradeoff between Increasing Fragility and Increasing Cost*

There is a range of "sweet spots," along this curve; the job of the engineer is to choose which spot along the curve makes sense for every tradeoff—consciously or unconsciously, wisely or unwisely.

The next two chapters investigate several more aspects of complexity in greater detail, particularly in relation to computer networks. They begin by examining the components of complexity in the next chapter—the moving parts that make up a network, and how they interact. Chapter 3, "Measuring Network Complexity," will investigate various attempts at measuring complexity in a network to examine the tools available in this space. Following those two chapters, the book will turn to more practical matters, with the aim of making network engineers conscious of the complexity tradeoffs they are handling in designing and deploying protocols, and designing and deploying networks. This exercise should lead to more wisdom in engineering choices as you journey to the center of complexity.

Chapter 2

Components of Complexity

Working on broken networks is always an exciting business to be in—particularly if you work for a large vendor where large broken networks are brought to your door every day. To survive the constant onslaught, you eventually develop a set of simple and quick patches or changes you can always rely on to settle a network down so you can start the process of actually troubleshooting the problem. For example, one set of steps network engineers dealing with failures in a distance-vector control plane might take to stabilize the network could be:

- Look at the routing protocol topology database.
- Determine how many paths, on average, there are to any given destination in the table.
- Configure interfaces as passive (so they won't exchange reachability information) until the average number of parallel paths is less than 4.

Let's take another example: assume that you're examining a network that won't converge, and you notice a lot of external routes in the protocol tables—say 75% or more of the routes in the table are externals, and they all seem to have a very short age. What's the first step you're likely to take in stabilizing the network? Find the redistribution points and replace any dynamic redistribution between protocols with redistribution of static routes.

But why should either of these techniques work as an initial step in getting a failed network up and running so further troubleshooting and design remediation steps can be taken? Because they attack all three of the major components of complexity in a large-scale network: the amount of state, the rate of state change, and the scope of interaction surfaces.

To build and manage resilient networks at scale engineers are going to manage complexity. While this is easy enough to say, it's hard to do. As with any engineering problem, the first step is to decide how to set the problem up. How can the problem be broken into a few smaller pieces, so each one can be managed separately? How do these pieces interact? Examining the problem of complexity with these three components of complexity in mind—state, speed, and surfaces—will help network designers and architects address complexity in an effective and balanced way. While there are a number of places you could begin looking at the complexity in this space, control plane convergence is a good place to begin, because it touches many of the issues, and many of the other network systems.

Network Convergence

Network convergence is a prototypical example from which to draw the various components of network complexity. It's an area of network engineering almost everyone who works in the networking field has encountered in some way, and the various components of complexity are fairly easy to tease out and understand as individual concepts within the realm of complexity.

Path Vector: A BGP Example

In the case of Border Gateway Protocol (BGP) convergence, the major components in convergence time include:

- The Minimum Route Advertisement Interval (MRAI): This timer is designed to prevent state changes from overwhelming the system, particularly in preventing positive feedback loops from forming (see Chapter 8, "How Complex Systems Fail").

- The amount of time it takes to process and complete the best path calculations, particularly in route servers, route reflectors, and other devices that handle a larger than normal set of BGP paths.

- The amount of time the BGP process on any particular speaker spends interacting with other processes in the device, such as the Routing Information Base (RIB) and other protocol processes.

Figure 2.1 illustrates BGP convergence.

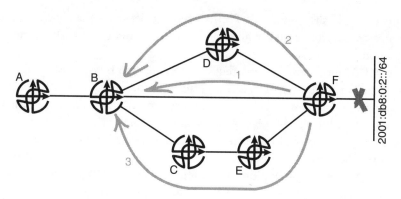

Figure 2.1 *BGP Convergence*

In this network, when the link from Router F to 2001:db8:0:2::/64 fails:

- Router F sends a withdraw to Routers D, E, and B. Router B, because this is its best path to 2001:db8:0:2::/64, will examine its available paths to this destination. Through the best path process, Router B will choose the path through Router D as the new best path, and send an advertisement with an explicit withdraw toward Router A.

- Routers D and E finish processing the loss of the path to 2001:db8:0:2::/64 next. Router D sends a withdraw to Router B; Router E sends a withdraw to Router C.

- Router B, on receiving the withdraw from Router D, examines its table and determines that the best path is now along the path [C,E,F]—note that Router C is still processing the withdraw it received from Router E at this point, so Router B still believes that the path through Router C is available. Router B determines that it should send a new update with an implicit withdraw to Router A, but it must now wait for the MRAI to time out before it can.

- Router C now finishes processing the withdraw it received from Router E, and sends a withdraw toward Router B.

- Router B examines its local table, and finds that it has no path toward 2001:db8:0:2::/64. It now transmits a withdraw to Router A, finishing the convergence process.

This example shows how BGP effectively works from the shortest path to the longest when converging. The same situation occurs when BGP learns a new destination.[1]

The MRAI increases the time required to converge by one MRAI timer for each "cycle" of increasing or decreasing the autonomous system (AS) Path. The processing time of running best path can also have a major impact on the time required for BGP to converge, especially in cases where the BGP speaker must process a large number of routes (such as a route server or route reflector). The time to run best path is also impacted by the interaction of the BGP process with other processes running on the router, such as the RIB process. Building a solid BGP implementation is not an easy task—there are only a handful of solid, widely used, BGP implementations in the world.

Distance Vector: An EIGRP Example

While Enhanced Interior Gateway Protocol (EIGRP) isn't as widely used as it once was, it's still worth looking at the EIGRP convergence process to gain a solid understanding of the way distributed control planes converge. Figure 2.2 illustrates a network used for discussing EIGRP convergence.

This process is fairly simple:

1. Router D discovers that it has lost its link to 2001:db8:0:2::/64 and examines its local table for an alternate route. Finding none, it sends a query to Router C, to discover if Router C has an alternate route. Router D places the route to 2001:db8:0:2::/64 in the *active* state while it awaits the response to this query.

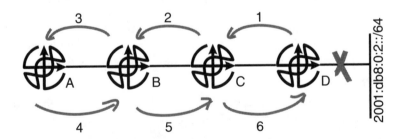

Figure 2.2 *EIGRP Convergence Processing*

1. Shivani Deshpande and Biplab Sikdar, "On the Impact of Route Processing and MRAI Timers on BGP Convergence Times," April 27, 2012, n.p., accessed July 8, 2015, http://www.ecse.rpi.edu/homepages/sikdar/papers/gbcom04s.pdf.

2. Router C receives this query and examines its local table to determine if it has an alternate route (other than through Router D). Finding none, it will then send a query to Router B, and place the route to 2001:db8:0:2::/64 into the active state while it waits for the response to this query.

3. Router B receives this query and examines its local table to determine if it has an alternate route (other than through Router C). Finding none, it will then send a query to Router A, and place the route to 2001:db8:0:2::/64 into the active state while it waits for the response to this query.

4. Router A receives this query and, finding no alternate route, nor any other neighbors that it can ask about this destination, removes the route from its local routing table and sends a reply to Router B.

5. Router B receives this reply, removes the destination from its local routing table, and sends a reply to Router C.

6. Router C receives the reply from Router B, removes the destination from its local routing table, and sends a reply to Router D.

7. Router D receives the reply from Router C and removes 2001:db8:0:2::/64 from its local routing table.

This might seem like a lot of work (and the worst possible case has intentionally been to illustrate the process from a speed of processing perspective), but each router can process the query or reply fairly rapidly, because there is little to do for each step. In fact, in typical EIGRP networks running "in the wild," the average amount of time required to converge per query hop is around 200 milliseconds.

Nonetheless, it is easy to see how the amount of state being processed could have a major impact on the time it takes to converge, and hence the stability of the network, as each router must process information about modifications in the network's topology in a serial way. Router A cannot, for instance, fully process the information it has about the loss of connection to 2001:db8:0:2::/64 until every other router within the scope of the query has already processed this information.

While each router might only need 200 milliseconds to process the topology change, a single event with hundreds or thousands of changes will cause each router in the query path to process the change for each reachable destination separately (much like BGP). Hence a large-scale change in reachability can put a good deal of stress on the processor and storage for every device impacted by the query.

Link State: OSPF and IS-IS Convergence

Link state protocols, such as OSPF and IS-IS, have a different set of convergence attributes; Figure 2.3 illustrates this process.

The steps illustrated are:

1. Router D discovers that 2001:db8:0:2::/64 is no longer reachable. In response to this change in the network topology, it will build a Link State Advertisement (LSA, for OSPF), or rebuild its Link State Protocol Data Unit (PDU; an LSP is a Link State Packet, which is similar to an LSA in OSPF), and advertise this new information toward Router C.

2. Router C, on receiving this new information, will simply forward a copy along to its neighbor, Router B, without processing the information. Router C will eventually process this information, but link state protocols typically flood first, and process later, to increase the speed at which the databases of all the devices participating in the control plane will be synchronized.

3. Router B, on receiving this new information, will simply forward a copy along to its neighbor, Router A, without processing the information.

4. At some point later in time (set by a timer within the link state protocol), Router D will run a local Shortest Path First (SPF) computation to determine what needs to be changed in the local routing table. The result will be Router D removing 2001:db8:0:2::/64 from its local routing table.

5. Shortly after Router D computes a new Shortest Path Tree (SPT), Router C will do likewise, adjusting its local routing table by removing 2001:db8:0:2::/64.

6. Shortly after Router C, Router B will perform the same computation, with the same results.

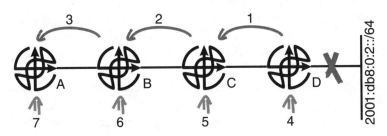

Figure 2.3 *Link State Convergence Processing*

7. Finally, Router A will perform the same computation, with the same results.

> **Note**
>
> This is a somewhat simplified view of the processing required to converge a link state control plane; more detail will be considered in the context of complexity later in this book. Readers can also look at books such as IS-IS for IP Networks[2] to understand link state processing more deeply.

In this case, the amount of state being carried in the packet impacts the processing time for a network topology change in:

- The amount of time it takes to transmit the link state information from router to router in the network. This would include serializing the packet onto the wire, clocking the packet off the wire, queuing the packet, etc. Any network topology update that requires more than one packet to flood in this way across the network will necessarily take longer. The more state required to describe the changes in the network topology, the larger the number of packets required to carry that information.

- The amount of time, processing power, and memory it takes to process the changes to the network topology will depend on the number of changes, or the amount of existing state. There are, of course, ways to optimize this processing (such as partial SPFs), almost to the point that the additional state can often only have a trivial effect on the time it takes to converge.

For link state protocols, there is still a connection between the sheer amount of state carried in the protocol and the time required for the routing protocol to converge when a change in the network topology occurs.

State

In large-scale systems, the sheer amount of state can be overwhelming—not only for the people working on the system, but also for the protocols and computer systems that must manage and process the information. Let's look at some of the reasons why the amount of state matters.

---

2. Russ White and Alvaro Retana, *IS-IS: Deployment in IP Networks*, 1st edition. (Boston: Addison-Wesley, 2003).

Amount of Information

The first of these factors is the amount of information that needs to be transferred across the network to converge.

Consider, for a moment, the amount of information contained in encapsulating a single BGP update. Based on packet format and historical information, assume that a single BGP update consumes about 1500 bytes (octets) of memory. At the time of this writing, the current full table size is over a half a million destinations, which will require at least 795MB that must be passed around between the routers in the network. This doesn't include TCP overhead, TLVs for formatting the data, and other transport requirements.

795MB of data might not seem like a lot in a world of 5GB presentations, but remember this is a distributed database running on a very large number of routers. How many? There are around 48,000 AS connected to the Internet at the time of this writing.[3] The number of BGP speakers in any given AS can be between ten and thousands; given there's no real way to know what the average number of speakers in a single AS is, let's use a conservative estimate, and call it 10 routers per AS. With these numbers, this 795MB table is being synchronized between some 480,000 devices. Doesn't sound so small now, does it?

This might all be impressive, but the average network isn't the Internet. Even so, a network of 1000 routers is keeping a multi-megabyte table synchronized across those 1000 routers in near real time—in seconds or milliseconds, rather than minutes, hours, or days.

For distance-vector protocols, the amount of information carried in the updates is also a factor, but in a different way. For instance, each parallel link in a network running a distance-vector protocol represents a completely new copy of the reachability information being carried between the two devices connected by these parallel links. These additional copies of the information can sometimes become desynchronized, or encounter other problems that cause an inconsistent view of reachability. These additional parallel links also represent potential feedback loops that can cause the network to never converge. Hence, in the example above, the network engineer might shut down parallel links to stabilize a distance-vector control plane. This can remove enough additional state from the network to allow the control plane to fully converge, bringing the network back into operation while a deeper analysis of the problems that brought the failure about can be investigated.

---

3. "Team Cymru Internet Monitor—BGP Unique ASN Count," n.p., accessed August 24, 2014, http://www.cymru.com/BGP/unique_asns.html.

The amount of information carried in link state updates impacts the operation of a link state protocol in much the same way. Not only does it take longer for the information to be flooded through the network, it also builds a bigger database across which the SPF algorithm needs to be run to construct a consistent view of the network topology. If the additional information is in nodes through which shortest paths pass, rather than just leaves along the edge of the network, the additional information can impact the speed at which SPF runs directly.

An Example of State Failure in the Real World

Most network failures are not pure "state-driven" events; there is almost always some combination of state, speed, and surface involved. There are a few, however, that are almost purely state driven, such as network meltdowns caused by a link bounce in a large-scale hub-and-spoke network. Figure 2.4 provides a basic network for discussion.

This network starts out with just a few spokes or remote sites, and grows over time. As new spokes are added, the amount of state climbs; so long as the amount of state climbs slowly, the control plane has ample opportunity to adjust to the small changes in reachability. A failure of the multipoint link at Router A, however, causes the entire distributed database to be revised at once—often overwhelming the ability of the control plane to cope. Consider the following sequence of events:

- The link at Router A fails, causing all the neighbor adjacencies to fail at the same time.

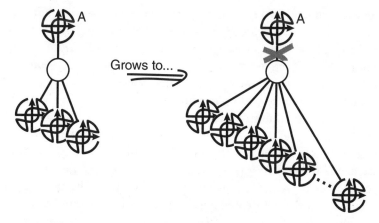

Figure 2.4 *Hub and Spoke Network Failure Example*

- The link is recovered, causing all of the routers connected to the hub and spoke network to attempt building an adjacency with Router A, the hub router.
- Some number of spoke routers successfully begin to form an adjacency with Router A.
- The spoke routers that have begun to successfully form an adjacency with Router A send their complete routing tables toward the hub to complete the formation of these adjacencies. This information overwhelms the input queue at Router A, causing hello and other adjacency formation packets to be dropped.
- These dropped packets cause the adjacency formation process to abort, restarting the cycle.

One possible way to resolve this constant attempt at forming a large number of adjacencies that cause all the adjacencies to fail, causing another round of attempting to form a large number of adjacencies in a short period of time, is to slow the process down. Start by allowing only a small number of spoke routers to form an adjacency. Once one set of adjacencies is formed successfully, allow another set of spoke routers to form an adjacency. Breaking the set of spoke routers allowed to form an adjacency into small groups controls the information flow across the network, keeping it below the level the hub router can process. Note that breaking the adjacency formation down into small groups emulates the process by which the network was built in the first place—in smaller chunks, over time.

Final Thoughts on State

If the routing protocol is viewed as a distributed, near real-time database, then the amount of time it takes for the database to converge is actually the amount of time the database is inconsistent. The example from EIGRP is particularly poignant: the EIGRP active timer is the amount of time you're willing to allow your network to remain unconverged, and hence (in the specific case of EIGRP), how long you're willing to allow packets to be dropped rather than forwarded to their final destination. BGP is similar to this, although traffic is more often routed suboptimally rather than dropped, with the expected results on jitter and delay. For a link state protocol, the amount of time the distributed database called the control plane remains inconsistent is the amount of time traffic can either be looped or dropped (depending on the type of topology change and the order of processing). State can be broken up into smaller chunks to be dealt with more efficiently, as shown in the example of the hub and spoke network failure.

Speed

The speed of change is, in most cases, actually a stronger predictor of network failure than the sheer amount of state in the system. So long as the state is relatively static, it isn't costing "on the wire" or processing on the network nodes; the static state is mostly a cost in the forwarding (or data) plane rather than in the control plane. Let's look at two examples of speed of state change having a major impact on network convergence.

The Network That Never Converges

Let's begin with a simple question: how long does it take for the global Internet to converge? In other words, if you remove a route from some random edge peering point, from an upstream provider's network, how long will it for "the rest of the Internet" to discover that this destination is no longer reachable? To make the problem simpler, let's assume that this route is removed at the edge of a tier 3 provider, rather than a tier 1 provider, so the route must propagate across four AS to be removed "everywhere" (in reality, the hop count would be longer than this because of the long tail distribution of AS hop count, but this example will stick with four hops here because it's a round number close to the average).

The convergence time question becomes, then—"how long does a BGP route take to propagate through four autonomous systems?" The answer is actually fairly simple, based on a lot of research and lab work: given no route dampening, BGP (roughly) converges based on the formula:

$$\text{Convergence} = (\text{Max AS Path Length} - \text{Min AS Path Length}) * \text{MRAI}$$

where MRAI is the minimum route advertisement interval, or the amount of time after advertising information about a particular destination before advertising more recent information about that same destination. If the route originally had an AS Path of 4 hops, and the route is now unreachable, and the MRAI is 30 seconds, then it will take, as a rule of thumb, around 2 minutes to remove the route from the global table.

What if the route is injected instead of being removed? This case deals with the time it takes for each BGP speaker—both internal and external, end to end in the entire global Internet—to receive the new routing information, process it, and then send it on to its peers. The MRAI impacts this process as illustrated in Figure 2.5.

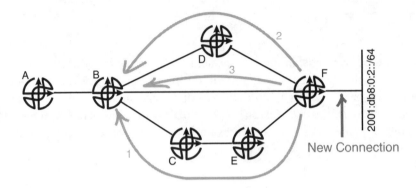

Figure 2.5 *BGP Convergence for Propagating a New Destination*

In this network, assuming the worst possible ordering of BGP advertisements, when 2001:db8:0:2::/64 is first connected to Router F:

1. Router F advertises the new destination to Router E, which then advertises this new route to Router C. Router C advertises this route to Router B, which then advertises the route to Router A. At this point, Router B sets the MRAI for this destination.

2. Router F also advertises this new destination to Router D, which then advertises the same destination to Router B. This advertisement arrives just a few moments after the advertisement from Router C, and wins the best path calculation at Router B. Router B, however, cannot advertise this new route to Router A until the MRAI timer expires. Once the MRAI timer expires, Router B advertises this shorter path to Router A.

3. Router F also advertises 2001:db8:0:2::/64 to Router B directly. This advertisement reaches Router B just moments after the MRAI timer expires, Router B has advertised the path through Router D to Router A, and has reset the MRAI timer. Router B must now wait until the MRAI timer expires (again) before it can advertise the new (and shorter) path to Router A.

This sequence of events has been observed in live networks (such as the global Internet). The MRAI, in this instance, causes the advertisement of newly reachable destinations to take minutes, rather than seconds.

Now, on the other side, how often do changes happen on the global Internet? Figure 2.6 is a chart taken from potaroo.net, a site that measures the state of the global routing table, at the time of writing.[4]

---

4. "The BGP Instability Report," n.p., accessed August 24, 2014, http://bgpupdates.potaroo.net/instability/bgpupd.html.

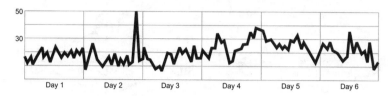

Figure 2.6 *Rate of Routing Table Change in the Global Internet*

Several observations are in order:

- The vertical axis represents the rate of change in the global *(default free zone)* Internet routing table per second. The average seems to be between 15 and 30 changes per second, with peaks that reach as high as 50 changes per second.

- The horizontal axis represents time, and is split up in this rendition of the data as occurring across days. Examining the information available across years of measurements indicates that this pattern exists across many years.

From the same data, it's apparent that the rate of convergence for any particular change in the global Internet table is measured in seconds or minutes (70 to 80 seconds would seem to be the average).

It's difficult to call a network with 15 to 50 changes per second in its routing table converged in any meaningful sense of the word. In fact, the Internet doesn't ever really converge—and it hasn't really converged in years. How, then can the Internet control plane provide reachability information reliable enough to make the Internet itself work? Why doesn't the Internet's control plane "crash," as might be expected in any normal network? Primarily the stability of the Internet's control plane is due to the relative stability of the "core," which moves most state changes to the edges of the network, and the strong division between internal and external routing information in any specific AS. This latter point is considered in the section, "Surfaces," in a few pages.

The Flapping Link

Flapping links are not as common as they used to be, particularly wide area links, but they can be devastating in their impact on convergence. Figure 2.7 illustrates a network for reference.

For each flap of the link between Routers A and B, Routers B, C, D, and E receive thousands of updates. Router F, however, consistently receives three times as many updates in the same time period—one of the many downfalls

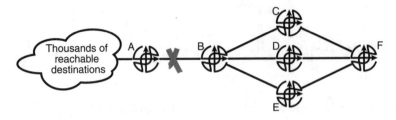

Figure 2.7 *Link Flaps and Speed-Based Network Failure*

of massively parallel topologies with distributed control planes. In real-world situations, Router F could fail in a way that prevents the network from ever converging. Depending on the configuration and scope of the failure domains in this network, Router F's failure (or even its inability to keep up with this constant flow of updated topology information) could bleed into the network beyond Router F, causing a general control plane failure.

The combination of the speed of a flapping link and parallel links that multiply the speed of topology updates can be fatal to a routing protocol.

Final Thoughts on Speed

It's not so much the speed of change that kills control planes, it's the unpredictability of the speed at which information changes combined with the amount of information changing in each time slice. The more random the rate of change, and the more random the amount of information changing, the harder it is to plan around the changes. Most network engineers, when designing a network, consider the way in which things should be interconnected, where services should be placed, and how to make things "simpler" for the human operator. What isn't often considered is the stability of the control plane; it's just a "given."

Speed is a crucial point to consider when dealing with network complexity; faster generally means more complex.

Surface

There is one more idea that mixes with the amount of state and the speed of change, either amplifying or dampening both, and hence impacting control plane stability: the surfaces across which different components or systems are interacting. Three basic concepts are involved in understanding interaction surfaces in complex systems; Figure 2.8 illustrates the first two.

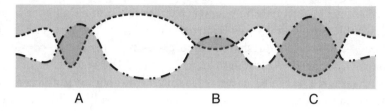

Figure 2.8 *Interaction Surfaces*

There are two basic concepts in interaction surfaces:

- **Interaction Depth.** The depth of interaction can be seen as how strongly the two systems or components interact. For instance, if one component relies on another component formatting data in a specific way, the two components must change in terms of the way that specific piece of data is formatted, in parallel. As the component that formats the data is changed, the component that needs to know how the data is formatted must also change. In the world of network architecture, this can be seen as the interaction between two different control planes, or the formatting of packets being inspected as they flow through the network. A single packet change format can cause hundreds or thousands of devices to require updates to read the new packet format correctly. Points A and C in Figure 2.8 illustrate deep interaction between the two components shown.

- **Interaction Breadth.** The number of places where two systems or components "touch" can be called the breadth of the interaction surface. The more places two systems or components interact, the more they will form a single, more complex system. In Figure 2.8, there are three points at which the two illustrated systems touch; one of these (point C) is wider than the other two, representing a number of interfaces located along a single task (or set of tasks).

A single example can be used to illustrate both concepts: two routing protocols configured on a set of routers throughout a network.

- Each protocol configured on a single router interacts with any other protocols on that same router through shared resources, such as memory and processor. Multiple protocols installed on a single router also share a common RIB (or set of RIBs), so that the removal of a route by one protocol can cause a reaction in the second protocol—perhaps advertising a replacement route, or removing reachability to a destination that was only reachable through the (now removed) destination. The first set of interactions—competition for shared resources—can generally be considered a narrowly scoped shallow interaction surface. The second set of interactions—shared and interactive reachability information through a shared RIB—can be considered a slightly broader, but still shallow, interaction surface.

- Configuring both routing protocols on every router in the network broadens the interaction surface, as there are more instances where the two protocols share processor and memory, as well as interacting through shared reachability information. This might not appear to be a large increase in complexity, but with every router in the network running both protocols, the opportunities for a single failure in either protocol to cause a large-scale outage is increased.

- Redistributing the two protocols to redistribute reachability information at one point in the network (on one router) increases the depth of interaction on that one router, increasing the complexity by some small amount.

- Redistributing the two protocols to redistribute reachability information on every router in the network increases the depth of interaction across the entire breadth of the interaction surface. This represents a large increase in the amount of complexity through the interaction surface between the two protocols.

The more the routing protocols rely on one another, or interact, the deeper the interaction surface. The more places the routing protocols interact, the broader the interaction surface.

Figure 2.9 illustrates the third basic concept involved in interaction surfaces: *overlapping interactions*.

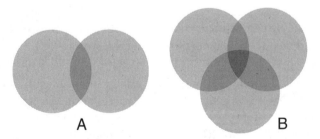

A   B

Figure 2.9 *Overlapping Interactions*

In Figure 2.9, set A illustrates two components or systems that overlap, or interact, while set B illustrates three. As more components or systems interact in a single set of interfaces, the overall system becomes more complex. An example of this in network engineering is, again, the interaction between devices that send packets and devices that process packets as they pass through the network.

- If a packet is simply forwarded based on the destination address, then each of the routers along the path is actually interacting with the sending and receiving hosts, but only in a very shallow way. Hence, the interaction overlap is high, but the depth of interaction is very shallow. The breadth of interaction would depend on the number of hops through which the packet must pass to travel from the source to the destination.

- If a packet is inspected by one device that requires state maintained between packets, and about return traffic, the interaction depth is fairly high between the sender, receiver, and control plane (as any packet format changes, or any network path changes, will need to be accounted for by the stateful packet inspection device). But if there is only one place in the network where this interaction is taking place, then there are only the three systems intersecting.

- Each point at which stateful packet inspection is added in the network increases the number of systems interacting, and hence the overlapping interactions.

The more overlapping components or systems, the more complex the overall system is.

The Hourglass Model

Complexity is necessary to provide the underlying robustness in real-world conditions—to repeat a statement by Alderson and Doyle first encountered in Chapter 1, "Defining Complexity":

> Specifically, we argue that complexity in highly organized systems arises primarily from design strategies intended to create robustness to uncertainty in their environments and component parts.[5]

---

5. David L. Alderson and John C. Doyle, "Contrasting Views of Complexity and Their Implications for Network-Centric Infrastructures," *IEEE Transactions on Systems, Man, and Cybernetics* 40, no. 4 (July 2010): 840.

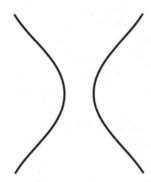

Figure 2.10 *The Hourglass Model*

Engineers are left with the problem of managing complexity. There is a simple model that is ubiquitous throughout the natural world, and is widely mimicked in the engineering world. While engineers don't often consciously apply this model, it's actually used all the time. What is this model? Figure 2.10 illustrates the hourglass model.

As an example, consider the four-layer model used so widely in the networking world. Figure 2.11 compares the commonly used four-layer model for network protocols to the hourglass model shown in Figure 2.10.

At the bottom layer, the physical transport system, there are a wide array of protocols, from Ethernet to Satellite. At the top layer, where information is marshalled and presented to applications, there are a wide array of protocols, from HTTP to TELNET (and thousands of others besides). However, a funny thing happens when you move toward the middle of the stack: the number of protocols decreases, creating an hourglass. Why does this work to control complexity? Going back through the three components of complexity—state,

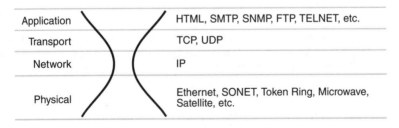

Figure 2.11 *The Hourglass Model Compared to the Four-Layer Network Model*

speed, and surface—exposes the relationship between the hourglass and complexity.

- *State* is divided by the hourglass into two distinct types of state: information about the network, and information about the data being transported across the network. While the upper layers are concerned with marshalling and presenting information in a usable way, the lower layers are concerned with discovering what connectivity exists and what the properties of that connectivity actually are. The lower layers don't need to know how to format an FTP frame, and the upper layers don't need to know how to carry a packet over Ethernet—state is reduced at both ends of the model.

- *Speed* is controlled by hiding information between layers. Just as parallel copies of the same information can be a "speed multiplier," hiding information can be a "speed reducer," or perhaps a set of brakes. If information can be handled at in one layer without involving the state of another layer, then the speed at which a new state is presented to any particular layer is reduced. For instance, an error in the data presented to an FTP client doesn't cause a change of state in the state of TCP, much less in the state of the Ethernet link.

- *Surfaces* are controlled by reducing the number of interaction points between the various components to precisely one—IP. This single interaction point can be well defined through a standard process, with changes in the one interaction point closely regulated to prevent massive rapid changes that will reflect up and down the protocol stack.

The layering of a stacked network model is, then, a direct attempt to control the complexity of the various interacting components of a network.

The Seven-Layer Model Is Dead

The seven-layer model is taught and used almost universally within the network engineering world——but its usefulness has been steadily decreasing over time. Two different problems plague the usefulness of the seven-layer model. *First,* the model is increasingly beset by the tendency to overlay protocol on top of protocol, and to avoid interaction with middle boxes by pushing ever greater amounts of information through a narrower channel. QUIC running over IPv6 running over Ethernet running over Virtual Extensible Local Area Network (VXLAN) running over IPv4 is difficult, at best, to describe using the seven-layer model; is Ethernet running on top of the VXLAN tunnel layer 2 in the model, or Layer 4? Should multiple seven-layer models be laid on top of one another to describe this situation? Is Multiprotocol Label Switching (MPLS) a Layer 2 protocol, or a Layer 3 protocol? Is it a tunnel, or not? These questions are difficult, if not impossible, to answer within the context of the seven-layer model. *Second,* to avoid deep interactions with middle boxes, many applications simply run over ports known to be "open" for most security devices and/or services. For instance, a large amount of the traffic crossing the Internet is passed through the HTTP protocol, using TCP port 80, even though the application may not be a website.

Both of these problems can be traced back to two sources. *First,* the seven-layer model overspecifies the data transport problem space. Rather than focusing purely on functionality, the seven-layer model also tries to carry in interaction points and locality. Layer 1 is not only a set of functionality, but also a location—a single physical link. Layer 3 is not only a set of functionality, but also a location—end-to-end (in theory). *Second,* the seven-layer model was really designed for a specific set of transport protocols—protocols that are no longer in wide use. Instead, the seven-layer model is used to describe a four-layer protocol stack, the TCP/IP suite of protocols.

Should engineers simply abandon network models, then? No—a better idea would be to rethink the set of models engineers use to describe the network. Rather than focusing on a host, or network device, centric view of the network transport system, it is better to break the system up using multiple models. One model can be used to describe transport, another to describe network devices, a third used to describe a host's interaction with the network, and a fourth used to describe the various types of control planes used to provide reachability information throughout the network. For transport models, a better focus would be the functions needed to provide a set of services, with iterative layers used at each locality. This would be more descriptive of the problems being brought to bear to solve specific problems in each case.

For more information on network models, see Chapter 4, "Models," in the Cisco Press title, *The Art of Network Architecture.*

Optimization

While state, speed, and surface will be used to describe complexity throughout this book, there is a fourth component engineers often need to take into account—optimization. Quite often, complexity is a tradeoff against optimization; increasing

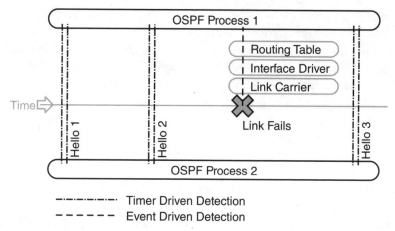

Figure 2.12 *Timer- and Event-Driven Detection*

complexity increases the optimization of the network, and reducing complexity reduces the optimization of the network. An illustration of this principle can be found in examining the choice between event-driven reactions and timer-driven reactions to changes in the network. Figure 2.12 illustrates timer- and event-driven detection.

In Figure 2.12, a timeline is shown from left to right. Over time, two OSPF processes are exchanging periodic hello packets—a classic example of a timer-driven detection system. If the link between the two OSPF processes fails, the two processes will recognize the failure through a loss of three hello packets, causing the adjacency to fail and the routes learned through the lost neighbor to be removed from the local database and routing table. A second detection process is also shown through the link carrier, interface driver, routing table, and into OSPF Process 1. This is an event-driven detection chain:

- If the link fails, carrier detection on the physical interface will fail. This will cause the physical interface to signal the interface driver that the failure has occurred.

- When the interface driver is notified, it will then signal the routing subsystem, which will remove any routes reachable through the now failed interface from any impacted RIB.

- When the RIB removes the effected routes, including the connected interface route, it will signal OSPF Process 1 of the failure. This will cause the OSPF process to remove any neighbors reachable through that interface from its local tables, and any link state database entries learned from this neighbor from its local tables.

Event-driven detection is more complex in this example, as the event must pass through multiple interfaces to reach OSPF Process 1. Each of these interfaces implies an interaction surface that must be managed; this interaction surface may, in fact, be deep, as the OSPF process may need to react differently depending on the link type, the type of failure, or other information provided from the lower layers. Event-driven detection also increases the speed of state change in the control plane; each link flap may be individually recorded in the OSPF process running over the link, and these flaps could well be transmitted throughout the control plane in the form of topology updates. The timer-based system is much simpler; the OSPF processes don't have a lot of knowledge about the underlying network being used to transport the hello packets, and the state of the adjacency is changed only at fixed intervals, dampening any potential feedback loops, and slowing down the rate of change in the control plane (speed).

The optimization tradeoff should be clear in this example, as well. The event-driven detection process will discover the downlink much faster, allowing the control plane to react to the failure by routing around the link—for instance—very quickly. This reduces the Mean Time to Repair (MTTR), and hence increases the overall network availability. In this case, then, the more complex event-driven process increases optimization, while opting for reduced complexity also incurs a reduction in network optimization.

It isn't always going to be the case that increasing optimization will require increasing complexity, or attempts to reduce complexity will always decrease optimization—but it is quite common. Examples of this tradeoff are scattered throughout this book.

A Final Thought

State, speed, and surface, and optimization—if you can get your thinking around these four components, you can get a solid grip on the problems involved in network complexity. Networks that never truly converge are becoming the norm rather than the exception; the traditional models are breaking down. The hourglass model provides a way forward through the complexity morass, if engineers can learn how to recognize complexity and manage it in all the various pieces of the network engineering puzzle.

Chapter 3

Measuring Network Complexity

Given these four fundamental aspects of complexity—state, speed, surface, and optimization—it only makes sense to measure these four points and generate a single number describing the overall complexity of a given design and deployment structure. It would be nice if there were some way to examine a proposed network design, or a proposed change to a network design, and be able to assign actual numbers to the complexity of each component so the complexity can be compared to any potential gain in performance, or the loss of complexity in one area can be compared to the gain in complexity in another. If it were only that simple.

As it turns out, the effort to measure complexity is, itself, quite complex.

Two problems rise to the surface when examining the problem of measuring and quantifying a network toward gaining an understanding of the overall system complexity. *First,* there is the sheer amount of information available. Given the current push toward big data analytics, and the ability to measure thousands to millions of interactions and data mining to discover important trends and artifacts, shouldn't something the size of an average network be an easy problem? Consider some of the various points of measurement just in trying to understand the interaction between the data flowing through each point in the network and the queuing mechanisms used to handle that traffic. This might include things such as:

- The amount of data flowing through each point in the network, including the input and output queue of each forwarding device.
- The depth and state of each queue of each forwarding device in the network.

- The source, destination, and other header information of each packet for-warded through the network.

- The number of packets dropped by each forwarding device, including the reason why they were dropped (tail drop, packet error, filtered, filtering rule, etc.).

Considering that the measurements themselves must pass through the network—and the measurements can easily contain more traffic than the measured traffic—the problems with measuring everything should quickly become apparent. How can you separate the measurement from the measured if the measurement is being carried on the same channel as what you are measuring? Added to this challenge are the states of each individual control plane system, and the components of those systems—things like the memory and processor utilization of each forwarding device, the state of each adjacency between each pair of devices participating in the control plane, and the flow of each reachability advertisement within the control plane. To make measuring the system complexity even more complex, the interactions between the systems must also somehow be taken into account—things like the impact of reachability information on the distribution and application of policy, any interdependencies between parallel control planes in terms of reachability information and system resources, and interactions between overlay and underlay control planes. Measuring not only the systems but also the interactions between the systems quickly becomes an intractable problem.

When measuring a system to understand its complexity level, some sort of sampling must take place. Sampling necessarily means that some information must be left out—which, in turn, means that any measurement of complexity along these lines is necessarily an abstract representation of the complexity, rather than a measure of the complexity itself.

To top all of this complexity off, there is very little agreement on the set of things to measure to create even an accurate abstract representation of the com-plexity of a network.

There is a second problem looming on the horizon just past this first one—a problem that's not so obvious, and actually makes the problem of measuring network complexity intractable. Network design represents ordered (or inten-tional or organized—these three terms are often used interchangeably) complex-ity, rather than unordered complexity. While data analytics deals with unordered data well enough, ordered complexity is an entirely different problem set.

Let's begin by examining some methods proposed to measure network com-plexity, and then consider ordered versus unordered complexity. Finally, several realms of complexity will be examined that will lead to practical applications.

Some Measures of Network Complexity

The difficulty of the task hasn't stopped researchers from attempting to measure network complexity. Quite the opposite—there are a number of methods that have been tried over the years. Each of these methods has contributed useful thinking to the problem space, and can actually be used to provide some insight into what network complexity looks like. Overall, though, none of these measurements will truly provide a complete view of the complexity of a network.

Let's look at three examples of network complexity measurements to get a feel for the space.

Network Complexity Index

The Network Complexity Index is described in "A Network Complexity Index for Networks of Networks"[1] by Bailey and Grossman (commonly called the NCI). The general idea is to tackle describing network complexity in two steps:

- Break the network down into subnetworks. As described in the original paper:

  Given a network N, we first divide the network into smaller sub-networks C[1], . . ., C[j], . . ., C[p] with the property that two nodes selected at random from the sub-network C[i] are more likely to be connected to each other than two nodes selected at random from outside the sub-network (N\C).

- Compute the complexity based on the size and number of the subnetworks. Again, as described in the original paper:

  Given the sub-communities of the network N, let X[j] denote the size of the j largest sub-community, so that the sequence X[1], . . . , X[p] is in decreasing order. In general, different communities may have the same size. We define the network complexity index B(N) of the network N as the solution of the following equation: B(N) = Max j, X[j] j

The equation given is a standard statistic used in evaluating the importance of scientific research known as the H-index. The H-index determines the impact of

---

1. Stewart Bailey and Robert L. Grossman, "A Network Complexity Index for Networks of Networks" (Infoblox, 2013), n.p., https://web.archive.org/web/20131001093751/http://flowforwarding.org/docs/Bailey%20-%20Grossman%20article%20on%20network%20complexity.pdf.

a particular piece of research by evaluating the number of citations of the work in a way that is similar to a web page search index using the number of links to a page to determine the importance or relevance of that page.

Seen this way, the NCI attempts to combine the connectivity within a network with the number of nodes within a network:

- The more the subcommunities, the more connection points there must be between these subcommunities, and hence the more complex the connection graph must be.

- The larger the subcommunities, the more nodes there are within the network; this again impacts the implied connectivity graph of the network

The size and scope of the connectivity graph, in turn, impacts the way information flows within the network, which also relates to the complexity of the network.

What the NCI Does Well

The NCI does a good job of producing a single number that describes the size and shape of a network in terms of nodes and communities, in turn implying the scope and complexity of the network interconnections. This single number, computed over time, can help network managers and designers understand the growth of a network in terms other than sheer size.

What the NCI Doesn't Do

From a network engineer's perspective, there are several practical problems with using the NCI as a single measure of network complexity. *First,* this isn't something you're going to compute on a napkin while you're eating dinner, or do rough calculations in your head around.[2] This is a math heavy computation that requires automated tools to compute. *Second,* other than measuring the growth and interconnectedness of a topology, it's hard to see how and where the NCI is useful in the real world. There's no obvious way to reduce network complexity as measured by the NCI other than reducing the number and size of the subcommunities in the network.

This second objection, however, leads to another shortcoming of the NCI: it doesn't really measure the complexity network operators interact with. It's quite

---

2. In fact, an entire project called Tapestry was built around measuring the NCI by gathering configurations automatically and running them through a processor. The project can be found on GitHub at https://github.com/FlowForwarding/tapestry.

common, in the real world, to find very large networks supporting only a few workloads that have been heavily optimized for that workload, and hence are not very complex from an engineer's point of view. It's also quite common, in the real world, to find small networks with a very diverse workload, and hence cannot be optimized for a single workload. These networks are more complex than their size indicates—the NCI would likely underestimate the complexity of these networks.

So what does the NCI miss? Just those pieces of network architecture that designers deal with most of the time, such as:

- Policy, expressed through configuration, metrics, protocols, and other methods
- Resilience, expressed through the amount of redundancy, fast convergence mechanisms, and other highly complex design components

So while the NCI is useful, it doesn't capture all the complexity of a single network in a way that can be usefully applied to real-world networks.

Modeling Design Complexity

In a set of slides presented to the Internet Research Task Force's Network Complexity Research Group, a group of researchers described a model for measuring and describing the complexity of enterprise routing design.[3] The process of measurement is as follows:

1. Decompose the network design into individual pieces, implemented as individual configuration components (across all devices in the network).

2. Build a network of connections between these individual components.

3. Measure this network to determine the complexity of the configuration.

Figure 3.1 is taken from these slides,[4] illustrating the linkages between the various configuration components.

---

3. Xin Sun, Sanjay G. Rao, and G.Xie Geoffrey, "Modeling Complexity of Enterprise Routing Design" (IRTF NCRG, November 5, 2012), n.p., accessed October 5, 2014, http://www.ietf.org/proceedings/85/slides/slides-85-ncrg-0.pdf.

4. Ibid.

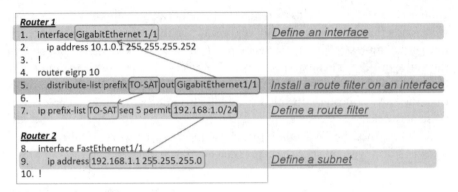

Figure 3.1 *Evaluating Linkages in a Network Configuration*

The more items configured, and the more dense the interconnection between the configurations (particularly between boxes), the more complex the design is determined to be. By examining these factors, the process yields a single number describing the complexity of the design. The presentation and the papers written by the same authors extend this concept to determining if the implemented design matches the design intent, given the design intent is stated in a way amenable to the process.

What Modeling Design Complexity Does Well

The concept of measuring not just the lines of configuration, but the interconnections between the lines of configuration, is extremely powerful. There is little doubt that much of complexity comes from the interrelated configurations spread throughout a network required to implement a single policy or to make a single protocol or process work. Looking at the interactions, or network of configurations, also takes the number of lines of configuration somewhat out of the picture as a measure of complexity. Because some devices can express a policy in a few simple lines, while others require a lot of configuration to express the same policy, this is a useful outcome.

What Modeling Design Complexity Doesn't Do

At the same time, however, the interconnections between lines of configuration can fall prey to the same problems just counting the number of lines of configuration can fall prey to—an entire policy might be represented by a single line of configuration on one device, while requiring a number of lines of policy on another. For instance, on Cisco IOS Software, the command *remove-private-as* is used to remove any private AS numbers in a BGP route advertisement. This single command essentially replaces a set of configuration commands that would necessarily be interconnected, such as a filter and an application of that filter to a particular set of BGP peers. Both configurations are valid and perform the same set of actions, but they would appear to have completely different complexity levels according to the measure as it's described. Further complicating the situation, different BGP implementations might use different sets of command to perform the same action, making one configuration appear more complex than another, although they're both implementing the same policy.

Another failing of the measure described above is that it's not always obvious what pieces fit together to make a policy. For instance, a configuration removing private AS numbers on every eBGP speaker in an AS might not appear to be related within the measurement; there is no specific point at which these multiple configurations overlap or interact in a way that's obvious, *unless you know the intent of the configuration*. Thus some policies might easily be missed as they consist of configurations with no obvious point at which they tie together.

Finally, it's difficult to assess how a single configuration used to implement multiple policies would be managed in this measure of network complexity— and yet, this is one of the thorniest problems to manage from a complexity standpoint, as this is precisely one of those difficult to manage interaction surfaces between otherwise unrelated policy implementations. How do the various policies measured interact? On this point, modeling design complexity is silent.

NetComplex

As previously discussed, the NCI measures complexity based on scale and perceived subcomponents; modeling design rates complexity on the network of interconnected lines of configuration. What about measuring complexity based on the amount of work needed to keep the distributed database that represents the network topology synchronized across all the devices participating in the control plane? This is precisely what NetComplex does. As Chun, Ratnasamy, and Kohler state:

> We conjecture that the complexity particular to networked systems arises from the need to ensure state is kept in sync with its distributed dependencies. The metric we develop in this paper reflects this viewpoint and we illustrate several systems for which this dependency centric approach appears to appropriately reflect system complexity.[5]

---

5. Byung-Gon Chun, Sylvia Ratnasamy, and Eddie Kohler, "NetComplex: A Complexity Metric for Networked System Designs" (5th Usenix Symposium on Networked Systems Design and Implementation NSDI 2008, April 2008), n.p., accessed October 5, 2014, http://berkeley.intel-research.net/sylvia/netcomp.pdf.

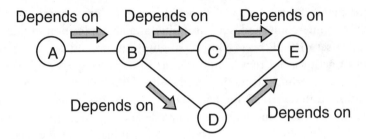

Figure 3.2 *Dependency and Complexity in NetComplex*

NetComplex evaluates the chain of dependent states in the network, assigns a metric to each dependency, and then calculates a single complexity measure based on these assigned metrics. Figure 3.2 illustrates dependency and complexity in NetComplex.

In this figure:

- Routers C and D depend on E to obtain a correct view of the network beyond Router E.

- Router B depends on Routers C, D, and E to obtain a correct view of the network beyond Router E.

- Router A depends on Routers B, C, D, and E to obtain a correct view of the network beyond Router E.

Hence, Router A "accumulates" the complexity of synchronization of information originating beyond E through the entire network. Through these dependencies, Router A is said to be linked to the remaining routers in the network. By examining these links, and combining them with the local state, the complexity of keeping the entire control plane synchronized can be given a single metric.

What NetComplex Does Well

By focusing on the amount of state and the way state is carried through the network, NetComplex does a good job of describing the complexity of a control plane. Based on this, NetComplex is useful for determining the additional complexity required to carry source routing information through the network, and forward based on this source routing information. Another place where Netcomplex would be useful is in putting a metric on the additional state information required to forward traffic on a per flow, rather than per destination/virtual topology basis.

What NetComplex Doesn't Do

NetComplex, however, is focused on the control plane within a single adminis-trative or failure domain. There is no way, for instance, to account for the infor-mation hidden through route aggregation, nor to differentiate between topology information and reachability (such as what happens at a link state flooding domain boundary). NetComplex doesn't work with policies, nor policy imple-mentation; nor does it deal with traffic flows, subnetwork scale, or network density.

Organized Complexity

Three different measures of network complexity have been examined at this point: NCI, modeling design complexity, and NetComplex. Each of these attempts to measure, in some way, at least some component of the four realms of network complexity—state, speed, surface, and optimization. None of them, however, measure everything in any one of these three domains, and none of them even come close to measuring overall network complexity. Why? The problem isn't just the ability to measure and process all the information needed to produce a single complexity number, it's embedded in the problem of network complexity itself.

Imagine, for a moment, a pool table with a set of balls on it. These specific balls are (at least nearly) perfect in their resilience, so they lose only infinitely small amounts of energy when they strike another object, and the bumpers on the sides of the table are designed in much the same way. There are no pockets in this table, either, so there is no place for the balls to leave the table. Now, place the balls on the table in some random distribution, and then strike one so it starts a chain reaction. The result will be a statistically random set of movements, each ball moving about the table, striking another ball or a bumper, retaining most of its energy, and then moving in a straight line in some other direction.

This particular problem is ripe for statistical regression analysis, or any other form of analysis data science can provide. The data scientist can tell you, based on a set of derived formulas, how often one ball will strike another, how long the system will take to run out of energy, what patterns will form in the ran-domly moving balls at what time—and many other things. Data science excels at finding patterns in seemingly random bits of data. In fact, it is often found that the data set must be larger to make an accurate prediction; the larger the data set, the more accurate characterization of it can be made, and the more accurate the predictions about the state of that data at some specific point in the future will be.

But let's change the situation somewhat. Let's take the same pool table, the same balls—all the same physical conditions. Only this time, someone has pre-planned the position and movement of every ball such that no two balls strike one another, even though they are all in motion. In fact, the movement of every ball is identical throughout the entire time the balls are in motion.

What can data science tell us about this particular situation? *Nothing.*

Simple observation can tell us which ball will be where at any point in time. Simple observation might even be able to provide a formula telling us where there will be clumps of balls on the table, or near misses. But statistical analysis cannot go much beyond a few simple facts here. What's more interesting is that statistical analysis cannot tell us what the point is in having these balls arranged just this way.

This is the problem of *organized complexity.*

As Warren Weaver noted in 1948:

> *This new method of dealing with disorganized complexity, so powerful an advance over the earlier two-variable methods, leaves a great field untouched. One is tempted to oversimplify, and say that scientific methodology went from one extreme to the other—from two variables to an astronomical number—and left untouched a great middle region. The importance of this middle region, moreover, does not depend primarily on the fact that the number of variables involved is moderate— large compared to two, but small compared to the number of atoms in a pinch of salt. The problems in this middle region, in fact, will often involve a considerable number of variables. The really important characteristic of the problems of this middle region, which science has as yet little explored or conquered, lies in the fact that these problems, as contrasted with the disorganized situations with which statistics can cope, show the essential feature of organization. In fact, one can refer to this group of problems as those of organized complexity.*[6]

This field of organized complexity exactly describes the situation engineers face in looking at computer networks. No matter what angle a computer network is approached from, the problem is both complex and organized.

- Protocols are designed with a specific set of goals in mind, a specific mind-set about how the problems approached should be solved, and a set of tradeoffs between current optimal use, future flexibility, supportability, and ease of implementation.

- Applications that run on top of a network are designed with a specific set of goals in mind.

---

6. Warren Weaver, "Science and Complexity," *American Scientist* 36 (1948): 539.

- Control planes that provide the metadata that make a computer network work are designed with a specific set of goals in mind.

- Protocols that carry information through the network, at every level, are designed with a specific set of goals in mind.

No matter which system within computer network is considered—from protocols to design to applications to metadata—each one was designed with a specific set of goals, a specific mindset about how to solve the problems at hand, and a specific set of tradeoffs. Some of these might be implicit, rather than explicit, but they are, nonetheless, intentional goals or targets.

A network is not just a single system that exhibits organized complexity, but a lot of different interlocking systems, each of which exhibits organized complexity, and all of which combined exhibit a set of goals as well (perhaps a more ephemeral set of goals, such as "making the business grow," but a set of goals nonetheless).

A Philosophical Aside

Within the realm of philosophy, there are those who believe that there is no such thing as organized complexity. Instead, what appears to be organized complexity is simply the result of emergence within any physical system once it becomes complex enough—that organization is somehow "built in" to the natural order, or into the way matter itself is formed and interacts. This school of thought believes that any and all actions can be traced back to some physical cause (for instance, that humans do not actually make decisions as much as decisions happen to humans). Whatever the reader's stand on this topic (and it is outside the scope of this book to argue the philosophical questions here), the practical result, in terms of network architecture, is: it doesn't matter. Networks are designed by people to solve a particular set of problems; no matter what is "behind" these designs, we must, to understand computer networks and their designs, get to the "why." Why did someone design this in this particular way? Why did someone make that particular tradeoff?

Network complexity, then, cannot simply be measured, computed, and "solved," in the traditional sense. Even everything could be measured in a single network, and even if all the information gathered through such measurement could be processed in a way that made some sense, it would still not be possible to fully express the complexity of a computer network in all its myriad parts—in essence because there is no way to measure or express intent.

Is This a Waste of Time?

None of this means it is wasting time to attempt to measure network complexity. What it does mean, however, is that the problem must be approached with a large dose of humility. Engineers need to be very careful about understanding the tradeoffs being made in every part of the design, and very intentional in remembering that there are limits to accurately predicting the outcome of any particular design decision.

Instead of "giving up," engineers should do everything possible to understand the complexity, to contain it, to minimize it, and to make intelligent tradeoffs—but there isn't, and won't ever be a silver bullet for complexity. As explained in Chapter 1, "Defining Complexity," there are sets of three out of which only two can be chosen, and there are curves where increasing complexity in one axis to solve a particular problem actually causes problems in another axis.

Measuring and managing complexity is not wasting time unless you believe you can actually *solve the problem*—because the "problem" cannot be "solved."

A Final Thought

This investigation of complexity has so far concluded:

- Complexity is necessary to solve difficult problems, particularly in the area of robust design.
- Complexity beyond a certain level actually causes brittleness—robust yet fragile.
- Complexity is difficult (or perhaps impossible) to measure in any meaningful way at the systemic level.
- There are a number of classes of problems where it is impossible to resolve for more than two of three goals (such as fast, cheap, high quality).

Given this set of points, it might seem like this is the end of the road. Network engineers are reliant on something that cannot be effectively measured—and measurement is always the first step in controlling and managing a problem set. There will never, in the end, be a single number or formula that can describe network complexity. Should we simply put on our pirate hats and proclaim, "Abandon hope all ye who enter here"? Or is there some way out of this corner?

There is, in fact, a reasonable way to approach complexity in the real world. Rather than trying to find an absolute "measure of complexity," or find some algorithm that will "solve" complexity, it's possible to construct a heuristic, or a method of looking at the problem set that will enable a path to a solution. The heuristic, in this case, is a two-part process.

First, expose the complexity tradeoffs inherent in network design. Exposing these tradeoffs will help engineers make intelligent choices about what is being gained, and what is being lost, when choosing any particular solution to a particular problem set. Every problem cannot be solved equally well; any solution applied at one point will increase complexity somewhere else.

To put it in other terms, network *engineers need to learn to be intentional about complexity.*

The next chapter will begin looking at three specific realms of complexity—operational, design, and protocol. In each of these cases, several places where designers must make tradeoffs to illustrate the process of bringing complexity out into the open will be considered. The closer engineers get to making intentional decisions about complexity when designing and managing networks, the more likely meeting the real-world demands placed on networks will be possible.

Chapter 4

Operational Complexity

This chapter addresses operational complexity in two stages. The first section explores the problem space; the second considers the various solutions, how they address the complexity issues, and tradeoffs involved in each one. While these sections will not be exhaustive, they will provide an overview of where to look for complexity in operations, and case studies of how to think through the various solutions available.

Exploring the Problem Space

This section considers two larger topics, each with two more specific use cases or areas of investigation. The first is the cost of human interaction with the network as a system. The interaction between people and the network reaches beyond the simple user interface piece of the puzzle, and into the way in which engineers can understand the network through a set of mental models, protocol operations, business and policy concepts, and other areas. Policy, in particular, comes to the fore in the second topic, an area rarely considered in network design, policy dispersion versus optimal traffic flow through the network.

The examples here are not an "end all, be all," description of the various sets of problems in this space, but rather an attempt to describe a minimal set of use cases that describe the space adequately.

The Cost of Human Interaction with the System

Humans interact with networks through a number of different workflows, including design, deployment, management, and troubleshooting. While each of these workflows is intended to result in one thing—the deployment of a new service or application on the network—they all must actually be completed through interaction with a large number of devices scattered throughout the network. A number of key principles can be inferred:

1. The number of devices that need to be touched by a human to perform an outcome correlates to the operational complexity of that network.

2. This operational complexity directly translates into Operational Expenditures (OPEX).

3. Reducing the operational complexity will result in leaner, more productive, higher Return on Investment (ROI) networks.

4. The number of devices affecting operational complexity includes both devices directly "touched" and devices "referenced" (as for example in a policy definition).

It will be useful to dive deeper into a couple of key cases to understand the root cause of this operational complexity that has the symptom of increased number of human interaction times.

Applying a Policy in the Network

For the first use case, consider an operator implementing a policy across all the edge devices in a network. The simplest way to understand this problem is to consider that the operator must touch each of the devices along the network edge. There are (at least) four major problems with such an approach to deploying this new policy manually:

- To deploy the new policy manually, the operator would need to touch each edge device in the network—potentially thousands of them. This could take thousands of hours of network engineering work, time that engineers could be thinking about more productive things, like the next wave of new equipment or design challenges.

- Over the time required to deploy this new policy, requirements (and hence the policy) could change. This isn't always an obvious result, but there are real-life situations in which multiple rollouts of new policies (or other network changes) were stopped midstream to manage the "tyranny of the immediate," and then never finished. The result is a network with a mishmash of policies deployed in a seemingly random fashion throughout the network.

- Even if the new policy is fully deployed over some period of time, the network will be in an inconsistent state during the deployment. This can make it difficult to troubleshoot network failures, lead to conflicting policies causing positive harm (such as the release of confidential information about customers), and cause many other unintended side effects.

- It's common enough for humans to make a mistake when configuring a large number of devices over a long period of time. The amount of time between mistakes woven into the configuration of network devices causing a network outage can be called the Mean Time Between Mistakes (MTBM). The MTBM can, just like the MTBF and MTTR, be tracked and managed—but manually configuring devices on a large scale will always result in mistakes creeping into configurations over time.

The Complexity of Large-Scale Manual Deployments

The scale of applying a policy, or some other new configuration, within large-scale network can be daunting—as an example, consider the following situation. A large enterprise has, over a number of years, attempted to convert from one routing protocol (IGRP) to another (EIGRP) on a locally contained campus network. However, this campus network is extremely dense; while it contains only around a hundred routers, it also happens to contain about a thousand low-speed links interconnecting those routers. Some parts of the network are traditional circuits (such as T1s), others are Frame Relay, while others are switched Token Ring segments, and still others are short-run Ethernet segments.

As IGRP and EIGRP aren't as well known as they once were, it's important to note a singular point: when EIGRP and IGRP processes are configured on a single router with the same autonomous system number, the two processes automatically redistribute between themselves, converting the metrics and other information between the two protocols such that all the routes redistributed appear to be internally learned. When the network engineering group first attempted to switch between the two protocols, they used this feature by simply configuring a number of routers with EIGRP and IGRP in the same AS.

At some point in this process, the network crashed. On recovering, the network engineering team left the network in the half-deployed state, with part of the network running both EIGRP and IGRP in the same AS. At this point, they decided to try a different path to conversion, configuring EIGRP alongside and intermingled with IGRP on a different set of routers, in different AS, and manually redistributing between them.

Again, at some point in *this* process (the second conversion attempt), the network crashed. On recovering, the network engineering team again left the network in the half-deployed state. Now all the routers are running IGRP in a single AS, some of the routers are configured with a different EIGRP AS on top of IGRP, and some other set of routers are configured with EIGRP in the same AS. In a final attempt to convert the network, the network engineering staff removed IGRP from yet another set of routers in the network, replacing it with EIGRP in a completely different AS from that deployed anyplace else in the network during short interval planned outages. Along the border between the EIGRP and IGRP sections of the network, they configured redistribution between the two protocols to maintain reachability during the conversion process.

Again, the network failed; the control plane simply would not converge. At this point things were dire. There were four sections in the network, one running IGRP, another running EIGRP alongside IGRP (routing across the same links for the same destinations) in the same AS, another running EIGRP alongside IGRP in a different AS, and another running EIGRP in a completely different AS with mutual redistribution. To add to the confusion (as if this weren't enough), the original network plan was laid out with multiple IGRP AS, each mutually redistributed into one another, rather than a single IGRP AS. At some point, the network ended up with each router having a close to unique configuration—because of three failed attempts to deploy a new, consistent routing protocol throughout.

The solution? Telnetting hop-by-hop through the network, a group of engineers removed every routing process on every router in the network. Once all dynamic routing had been removed, the network was rebuilt, again using Telnet hop-by-hop, configuring EIGRP in a single, common, AS throughout the entire network.

The lesson is this: manual deployments at scale are hard. When the deployment hits the wall and the network fails, suddenly the tyranny of the immediate kicks in. The doors must open, and the business must bring in revenue, so the network is stabilized enough to get mission critical applications running again, and the attempt is abandoned for a few more days (which can easily turn into months and years). The end result is often a mess of failed deployments, difficult to manage and impossible to troubleshoot. Sometimes the only solution is simply to "start over."

Troubleshooting a Network

A second use case of interest is troubleshooting a network failure, which directly impacts one of the measures of network availability, the MTTR. The process of troubleshooting a large-scale system is often as much an art as it is an engineering skill, including multiple phases or areas of work:

- Problem identification, which normally involves some form of half splitting and comparison of expected (or ideal) state with actual state. Identifying the problem often consumes more than half the troubleshooting process (it's not knowing what to strike with the hammer, it's knowing where to strike it that matters).

- Problem remediation, which normally involves replacing or reconfiguring the device. Often this is undertaken in a way that provides a temporary, rather than permanent, fix. Note that while a temporary fix is in place, the network is subject to the same problems described above in the policy deployment scenario—if the tyranny of the immediate takes over, and the temporary fix is never replaced or verified, the network can build up a "layer of fixes" or technical debt that causes a large number of problems later on.

- Root cause analysis, which normally involves taking a deeper look at the problem symptoms, the temporary fix, and any further information gathered off the network to go deeper than "this is the problem." Root cause analysis looks for when changes that caused problems were made, and why any change management process didn't catch the error. The point of root cause analysis is to verify that the temp fix is the correct solution or replace it with a more permanent solution, and to try and ensure the problem doesn't occur again in the future.

Where to Strike: The Apocryphal Story of the Engineer and the Hammer

For readers unfamiliar with the apocryphal story of the engineer and the hammer from the first bullet point above, one form is repeated here. There was once an engineer who worked on a particular piece of machinery for twenty years, and then decided to retire. The machine worked without him fine for some time, but then one day developed some sort of problem no one could diagnose or repair. Many top experts were brought in, until finally the company gave up and hired the retiree back in as a consultant. On arriving at the site, he listened for a moment to the noise the machine was making, picked up a hammer, and whacked it once. The noise went away, and the machine began operating properly. A few days later the company received a bill for $10,000. The accounting department objects, sending him an email stating they need to understand how picking up a hammer to hit the machine is really worth this amount of money. The retiree sends back a new bill, this time itemized. It says, "$1: hitting machine with hammer. $9,999: knowing where to hit machine with hammer."

Several points come into play when troubleshooting a network problem in regard to complexity, including:

- The number of devices the operator must touch to troubleshoot the problem. This is similar in scope and concept as the number of devices the operator must touch to deploy a policy.

- The number of places measurements can be taken in the network, and how difficult it is to take those measurements.

- The amount of information available to define what the network normally looks like, and hence answer the question, "what's changed?"

To put these into perspective, consider a specific use case. Consider a flat IP network in which a source node loses connectivity to a destination node. In this example, assume there are a few devices between source and destination. The engineer tasked with troubleshooting this problem could potentially access each device (say by accessing each device hop-by-hop through the routers along the path through which the traffic should travel, starting with the default gateway) and issue a number of commands to understand the node's state and determine which of the nodes in the path is causing the outage. As the network grows in scale and complexity, the path through the network becomes harder to trace, and the number of devices to hop through may become close to impossible in real time (as the error is occurring). If the network grows beyond a single administration domain, gathering information from each device along the path may become impossible due to access restrictions. The larger and more complex the network is, the more difficult it will be to troubleshoot using manual methods.

Policy Dispersion Versus Optimal Traffic Handling

Network designers don't often think about the relationship between control plane complexity and optimal utilization, but there is a clear link through the concept of policy dispersion. Policy dispersion is nothing more than one of the

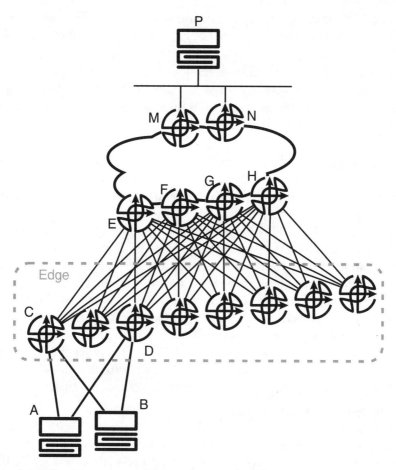

Figure 4.1 *Policy Dispersion and Optimal Network Utilization*

costs involved in the human interaction with the network, as outlined in the pre-vious section—the number of devices that require configuration to implement a specific policy. A specific example will help in understanding the scope of the problem. Use the network in Figure 4.1 for this example.

Assume three sets of policies need to be applied to incoming traffic:

- A quality of service policy classifying large file transfers originating from Host A so these flows are placed into a lower classification queue along the path.

- A quality of service policy classifying smaller file transfers originating from Host B so these flows are placed in a medium priority queue along the path.

- A quality of service policy classifying voice traffic originating from any host connected to any router in the "Edge" box into a high priority queue.

The concern here is not with how these policies might be implemented, but where they might be implemented—and the tradeoffs involved in deciding where to implement them. There are three places these policies can be implemented in the network illustrated:

- The most natural place to deploy these policies would be along the edge of the network, (Routers C and D in the example), and potentially all the other devices at the same level in the hierarchy. This design has the advantage of enforcing the policy on the links between the edge devices and Routers E, F, G, and H (and the rest of the network), so traffic is handled optimally all along the path. The disadvantage of this solution is the configuration of the edge routers becomes more complex as additional configuration is added to implement the policy—and there are (potentially) a large number of edge devices (in this case there are only ten, but in large-scale networks there could be many thousands). The number of devices on which the policy must be configured can be traded off against the uniformity of the configuration for all edge devices throughout the network, of course, but this doesn't "solve" the complexity problem, it just moves the complexity from one place to another in the operational chain.

- The first alternative would be to implement these policies at Routers E, F, G, and H. In this case, the number of routers across which the policies must be synchronized is much smaller, but the links between the edge routers and these four routers will not be used optimally by the traffic flows being generated by the hosts. The tradeoff is there are only four routers on which the policies must be implemented and maintained—making the implementation and synchronization of policies easier.

- The second alternative would be to implement these policies at Routers M and N, so they primarily control the traffic flowing along the Ethernet link connecting the destination host to the network. This increases the length of each path that will be used suboptimally, and also decreases the number of devices on which the policies must be configured and managed.

The answer, in this case, might appear to be simple—configure the policies along the edge of the network. In larger networks with a number of edge modules, however, the choice becomes more complicated.

If there are thousands of edge devices, and each edge device is configured with the same policies to ensure consistency of application and configuration, as well as optimal network usage throughout the network, how many devices must have synchronized configurations, and what is the cost of a mistake? If every edge device is configured with just the policy it needs, then what is the cost of maintaining a thousand different configurations, and what is the cost of a mistake?

Which specific areas of the network need to enforce optimal traffic flow, and why? In this small (and contrived) example, do the links between the edge routers and Routers E, F, G, and H really need to be policy controlled? Would it be more efficient to simply throw bandwidth at the problem of quality of service along the first layer of hierarchy so the relevant policies can be implemented on a smaller number of devices further into the network?

These questions aren't as easy to answer as they might first appear. To see why, turn to some of the mechanisms used in network design to manage the operational complexities previously considered.

Solving the Management Complexity Problem

If you're an experienced network engineer, by the time you get to this point, a voice in your head should be screaming "automate it!" The problems of human interaction with the network and policy dispersion through the network are, in fact, addressable through automated management tools—and this is certainly a good option in many cases. However, there is a historical tendency in network design and engineering to throw complexity over the cubicle wall onto the network operations, implying "the network management system will manage that problem." Moving complexity from the network design or the protocol into the network management system doesn't really reduce complexity; it just hides it behind a department division (or cubicle) wall.

This tendency is further exacerbated when network engineers and designers consider only a part of the overall network when trying to reduce complexity, instead of taking a systemic architectural approach in which the moving of complexity from module to module is quite evident. Only by looking at the overall system can you see the full impact of removing complexity from one discrete area.

Three different mechanisms for managing operational complexity can illustrate this in more detail. Automation, because it is the favorite tool of all large-scale networks, will be considered first, followed by modularity, and finally adding protocol complexity to reduce management complexity.

Automation as a Solution to Management Complexity

Consider the example given in the previous section—deploying a set of quality of service policies. The basic choice in that situation was to either:

- Deploy the policy closer to the network edge on more devices, thus making more optimal use of the available bandwidth, but managing the policy on a larger number of devices.
- Deploy the policy closer to the core of the network, reducing the number of devices on which the policy must be managed, but (potentially) using the available bandwidth less efficiently.

Hence, the solutions available point to a tradeoff between managing complexity and optimal network utilization (a tradeoff that's actually quite common in network design decisions). Automation appears to provide a "third way" out of this situation, allowing the policy to be placed on the edge devices without manual intervention, thus resolving the complexity tradeoff; however, it's not that simple. There is no "silver bullet" for the complexity curve. Tradeoffs will be considered in the following sections.

Brittleness

Automated systems take the "human out of the reaction." While this does provide consistency in the management process, it also takes the recognition of problems and issues out of the management process, as well. This removal of human interaction can result in what might be called ossification (the word used to describe the process of material becoming fossilized). The result can be a hard, but brittle, material—*robust yet fragile* is the term used to describe this in Chapter 1, "Defining Complexity."

Automation is brittle because automated processes can't respond to every possible failure mode or situation—because the human designers of such systems can't imagine every possible failure mode or situation. The brittleness of an automated system can be offset by periodic human oversight and better design, but such interactions must be managed, increasing complexity in the process of deploying a system designed to reduce complexity. There is a clear tradeoff here that needs to be managed when considering automated solutions to solve management complexity problems.

An example of this situation might be seen when deploying an orchestration system to manage tunneled overlays in a data center fabric. Applications can be given the ability to bring up new tunneled paths across the fabric through the orchestration system fairly easily—over time thousands (or tens of thousands) or such tunnels can be built without any human intervention. But what happens when an application builds enough tunnels to overcome the ability of any particular device's forwarding table to manage the set of tunnels overlaid onto the topology? The best case is a tunnel creation process fails, causing a human operator to look at the situation and try to find out what's going on. The worst is a complete network failure due to an overloaded forwarding place.

Ossification also leads to brittleness in another way—the assumption that "if it exists, it is needed by someone." In a purely automated solution, it is often difficult to trace down why a particular tunnel (in this example) was configured through the various system log files. How can the operator be certain there isn't an ever increasing set of unused tunnels that are needlessly wasting network resources due to incorrect cleanup (or garbage collection) processes?

Network State

Automation systems are, in a sense, abstractions of the network state. Rather than dealing directly with configurations or the current running state of any given device, the network operator deals with a piece of software that interprets intended state into actual state. This added layer of abstraction is what gives network automation its power to cut through complex configurations on a large number of devices.

The other side of this abstraction, however, is losing touch with the real state of the network. An engineer looking at the configuration of a single device might need to trace through a number of processes and pieces of code to understand how and why a particular configuration is the way it is. This can be problematic in large-scale outages, or when time is at a premium in tracing down a network outage. Again, this can be resolved by taking great care with documentation; however, documenting the processes whereby a particular configuration is installed on a particular device is a form of complexity on its own.

A second problem in this space is the failure to single source, or to have a canonical source of truth about what the network configuration should be and why it's configured this way (connecting intent to deployment). Engineers are bound to examine the actual configuration of the devices deployed in the network first to understand what is actual and intended. They might look at the comments in an automation framework second, and then finally into some form of actual documentation stored in a repository. There is a clear tendency for documentation stored in different locations, and managed within different time scales, to diverge over time. With no "single source of truth," it's hard to know precisely what any particular configuration was designed to do, nor how it should actually be deployed. Because of this, well-documented systems can actually provide a false view of the state of the network—a situation sometimes worse than having no (or minimal) documentation.

Managing the Management System

Anyone who has ever worked on a large-scale system development from a software perspective can tell you the difficulties involved—tracking changes to the codebase, testing the code before it reaches production, managing the entire feature development process—each of these has its own set of complex problems to solve. When a network automation project begins as a "side project" on the whiteboard with a couple of network engineers, it's hard to imagine the final system, years later, with version control, a full blown smoke test system, a lab environment, and so on.

While automation can be a huge benefit for controlling the complexity of network devices, it can also be a source of endless complexity on its own. Vendors have, for years, promised to make the process of managing equipment easier for automation systems; there is a constant swing between open interfaces and revenue projection. Perhaps software defined networks and other, newer, models will provide the keys to unlocking simpler automated management, but there are definite tradeoffs in this area the network engineer should be aware of.

Final Thoughts on Automation as a Solution

Automation of network device configuration might be seen as similar to automating many other tasks in a network. Each solution has plusses and minuses, and each solution has its own set of complexities.

The three areas discussed previously—brittleness, network state, and managing the management system—are factors that need to be considered when deciding to automate any particular network configuration task, and when building automation systems.

Modularity as a Solution to Management Complexity

Modularity is often used as a mechanism to break networks up a number of failure domains, but it's also a useful mechanism to manage operation complexity. Modularizing networks has many benefits, including the ability to constrain the scope of network structures, constrain the (adverse) effects of network changes, and allow for modules that are not only reusable but also can evolve somewhat independently. As a corollary, modularizing networks reduces the number of elements, protocols, and the amount of information that humans have to deal with when interacting with these networks.

Returning to the previous example, determining whether to distribute a set of quality of service policies to the edge of a network on a wide array of devices, or on a smaller set of devices closer to the network core. One of the issues considered in that example was the problem of either:

> Distributing the policy to every edge device, and thus distributing the policy configuration to a large number of devices where the policy isn't needed
>
> or
>
> Distributing the policy only to the set of devices where the policy is needed, but then dealing with a lack of consistency throughout the network

Modularity helps to resolve this problem by breaking devices up into modules. Each module can then have a set of policies that are applied uniformly across all the edge devices in the module. So long as a network engineer examining the device can locate the module in which the device is configured, a common or standard set of configurations should be readily apparent.

In fact, in this sense modularity is an adjunct to the abstraction of service types necessary to the automation of network configuration. Treating each device as a "single case" in a network automation system imports the complexity of thousands of configurations back into the automation system itself—network automation only makes sense if it's possible to separate off a relatively small number of "devices classes," each of which can be abstracted into a single configuration. This is what modularity helps to achieve—not only can a device be classified as an edge or core device, it can be classified as an edge device connecting a user or process that connects to accounting systems, for instance (because the device is located in an edge module used primarily by the accounting office).

This greater degree of precision allows more, rather than less, "cookie cutter" configurations to be designed and used throughout the network. The idea, from an operational complexity perspective, is to be able to group in modules and templates those device roles, to further be able to interact with the aggregate. While an operator typically will not be saying "apply policy X to all edge devices," he or she could be saying "apply policy X to all edge devices" that provide Layer 3 Virtual Private Network (L3VPN) service and have more than Y number of subscribers.

Modularity, however, is not without its complexity tradeoffs. Modularity can be taken to extremes in one of three directions:

- *First,* modularity might be taken to the extreme of attempting to build the perfect configuration for every possible corner case. If this path is taken, the final module size is often one. But rather than treating each device as an individual configuration, the result is a layering of policy on top of policy, and exception on top of exception, to the point where the final device configuration is not only unique, it is uniquely created through a unique set of rules. Each rule might apply to a wide array of devices, but each device represents a unique combination of those rules. This actually causes more problems than it solves, as it introduces another entire realm of interaction surfaces into the network—policy to policy, or domain to domain.

- *Second,* modularity might be taken to the extreme of managing down the array of possible policies and configurations to the minimum at the expense of the actual applications and services using the network. In this case, an application developer or user might be told they cannot deploy a particular service or application on the network because it would be too difficult to adjust the network policy around it. Another way of putting this would be, "this application can be deployed, but the application will run in a suboptimal way because there's no easy way to adjust our tools and modules to support the policy requirements for optimization." There will, of course, always be some set of applications that will run suboptimally on a network with a small set of consistent policies, but there must also always be a balance sought between the complexity of policy, the "leakiness" of the abstractions used to modularize the network, and the actual applications and services running on the network.

- *Finally,* modularity can be taken to the extreme of perfectly clean APIs, or perfect interaction surfaces, creating hard sided silos that cannot be broken down. This produces another form of brittleness through ossification in the network design; once the silos are set up, there is no space or way for the network to grow and resolve new business problems. The business becomes, in effect, a victim of complexity reduction in the network operations realm—perhaps a prime negative example of "throwing complexity over the cube wall."

Protocol Complexity versus Management Complexity

Return, for the moment, to the problem of human interaction in troubleshooting a network, application, or service failure. Assume the network operator needs to determine what path is traffic taking between two specific hosts. One way the operator could determine this is to start at the host, determining the default gateway for that specific host. Once at the default gateway, the operator could then examine the local forwarding table to find the next hop; moving to this next hop device, the operator could trace the path of the traffic through the network.

Alternatively, the operator could use a **traceroute** from the source node only, and more quickly and efficiently have a potential identification of where the path is broken. It would be useful to analyze this case in some more depth. A single tool added to the operator toolset is dramatically improving the time it takes to detect the failure, and also massively reduces the number of devices and commands that the operator needs to interact with. The application **traceroute** is leveraging specific protocol behavior [i.e., expiration of the Time-to-Live/Hop Limit, generation of Internet Control Message Protocol (ICMP) messages], which is arguably more protocol complexity. The end result is that the number of devices touched by the operator decreases to one. This makes for a solid example of the shifts in complexity and the tradeoffs: shifting complexity from operational complexity to protocol complexity dramatically improves the end result.

Consider a slightly more comprehensive case that illustrates similar results. Assume you are troubleshooting a broken MPLS Label Switched Path (LSP). An operator can use the same application, **traceroute,** and have not only a potential identification of the problem node, but also he or she could trace the MPLS label stack throughout the path with the use of ICMP Extensions for MPLS (RFC4950).[1] In this case, however, the operator could also choose to use another tool: Detecting MPLS Data Plane Failures (RFC4379).[2] This is a more complex approach from a protocol complexity standpoint, but is one that can provide much more granular problem cause identification, and more comprehensively can explore equal cost multipaths. In other words, using this new tool, MPLS LSP Ping/Traceroute, can result in faster and better troubleshooting, specifically a more comprehensive path coverage and actual problem cause reporting.

To finalize this use case, continue with the MPLS LSP example and now assume that there is RSVP-TE (node or path) protection deployed in the network, and there is also bidirectional forwarding detection in place for rapid fault detection. These protocols will be explored more fully in Chapter 7, "Protocol Complexity," but it is also interesting to see their operational implications. A rapid fault detection and automatic fault remediation (or bypass) can actually be seen as "proactive troubleshooting," in which no human intervention resulted in an outage prevented and allows more time for an operator to diagnose and fix the root cause.

As with all things in the world of complexity, however, there are a number of tradeoffs in the real world.

- The protocol becomes another "thing" which must be managed within the context of the network. To return to an earlier example, routing protocols reduce complexity by removing the requirement to manually configure full reachability information on every router in the network. On the other hand, routing protocols inject their own complexity into the network in operational terms, including policy, aggregation, operation, and other issues.

---

1. Ron Bonica et al., "ICMP Extensions for Multiprotocol Label Switching" (IETF, August 2007), accessed September 15, 2015, https://www.rfc-editor.org/rfc/rfc4950.txt.
2. K. Kompella and G. Swallow, "Detecting Multi-Protocol Label Switched (MPLS) Data Plane Failures" (IETF, February 2006), accessed September 15, 2015, https://www.rfc-editor.org/rfc/rfc4379.txt.

- The protocol is, in effect, a "leaky abstraction." While **traceroute,** for instance, can expose the path through the network from one host to another, it might not expose the path a particular application's or service's path will really take. For instance, voice traffic might be directed onto a different set of links than network management traffic for quality of service reasons.

Failures in Traceroute without Traffic Engineering

It's worth mentioning that it doesn't take policy-based routing or traffic engineering to cause problems of the type described here. Assume, for instance, that you run a traceroute from a device to discover the source of a large delay along the path. The result looks something like this:

```
C:\>tracert example.com
1 <1 ms <1 ms <1 ms 192.0.2.45
2 4 ms 3 ms 11 ms 192.0.2.150
3 20 ms 4 ms 3 ms 198.51.100.36
4 * * * Request timed out.
5 * * * Request timed out.
6 7 ms 7 ms 7 ms 203.0.113.49
```

The two "starred" hops certainly look suspicious, don't they? In reality, though, they could mean anything—or nothing. Three specific points are worth noting. *First,* not every device along a path will decrement the TTL on an IP packet. Data link layer firewalls that connect as switches rather than routers will pass traffic through without modifying the TTL, for instance. *Second,* tunnels may appear as a single hop or many. A device that switches a packet based on an outer tunnel header will not (most of the time) do anything with the inner header TTL, which means a large set of devices can appear to be a single device. *Third,* the return path is not shown in the output of a *traceroute*—and yet the return path has as much to do with network performance as the outbound path.

In all three of these cases—and many others besides—the network has been abstracted to appear simpler than it actually is. Hops that do exist are not exposed, and half of the entire round trip path is not shown at all. These abstractions leak, however, in impacting the performance of applications carrying traffic over the network. This lack of visibility into the actual operation of the network can have a major impact on finding and resolving problems, as well as in understanding the actual operation of the network.

A Final Thought

This chapter has covered both the problem space and some solutions for the problem of operational complexity. The two earlier examples of the problem space are the cost of human interaction with the network, and policy dispersion versus optimal network usage. Both of these problems illustrate a single point—the scale of a network relates as much to the complexity of the services offered as it does to the number of devices physically interconnected by the network. A large number of devices, each serving a similar purpose, and therefore with few configuration differences to support a wide array of policies, have a completely different set of scaling issues than a moderately sized network carrying a wide array of services. This, if nothing else, is a useful takeaway from examining management complexity in a network—the problem of scale doesn't have a single axis, but rather at least two axes.

After examining some of the problem space, this chapter then looked at some of the potential solutions to the complexity problems, including automation, modularity, and protocol complexity (or adding additional protocols). Each of these has tradeoffs, however, from brittleness to state to adding more surface interactions and systems that must be managed. In each of these cases, some complexity is being "tossed over the cubicle wall" to some other place to be managed. Automation is, of course, a requirement in the operation of truly large-scale networks—but it's important not to use automation as a thin coat of paint over what is an otherwise complex system. Tossing complexity over the cubicle wall, to someone on a development operations team, or a nearby friendly coder, might make the network seem simpler, but the complexity required to solve real-world problems doesn't ever go away.

While this chapter isn't a major focus of this book, it does, hopefully, provide some thinking material for network engineers to consider, and some places for engineers to look for complexity tradeoffs. The next chapter moves from operational complexity to design complexity. Many of the same problems, solutions, and tradeoffs will appear, but expressed from a different view—and in a different domain.

Chapter 5

Design Complexity

Anyone who's been in the network or operations world for a long time has a story about a network topology that was simply overwhelming. Like the time the network designer for one large company stood in front of a flip chart of over a hundred pages hung on the wall of a conference room explaining the ins and outs of his network's physical layer topology. Or the network that was built with hundreds of T1 speed links through a single campus because the bandwidth requirements had long ago overrun the capacity of ten or fifteen T1s in parallel, but the local telco wouldn't offer any sort of larger link.

These large-scale failures in network design are often trotted out as the worst of the worst in complex networks because network complexity is often equated with topological complexity—how many links are there, where are they placed, how many loops, etc. The more highly meshed the topology, the more complex the network (if it's easier to find your way through your child's room than your network topology—or if your network is meshier than your child's room, you know you have a problem).

Equating topological complexity with design complexity, however, we are limiting our field of view in some very less than useful ways—because the topology doesn't stand alone in terms of complexity. It's quite easy to build a topology that is very dense, and has a lot of nodes, and yet isn't all that complex. Think, for instance, of a typical folded single stage spine-and-leaf topology. There are a lot of connections, a lot of links, and a lot of devices—but the topology is fairly easy to understand, and fairly easy to explain.

So why and how does a difficult to understand topology relate to network design complexity? Beyond the gut visual reaction, what else is there that ties complexity and spaghetti-like topologies together?

The one that we'll consider in this chapter is the topology's relationship with the control plane, as this is probably one of the more difficult surface interactions to manage. The two surfaces interacting—the layer that is transporting packets (such as the physical layer or a tunnel) and the control plane—are very complex systems on their own, each consisting of a number of subsystems, and hence presenting their own deep complexity problems. Combine two complex systems along a large, ill-defined, and oft-changing interaction surface, and you end up with more complexity than you want to deal with.

Three primary areas where the control plane interacts with the transport layer's topology are as follows:

- The amount of control plane state.
- The rate of control plane state change.
- The scope of propagation through which any change in the topology must be carried—how far a topological change must be carried within the control plane.

It's interesting to consider these three points in relation to the components of complexity back in Chapter 2, "Components of Complexity."

- **State:** How does the topology contribute to, or take away from, the amount of state the control plane is handling?
- **Speed:** How does the topology contribute to, or take away from, the speed at which the control plane must react to changes, or even the rate at which changes in the topology are reported to the control plane?
- **Surface:** How many devices in the control plane does a change in the topology impact? How deep is the interaction between the control plane and the data plane, or the topology? How many places do control plane components interact?

While there are a lot of different points we could examine to understand these interactions in some detail, we'll limit ourselves to four (otherwise, we could have an entire stack of books, rather than a single chapter).

The first example is control plane state versus stretch—a clear example of how the amount of information carried by the control plane, and the rate of change in the control plane, can be traded off against the efficiency of the network.

The second example will be topology versus speed of convergence. Not only will we look at the relationship between resilience and redundancy here, we'll also look at the relationship between topology and resilience.

The third example, fast convergence, continues the theme of convergence speed, and hence network performance, as a source of complexity—and the tradeoffs surrounding convergence.

Our final example will be virtualization versus design complexity. This one won't be so obvious to most network engineers, even after many years of practice, but there is a definite relationship between complexity and the various forms of virtualization network engineers practice.

Control Plane State versus Stretch

What is network stretch? In the simplest terms possible, it is the difference between the shortest path in a network and the path traffic between two points actually takes. Figure 5.1 illustrates this concept.

Assuming that the cost of each link in this network is the same, the shortest physical path between Routers A and C will also be the shortest logical path: [A,B,C]. What happens, however, if we change the metric on the [A,B] link to 3? The shortest physical path is still [A,B,C], but the shortest logical path is now [A,D,E,C]. The differential between the shortest physical path and the shortest logical path is the distance a packet being forwarded between Routers A and C must travel—in this case, the stretch can be calculated as (4 [A,D,E,C])–(3 [A,B,C]), for a stretch of 1.

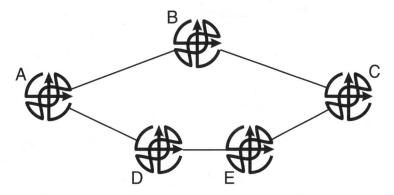

Figure 5.1 *Stretch, Illustrated*

How is stretch measured

Should stretch be measured in terms of hop count, the summary of the metrics, the delay through the network, or some other way? It depends on what is most important in any given situation, but the most common way is by comparing hop counts through the network, as is used in the examples here for simplicity. In some cases, it might be more important to consider the metric along two paths, the delay along two paths, or some other metric, but the important point is to measure it consistently across every possible path to allow for accurate comparison between paths.

Several points are worth noting about stretch:

- It's sometimes difficult to differentiate between the physical topology and the logical topology. In this case, was the [A,B] link metric increased because the link is actually a slower link? If so, whether this is an example of stretch, or an example of simply bringing the logical topology in line with the physical topology is debatable.

- In line with this observation, it's much easier to define policy in terms of stretch than almost any other way. Policy is any configuration that increases the stretch of a network. Using Policy Based Routing, or Traffic Engineering, to push traffic off the shortest physical path and onto a longer logical path to reduce congestion on specific links, for instance, is a policy—it increases stretch.

- Increasing stretch is not always a bad thing. Understanding the concept of stretch simply helps us understand various other concepts, and put a framework around complexity tradeoffs. The shortest path, physically speaking, isn't always the best path.

- Stretch, in this illustration, is very simple—it impacts every destination, and every packet flowing through the network. In the real world, things aren't so simple. Stretch is actually per source/destination pair, making it very difficult to measure on a network wide basis.

With all of this in mind, let's look at two specific examples of the tradeoff between stretch and optimization.

Aggregation versus Stretch

Aggregation is a technique used to reduce not only the amount of information carried in the control plane, but also the rate of state change in the control plane. Aggregation is built into IP (both IPv4 and IPv6)—even a single subnet contains multiple host addresses. By connecting a single broadcast segment to a set of hosts, the IP routing protocol doesn't need to manage Layer 2 reachability, nor individual host addresses.

> **Note**
>
> Host addresses are sometimes used to provide mobility within a larger network, particularly data center fabrics and mobile ad-hoc networks—an illustration of the state versus stretch tradeoff we won't consider here.

Aggregation within the control plane can also cause stretch, as Figure 5.2 shows.

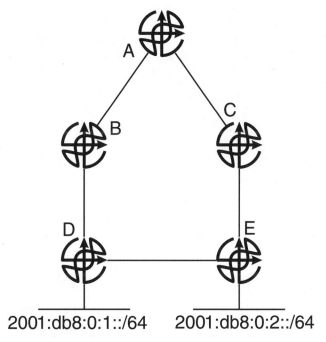

Figure 5.2 *Aggregation and Stretch*

> **Note**
>
> Most routing protocols take into account the metrics of an aggregate's components to provide as close to optimal routing as possible at an aggregation edge of this type. However, it's still common for stretch to be introduced into the network even with these counter measures. This example dispenses with taking component metric into account to make the principle easier to illustrate.

Two different situations illustrate increasing stretch through route aggregation:

- Assume the [A,B] link has a cost of 2, and all the other links in this network have a cost of 1. If Routers B and C both aggregate to 2001:db8::/61, then the path through [A,C] would be preferred for everything within the aggregate. Traffic destined to 2001:db8:0:1::/64 will pass along the path [A,C,E,D] to reach its destination, even though the shortest (physical) path is [A,B,D]. The stretch for 2001:db8:0:2::/64 isn't changed, but the stretch for 2001:db8:0:1::/64 is increased by one.

- Assume all the links in the network have a cost of 1. If Routers B and C both aggregate to 2001:db8::/61, then Router A will somehow load share traffic toward the two subnets behind Routers D and E across the two equal cost paths it has available. Given perfect load sharing, 50% of the traffic destined to 2001:db8:0:1::/64 will flow along [A,C,E,D], with a stretch of 1, and 50% of the traffic destined to 2001:db8:0:2::/64 will flow along [A,B,D,E], with a stretch of 1.

The question that should come to mind about now is this—so what? The amount of control plane state is decreased through aggregation (both the actual amount of state and the rate of change in that state), which clearly reduces complexity. There are three outcomes being traded off here:

- Implementing aggregation breaks up failure domains, improving the stability and resilience of the control plane (and hence of the entire network).

- Implementing aggregation requires designing, configuring, and maintaining the set of policies around the aggregation itself. This is additional complexity.

- Implementing aggregation in this network causes what would normally be two redundant links to become a single point of failure. If Router B is the preferred route to the aggregate 2001:0db8::/61, and the link between

Routers D and E fails, 2001:0db8:0001::/64 will become unreachable from Router A. Traffic destined to this prefix will be forwarded to Router C, because the aggregate covers this address space, and then dropped because Router C will have no route to the specific subnet. To remedy this, a new path must be installed providing an alternate path to Router D from Router C. Normally, this link would be installed between Routers B and C, and configured so it is "behind" the aggregation, rather than "in front of" the aggregation (aggregation must be configured toward Router A from Router C's perspective, not Router B). Solving this aggregation black hole problem increases complexity in several areas.

- Increasing stretch increases the complexity of the data plane by pushing traffic through more hops, and hence more queues, etc.

- Increasing stretch disconnects the obvious/apparent operation of the network from the way the network actually works. As policies are implemented that increase stretch, it becomes more difficult to look at the network topology and understand how traffic flows through the network. This increases the complexity and difficulty of troubleshooting various problems that might (in fact, almost certainly will) arise in operating the network.

- Increasing stretch increases the overall utilization of the network without any actual increase in the amount of traffic being carried through the network. In the example given in Figure 5.1, traffic that would normally take a two-hop path is directed along a three-hop path, which means one more link and one more router are involved in forwarding and switching the packets in the flow(s) across the network. In purely mathematical terms, increasing stretch decreases the overall efficiency of the network by increasing the number of devices and links used to forward any particular flow.

This last bullet is an interesting point—for it cuts to the heart of our next comparison of stretch versus control plane state, how traffic engineering impacts complexity.

Traffic Engineering

Let's look at a more specific example of trading state for traffic engineering. We'll use the network in Figure 5.3 as an example.

Assume that every link in this network has a cost of 1; the shortest path between 2001:db8:0:1::/64 and 2001:db8:0:2::/64 is [A,B,F]. However, the

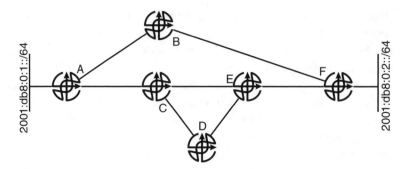

Figure 5.3 *Traffic Engineering, State, and Stretch*

network administrator doesn't want traffic between these two subnets traveling along that path—for instance, perhaps the traffic being exchanged is a high bandwidth file transfer stream, and the [A,B] link is already used for a video stream. To prevent the two streams from "colliding," causing quality of service issues, the network administrator implements some form of policy-based routing at Router A that redirects the file transfer traffic through the path [A,C,E,F].

Consider what this involves:

- A policy must now be created and installed on Routers A and F to redirect this specific traffic around the [A,B,F] path.

- The stretch for the file transfer traffic has been increased by one.

- This additional stretch means the traffic is now going to pass through four hops, rather than three, which means four input queues, four output queues, four forwarding tables, etc., must be managed, instead of three.

- The path of any given stream through the network is no longer obvious from the topology; to understand the path of a specific stream, a network engineer troubleshooting problems must examine the control plane policies to determine what will happen in each specific case.

Each of these is an added bit of complexity—in fact, both the data plane and the control plane complexity have increased through this exercise. So what have we gained? Why do this sort of traffic engineering?

Because even though the overall efficiency of the network (in terms of utilization) has decreased by redirecting some traffic along a path with some stretch, the overall utilization rate of the network has increased in terms of its ability to handle load, or rather to support a specific set of applications. To put this in other terms, the network now has a higher utilization rate even though the overall efficiency is lower. This prevents the network operator from being forced to install new links, or upgrade capacity—both good things from the operator's point of view.

State versus Stretch: Some Final Thoughts

So in the case of state versus stretch, any time we are increasing stretch, we are implementing some sort of policy, and any time we are implementing a policy, we are increasing complexity in some way. On the other hand, creating stretch through policy is often necessary to either reduce state in the control plane, or to improve overall network utilization.

State versus stretch is, then, a set of tradeoffs. There is no absolutely right answer to the question, "Should I implement this policy that increases stretch?" The right answer is always going to depend on the goals and the projected consequences. Before we jump into the next section considering the tradeoff between topology design and convergence, it's important to tie state versus stretch back to the state, speed, surface framework outlined in Chapter 2, "Components of Complexity":

- **State:** The amount of information in the control plane is either decreased through aggregation, or increased through traffic engineering. In the one case, the amount of control plane complexity is decreasing, while the network complexity (in the data plane) is increasing, at least in some amount.

- **Speed:** Aggregation reduces the speed at which the control plane must react by hiding changes in the network. Chapter 6, "Managing Design Complexity," looks at this in more detail. Adding more state to the control plane to engineer traffic has an effect that's the opposite of aggregation; a single link failure can mean multiple updates in the control plane, so the control plane must react more quickly.

- **Surface:** Aggregation reduces the interaction surface between the control plane and the topology in some ways—by hiding some parts of the topology from the control plane—and increases the interaction surface in other ways—by implementing control plane policy that must coincide with specific topological features within the network. Traffic engineering increases the interaction surface between the control plane and topology.

The state, speed, and surface framework proves useful in diagnosing the various points where complexity has increased, where complexity has decreased, and where the tradeoffs lie.

Topology versus Speed of Convergence

Stretch isn't the only place where the network topology and the control plane interact with one another. The actual layout of the topology is a (often not so obvious) point of interaction, as well. Let's consider two specific examples of interactions between the topology and the control plane: ring topology convergence, and redundancy versus resilience.

Ring Topology Convergence

Ring topologies, such as the one illustrated in Figure 5.4, have a fairly specific set of convergence characteristics.

If the [D, 2001:db8:0:1::/64] link fails, what is the convergence process for a distance vector protocol on this topology?

1. Router D discovers the failure.

2. Router D advertises the failure to Routers C and E.

3. Routers C and E advertise the loss of the link to 2001:db8:0:1::/64 to B and F.

4. Routers B and F advertise the loss of the link to 2001:db8:0:1::/64 to Router A.

5. The route to 2001:db8:0:1::/64 is removed from all the local routing tables, and traffic destined to this subnet is dropped.

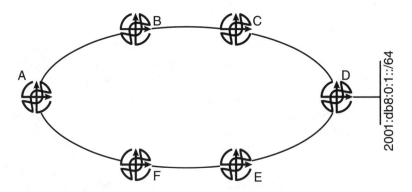

Figure 5.4 *Ring Topology Convergence*

What about with a link state protocol?

1. Router D discovers the failure.

2. Router D floods modified link state information to the rest of the routers in the network (or at least within the flooding domain).

3. Each router then sets a timer to delay running SPF.

4. As each router runs SPF, it will recalculate the best path to 2001:db8:0:1::/64 and install it.

5. As routers in the ring run SPF at different times, they will install the new path toward this destination at different times, resulting in microloops while the routing tables throughout the ring are in an inconsistent state. (Note this won't happen with a route removal, as in this case.)

6. After some period of time, all routers have run SPF, recalculated their best paths to the destination, and installed the routes.

So no matter which type of routing protocol you're using, there is some time lag as the information about changes to specific destination is propagated and acted on through the ring. You essentially have your choice between dropping or looping traffic during convergence.

Why, then, do network designers often use rings? The primary reasons are as follows:

- Rings are the least connection rich topology that offers a secondary path (a two connected graph, in more formal terms).

- Because rings are not connection rich, there are no scaling issues with the number of neighbors, etc., on a ring topology—no matter how large the ring grows, each router will only have two neighbors.

- Rings are good for spanning long geographic distances with a minimal set of (expensive) links.

- In terms of complexity, ring topologies add a lot less load to the network's (routed or IP) control plane.

Triangles (any part of a larger topology with three hops) converge much faster than rings (any part of a topology with four or more hops), but triangles place a lot more load on the control plane—particularly in terms of the amount of information each node receives. Here, then, we have a clear complexity tradeoff in the interaction between topologies, control planes, and convergence speed.

Let's go to the opposite end of the network topology spectrum and example very densely connected topologies.

Redundancy versus Resilience

Assume that you need to build a network with six nines of reliability (99.9999% uptime), and the only links you have available have an average downtime of about 3.5 days in any given year (99% reliability). The easy solution to providing high availability with low reliability parts is to put many of them in parallel. Table 5.1 shows the relationship between increasing the number of parallel units and the reliability of the system.

Calculating Availability

How did we find these numbers? The formula for parallel and series availability is simple if you have availability numbers for each component. For series components, simply multiply the availability for each series component together. For instance, to find the availability of two 99% available links tied together back to back, multiply the two availabilities together:

```
A == A₁ * A₂
A == 0.99 * 0.99
A == 0.9801 == 98% available
```

For components in parallel, use the following formula:

```
A == 1 - ((1 - A₁) * (1 - A₂))
A == 1 - ((1 - 0.99) * (1 - 0.99))
A == 1 - (0.01 * 0.01)
A == 1 - 0.0001
A == 0.9999 == 99.99% available
```

Table 5.1 *Availability versus Redundancy*

Number of Links in Parallel	Combined Availability (%)	Projected Downtime/Year
1	99	3.69 days
2	99.99	52 minutes
3	99.9999	31 seconds

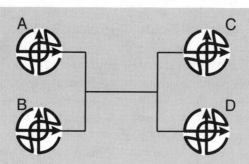

Figure 5.5 *Computing Parallel and Series Availability*

If you're combining parallel (side-by-side) and series (back-to-back) components, then compute in pieces, starting from the smallest groupings either in parallel or series, and, as you replace the smaller sections with larger ones, treating a group of components as a single component. Figure 5.5 is used to illustrate computing the availability of a system with both parallel and series components.

If Routers A, B, C, and D all had individual availability rates of 99%, you would compute the availability of all four routers (ignoring the links) using the following formula:

```
(A,B) == 1 - ((1 - A) * (1 - B))
(A,B) == 1 - ((1 - 0.99) * (1 - 0.99)
(A,B) == 1 - (0.01 * 0.01)
(A,B) == 1 - 0.0001
(A,B) == 0.9999 == 99.99% available
```

Given the availability of the pair of routers (A,B) is going to be the same as the availability of the pair of routers (C,D), you can now compute the availability of the four routers by computing the availability of (A,B) in serial with (C,D):

```
Availability == (A,B) * (C,D)
A == 0.9999 * 0.9999
A == 0.9998 == 99.98% available
```

So the combined systems (ignoring the links) would have three nines of availability.

Easy—just make certain that there are at least three links in parallel anyplace in the network, and you have six nines of reliability, right? Well, maybe. Let's add in redundancy for our routers, and then try to build something out of it. Figure 5.6 illustrates a triple redundant full mesh topology.

This design certainly meets the six nines requirement from the perspective of links and routers—but how fast is the control plane going to converge? It might even work under "ideal" conditions, but when one link fails in a way that causes a rapid flap, interesting problems are going to result from this sort of design. In lab testing done on EIGRP, the protocol actually started losing convergence speed at around four parallel links (on a very simple topology with tens of thousands of routes).

Link state protocol convergence could be hampered by the number of control plane traffic flooded through the network. For instance, if the (A,2001:db8:0:1::/64) link fails, the modified link state update will be flooded throughout the triple full mesh multiple times, unless some sort of flooding

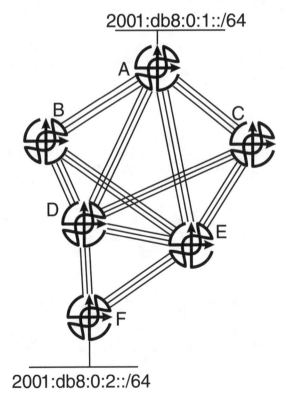

Figure 5.6 *A Triple Redundant Full Mesh Topology*

reduction mechanism is used. This is, in fact, why mesh groups exist in IS-IS and OSPF—to prevent large flooding events on full mesh networks. Beyond this, the number and location of microloops created during convergence on this topology could be large and difficult to predict.

One way to lower the complexity of this type of topology, while maintaining triple redundancy for resilience, might be to treat each of the sets of links between the routers as a single link—this would be possible using a technology like Link Aggregation Groups (LAGs), for instance. Observant readers are already going to realize that there are tradeoffs here, as well. First, the LAG has its own control plane, and makes modifications to the forwarding plane, to ensure equal use of each of the parallel circuits. These will interact with the overlaying IP routing protocol, creating another interaction surface. One example of the difficulty in managing this interaction surface is deciding how to handle the failure of a single link out of the three available between any two routers. Should the metric on the single aggregated link be modified in the routing protocol? Or should the link be used at equal cost anyway? What are the implications of each solution from a traffic flow and loading perspective? These are, as always, not easy questions to answer—while such a solution might fit a particular situation well, then, there are always tradeoffs to consider in terms of complexity and optimization of traffic flow through the network.

So it depends on a lot of factors, but the routing protocol here is probably not going to converge within the six nines requirement in all possible conditions without some serious tuning of timers, and potentially some reduction of control plane state along the way.

The tradeoff here is between redundancy and resilience—while it might seem that adding redundant links will always increase network resilience, this simply isn't the case in the real world. Each redundant link adds a bit more control plane state, and a bit more load during convergence. Each added bit of load slows down the convergence speed of the control plane, and, in some cases, can even cause the control plane to fail to converge.

Topology versus Speed of Convergence: Some Final Thoughts

Let's go back to our state, speed, and surface model to see how and where the topology versus speed tradeoff fits. They will be presented in a slightly different order here.

- **State:** As the redundancy built into the network increases, the number of links and the number of adjacencies/peering sessions must increase to discover the additional links and neighbor relationships across those links.

This, in turn, increases both the amount of information carried in the control plane and the number of replications of that data throughout the network.

- **Surface:** As the number of devices in the network increases, the number of adjacencies or peering relationships among devices participating in the control plane must also increase. The increase in peering relationships represents an increase in interaction surfaces. Any particular piece of information must be carried through more devices.

- **Speed:** As the redundancy built into the network increases, the number of times any particular piece of information about the state of the network must be replicated increases. If any change in the topology requires the control plane to converge so the state of the internal databases matches the state of the real world (in topological terms), each additional piece of information included in the total state either requires convergence to take longer, or a larger amount of state to be distributed and calculated across in the same amount of time. If we expect the network to converge in the same amount of time or faster with more information, then we are expecting the control plane to process information more quickly. Larger databases processed in the same amount of time (or faster) require more speed, or more transactions per second.

This last point on speed will operate as a segue into the next section investigating the relationship of speed and complexity—fast convergence.

Fast Convergence versus Complexity

When networking technology first became widespread, fast convergence meant fast enough to allow a file transfer or email to make its way through the network without too much interruption. As networks have become faster, the applications deployed on top of them have been built around the faster speeds and higher availability networks can deliver. Once acceptable convergence speeds are now considered too slow for many applications. Consider the following illustration showing the theoretical convergence times of various routing protocols as they were originally deployed, using default timers and no "tricks," such as loop-free alternates (LFAs) or fast reroute mechanisms. Figure 5.7 illustrates routing protocol convergence speeds with default timers and "No Tricks."

Let's look at each protocol to get a sense for the convergence times shown here.

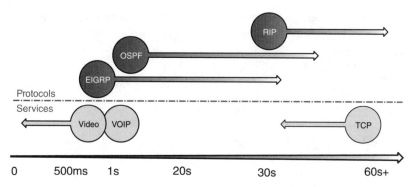

Figure 5.7 *Routing Protocol Convergence Speeds with Default Timers and "No Tricks"*

- Routing Information Protocol (RIP) uses a periodic update to inform neighbors about a change in reachability (RIP doesn't really carry topology information, though some information about the topology can be inferred from the database). The "default" timer for this periodic update is 30 seconds; on average (statistically), any given change in reachability will wait 15 seconds before being advertised to a neighboring router. The average time to notify the entire network of a change in reachability, then, is the maximum number of hops the reachability change must travel multiplied by 15 seconds. For large networks, this could mean two or three minutes.

- OSPF is a link state protocol, so any change in topology and/or reachability is flooded through the entire network. Every router that receives an updated LSA will compute the SPT (calculated using SPF) independently, which means (theoretically) in parallel with all the other routers in the flooding domain. The original timers that impacted OSPF convergence are the LSA generation timer and the SPF calculation timer. These two timers, combined, result in a minimum convergence time for standard, unaltered OSPF of around one second. The maximum convergence time is shown here to be around 30 seconds, the maximum amount of time a neighbor failure will take to be discovered and advertised throughout the network.

- EIGRP is a distance vector protocol that holds one hop of topology information in a local database, using this information to precalculate loop-free paths where possible. If an alternate loop-free path is available, EIGRP can converge in less than 100 milliseconds (ms) after a link failure has been detected. In the absence of a LFA (called a Feasible Successor, or FS), EIGRP will propagate a query through the network; on average, this query will require about 200 ms per hop to process. The average amount of time EIGRP requires to converge is, then, 200 ms multiplied by the number of routers that must participate in the query process—a number regulated by network design and configuration. The maximum convergence time is set by the EIGRP Stuck in Active timer, which is normally around 90 seconds.

> **Note**
>
> Why is SPT calculation theoretically in parallel? Because of slight differences in the rate at which one router can flood packets to each of its neighbors, and the cumulative time required to flood new information through a multihop network, there is no way to ensure all the routers in the network receive new topology information at precisely the same moment. Given this, there is also no way to ensure that every router in the network will begin calculating a new SPT at precisely the same moment. This is, ultimately, the cause of microloops during link state protocol convergence.

As you can see from the application requirements shown in Figure 5.7, these convergence times just won't supply what is expected out of networks today. How can convergence times for these protocols be improved? The first step in the process was to move from *talking to talking faster*.

Improving Convergence with Intelligent Timers: Talk Faster

If we want to improve the convergence of a routing protocol, where would be the easiest place to start? Given the focus on the interaction between the various timers, the distribution of routing information, and the calculation of new forwarding tables, the most obvious place to begin would be with the timers the protocols use to determine when to advertise new pieces of information. To better understand the problem, we face when shortening these timers, we need to understand why the timers are there in the first place. Let's consider OSPF running on the network shown in Figure 5.8.

Just to illustrate the point, assume the 2001:db8:0:1::/64 link is flapping so it fails, then reconnects, every 200 or 300 ms. What happens if Router A generates a new LSA each time this link changes state? Routers B and C would be flooded with routing updates, taking up bandwidth and buffer space. To prevent this from happening, OSPF is designed with a minimal amount of time a router will wait before advertising a link state change—the *LSA generation timer*. If the LSA generation timer is set fairly high, rapid status changes in locally connected links will be damped—constant flaps like the one described here will not cause

Figure 5.8 *A Simple OSPF Network*

a constant flood of LSAs flooded through the network. On the other hand, setting the LSA generation timer too high will cause the network to converge more slowly. How do we resolve this problem?

The solution is to use a variable timer—allow Router A to advertise the new link state very quickly (or even immediately) when the 2001:db8:0:1::/64 link changes state, but then "back off," so that Router A must wait some longer period of time before advertising the next link state change. This will allow the network to converge quickly for single changes, but dampen the effect of a large number of changes happening over a short period of time.

This is precisely what exponential backoff, a feature now included in most OSPF implementations, does. The timer is set to a very low number, and increased each time a new event occurs, until it reaches some maximum amount of time between new advertisements. As time passes with no events occurring, the timer is reduced until it eventually reaches the minimum again. Figure 5.9 illustrates the exponential backoff timer operation.

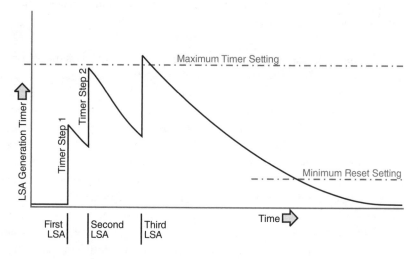

Figure 5.9 *Exponential Backoff Timer Operation*

In Figure 5.9, the first failure of 2001:db8:0:1::/64 causes Router A to generate an LSA (close to) immediately, so the rest of the network is informed as quickly as possible. Router A, after sending this LSA, modifies its LSA generation timer to *Timer Step 1*. Router A then immediately begins "decaying" the LSA generation timer, reducing it slowly as time passes without any new link state changes. After a few moments, however, the second topology change occurs. Router A now waits until the timer expires, sends out a new LSA, and adds more time to the timer, increasing it to *Timer Step 2* in the illustration. Again, Router A begins reducing the timer slowly while the 2001:db8:0:1::/64 link remains stable. A third state change, however, causes Router A to wait until the timer expires, transmit a new LSA, and, again, add more time to the timer value. At this point, the *maximum timer setting* has been reached—no matter how many future failures occur, the timer will never be set any higher than this value.

This type of exponential backoff can be applied to the interval between SPT calculations, as well, to provide fast reaction for small numbers of changes without overloading the network with updated information and processing requirements.

> **Note**
>
> If this looks similar to a chart for BGP dampening, that's because it is—dampening and exponential backoff use the same principles and techniques to promote network stability while allowing for fast notification of small changes in reachability or topology.

Several points are worth considering in the relationship between talking faster and complexity.

- Only a minimal amount of state is added to the control plane—in fact, no new state is added to the control plane state carried between routers at all. A number of additional timers must be added to the control plane protocol implementation (this can be quite complex, of course, depending on the granularity at which the timers must operate—per neighbor/peer, per prefix, etc.), but this is all opaque to the "on the wire" protocol itself. There may—or may not—be more traffic on the wire to provide for faster convergence, depending on how the timers are set. In older networks, with lower transmissions speeds, these additional packets could have a large impact on the operation of the network itself. In more modern, higher speed links, this additional traffic is minimal against the gains in convergence speed. These sorts of timer modifications, done correctly, might increase the *speed* of operations in the control plane, the speed at which the control plane is propagating state throughout the network. Increasing the spacing of advertising events as the rate of events increases (exponential backoff), mitigates the speed of operations to the point that little additional complexity is added if the two techniques are combined.

- Perhaps the most complexity is added through exponential backoff timers along the interaction *surfaces* in the control plane. Rather than having a lot of devices with fairly consistent timers, the operator now has a lot of devices, each with fairly independent timers that could be running at different rates. This makes it harder to predict, at any given moment, precisely what the state of the network is, introducing a more "quantum state" nature to the mix when troubleshooting or determining what control plane behavior will be in specific situations. Multiple failure situations will now produce a different chain of events than single failure situations, potentially causing difficult to trace race conditions and other artifacts of complex surface interactions.

Note

As with all control plane modifications, there is a definite tradeoff to be considered when configuring exponential backoff as a mechanism to provide faster convergence. For instance, a single misbehaving device (or an attacker) can, by injecting false changes to the topology into the control plane, conceivably, force the exponential backoff timers to remain high (near the maximum timer setting in Figure 5.9). If these timers are forced to remain higher than they should be, the network will react too slowly to real changes, potentially causing application failures. This might seem to be far-fetched, but it's also not something the typical network administrator is going to look for when troubleshooting application performance issues.

Modifying the convergence timers in routing protocols, then, typically provides a lot of gain in terms of convergence time without having a huge complexity impact.

Removing Timers from Convergence: Precompute

What's next after talking and talking faster? If making the timers more intelligent can dramatically improve convergence time, then what about simply taking the timers out of convergence altogether? This is what precomputed LFA paths does. Figure 5.10 will be used to illustrate how this works.

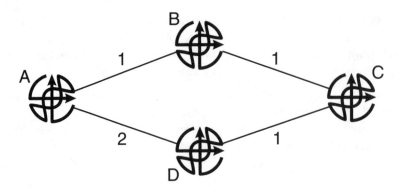

Figure 5.10 *Precompute Example for Fast Convergence*

In this network, Router A has two paths to reach destinations behind Router C: via Router B with a total cost of 2, and via Router D with a total cost of 3. In this case, Router A will obviously choose the path through Router B with a total cost of 2. But why couldn't Router A install the route through Router D as a backup path? It's obvious the path is loop free.

This is, in fact, what precomputing does—discover alternate loop-free paths and install them as a locally available backup path. The key point to remember is that routers can't "see" the network like a network engineer, with an actual diagram of the network end-to-end on which to map out alternate paths to reach a single destination (and it's not so simple as to find the alternate paths on a map, anyway—the cost of the path makes a big difference, as we'll see in the next section). All the router can do is examine the cost of the two paths, especially the cost being advertised by the next hop of any alternate route, to determine if the path should actually be used as a LFA.

In this case, Router A can look at Router D's cost and determine that the path through Router D cannot be a loop, because the cost of Router D's path is less than the cost of Router A's path. In EIGRP terms, this is called the feasibility test; if the neighbor's Reported Distance (the cost at Router D) is less than the local Feasible Distance (the best path at Router A), then the path is loop free, and can be used as a backup. OSPF and IS–IS calculate LFAs in much the same way, by calculating the cost to any given destination from the neighbor's point of view to decide if the path is loop free or not.

Let's consider the precomputation of LFA paths in complexity terms.

- Like timer modification, precomputing LFA paths doesn't add anything to the *state* carried through the network in the control plane. All the information required to compute these alternate paths is available in information already carried by the control plane, both with EIGRP and with link state protocols, so there is no reason to add any new information. Precomputing alternate paths does, of course, increase the internal state for any specific implementation, introducing new code paths that need to be tested.

- Precomputation has little to no impact on the *speed* at which the control plane operates—if anything, if most paths through a network can be protected through precomputation, the timer modifications discussed in the previous section may become less important, allowing convergence speeds to become "lazier," and the pace of notifications in the control plane to be slower.

- Perhaps the most complexity is added through precomputation—as was true with exponential backoff timers—along the interaction *surfaces* in the control plane. This is true along two dimensions—control plane operation and operational state. Control plane operation is made more complex by the possibility that a single or multiple failures may cause overlapping precomputed paths to come into play, causing unanticipated states in the network. Race and other conditions are a possible side effect that must be considered (and possibly tested for). From an operational state perspective, precomputed paths add one more bit of internal state to each forwarding device operators must pay attention to—what is the alternate path, is the network in a state between switching to the alternate path and calculating a new best path, for instance. In the case of two failures occurring at or near the same time, it's difficult for an operator to predict the outcome, and hence to know how the network will actually converge (will it converge within the required bounds).

As was the case in modifying timers to improve protocol convergence, precomputing paths offers a lot of gains against very small increases in apparent complexity. In fact, EIGRP Feasible Successors, a form of precomputed paths, have been deployed in many large-scale networks for many years with little noticeable increases in complexity.

Working around Topology: Tunneling to the Loop-Free Alternate

What happens if the metrics in Figure 5.10 are changed slightly, throwing in an extra router, and resulting in the network illustrated in Figure 5.11?

Router A still has two paths to every destination beyond Router C, such as 2001:db8:0:1::/64, but the path via Router D cannot be used as a LFA. Why? If the path to 2001:db8:0:1::/64 through Router B fails, and Router A switches to

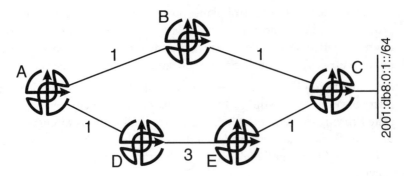

Figure 5.11 *The Loop-Free Alternate That Isn't*

the alternate path through Router D, where will Router D forward this traffic? Router D has two paths to 2001:db8:0:1::/64; through Router E with a cost of 4, and through Router A with a cost of 3. Router D will, then, forward any traffic Router A sends it with a destination of 2001:db8:0:1::/64 back to Router A.

Router A using Router D as a LFA, in this case, actually results in a routing loop during the time between the failure of the path through Router B, and the time when Router D recomputes its best path and starts using the path through Router E to reach2001:db8:0:1::/64. This is called a *microloop,* because the loop is caused by the control plane, and it tends to be for a very short duration (it isn't a permanent loop).

How can we resolve this? The most obvious answer is to simply not use the path through Router D as a backup path—but we're trying to provide for fast rerouting of traffic in the case of a change in the network's topology, not dropped packets. Fast reroute solutions can solve this problem by tunneling past Router D, to some point in the network where the traffic won't be forwarded (looped) back toward Router A. There are several ways to accomplish this:

- Compute the SPT from the perspective of a wider ring of neighbors until you find a point several hops away where you can tunnel traffic to without it looping back to yourself. Most mechanisms that do this stop searching at two hops (your neighbor's neighbor), because this finds the vast majority of all alternate paths available in this way.

- Advertise reachability to 2001:db8:0:1::/64 through Routers D and E to Router A.[1]

---

1. See, as an example S. Bryant, S. Previdi, and M. Shand, "A Framework for IP and MPLS Fast Reroute Using Not-Via Addresses" (IETF, August 2013), accessed September 15, 2015, https://www.rfc-editor.org/rfc/rfc6981.txt.

- Compute an alternate topology using an algorithm such as depth first searching with a random walk, or others.[2]

- Compute a reverse tree from the destination toward the local router; find a point on this reverse tree that is not on the current best path from the local router toward the destination.[3]

Once the remote point where traffic can be safely tunneled is found, some form of tunnel must be automatically created to use as a backup path. This tunnel must be inserted in the local forwarding table with a very high metric, or inserted in such a way as to prevent it from being used until the set of primary (nontunneled) paths have been removed from the table. The end point of the tunnel must also have a tunnel tail end though which to handle packets being forwarded down this path, preferably something that is autoconfigured to reduce network management and configuration overhead.

Returning to the state, speed, surface, optimization model developed up to this point will help expose what new complexities these types of tunneled fast reroute add to the network.

- Tunneled solutions add *state* in a number of ways. *First,* there is the additional internal and implementation state, both of which add complexity. This state includes additional processing required to recalculate any tunneled backup paths when the network topology changes. *Second,* some mechanisms require the advertisement of additional control plane state explicitly (such as NotVia), which adds control plane protocol complexity. *Third,* if the tunneling protocol used to build the fast reroute backup paths are not currently deployed in the network, they must be deployed—adding additional protocols to the stack, configurations, etc. *Finally,* the provisioning (or autoprovisioning) tunnel endpoints throughout the network increases complexity by increasing configuration.

- Tunneled fast reroute mechanisms don't increase the *speed* at which the control plane operates, nor the speed at which changes occur in the network topology. In fact, fast reroute can actually reduce the speed of

---

2. See, as an example A. Atlas et al., "An Architecture for IP/LDP Fast-Reroute Using Maximally Redundant Trees" (IETF, July 2015), accessed September 15, 2015, https://www.ietf.org/id/draft-ietf-rtgwg-mrt-frr-architecture-06.txt.

3. For further information, see Chapter 8, "Weathering Storms," in *The Art of Network Architecture: Business-Driven Design*, 1st edition. (Indianapolis, Indiana: Cisco Press, 2014).

updates by reducing the need for the fancy and tuned timers described above. In this case, tunneled fast reroute mechanisms can be a way to reduce complexity.

- Tunneled solutions increase the size and depth of interaction surfaces in a number of ways. In fact, this is probably the primary way in which these solutions increase network complexity. A few examples will suffice— *First,* determining the traffic patterns in a network is much more complex, particularly during network outages. For networks that value a high level of utilization (rather than overbuilding and ignoring quality of service), this adds a number of factors to consider when planning, configuring, and managing quality of service issues. *Second,* because traffic can travel over tunnels during transient states to a point multiple hops away in the network, following the flow of a particular stream or flow can become much more difficult. In networks with constant topology change, this can become an overwhelming challenge. *Third,* operators must remember to look in more than one place when determining where traffic is flowing and why—there is more to the control plane than just what is in the current forwarding table. *Finally,* tunneled mechanisms require that a large number of devices be capable of dynamically terminating tunnels to reroute traffic. Each of these dynamically open tunnel tail ends are potential security threats and additional management complexity.

Some Final Thoughts on Fast Convergence

It should be obvious by now that moving from default timers, to precalculated LFAs, to tunneled LFAs, involves two somewhat small steps up in complexity, and one final step that's a bit larger in complexity. Figure 5.12 illustrates this concept.

Note

Tunneled and precomputed LFAs are close to identical in the speed of convergence offered by each solution, so they are shown close together in Figure 5.12. The primary tradeoff between these two is the amount of control plane complexity versus the types of topologies each will cover. Tunneled LFAs can cover just about every topology (with some exceptions—nonplanar topologies aren't always covered by every tunneled LFA technology), at the cost of more complexity in the control plane.

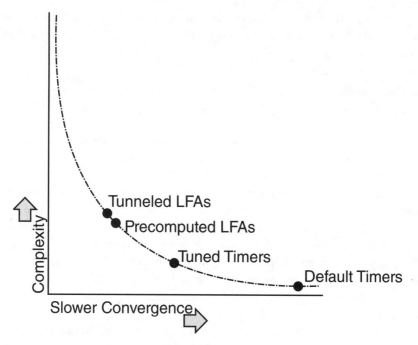

Figure 5.12 *Complexity versus Convergence*

You might place each specific solution in a different place on this curve—it all depends on the requirements of the network you're working on, and how you perceive the added complexity of moving to ever faster convergence. Either way, movement along the continuum of talk, talk faster, precompute, and tunnel adds another layer of interconnected entities into the network as a system, another set of interaction surfaces, and another group of uncertainty points. While each one appears to be fairly simple on the surface, complexity can add up very quickly when trying to converge quickly. The tradeoffs here are real, persistent, and urgent.

Will there ever be any end to the fast convergence game? Let's put the question the other way around. Networks are, in essence, a sop to human impatience. The problem network engineers face is that there is no apparent end point in human impatience—no matter how fast something is, it can always be faster. As noted in the beginning of this chapter, email and file transfer work fine with moderately fast control plane convergence. Voice and video, however, put higher expectations on the network. High-speed trading in the stock market and real-time medical uses place even harder requirements on network convergence. As machine to machine and other applications are deployed across networks, they are likely to push ever increasing convergence speeds, until engineers have simply reached the limit of what can be done to make a network control plane converge faster. In short, there is probably no end in sight for trying to make the network converge more quickly.

Virtualization versus Design Complexity

Virtualization is one of those "always new" technologies in the world of networking. It was new when Frame Relay first provisioned virtual circuits, it was new again when Asynchronous Transfer Mode (ATM) was first proposed, it was new when VLANs on Ethernet were proposed, and it was new when MPLS originally known as tag switching) was proposed, and it will be new again in some future instance. Why is virtualization such a popular and perennial topic in network engineering? Because it provides a way to hide information (more on information hiding can be found in Chapter 6, "Managing Design Complexity"), which allows network operators to resolve complex problems in apparently simple ways. To understand the reasoning behind virtualization, let's look at a simple use case using the network illustrated in Figure 5.13.

Assume we want to be certain that Hosts A and F can talk to one another, and Hosts B and E can talk to one another, but Hosts A and B cannot, nor A and E, nor B and F, nor E and F. We could, of course, set up filters at all the interfaces through the network to ensure traffic can only pass between the hosts we've decided should communicate, and traffic cannot pass between hosts we don't want to communicate. This would take a lot of management and configuration effort, however—it's simpler to create two virtual topologies on which only devices within each virtual topology can communicate, and attach the right set of hosts to each virtual topology.

In this case, we could include E, it's upstream router, D, the [D,E] link, B's upstream router, C, the [B,C] link, and B, on one topology. On the other topology

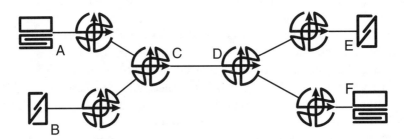

Figure 5.13 *Virtualization Use Case*

we could include A, A's upstream router, C, the [A,C] link, D, F's upstream router, [D,F] link, and F. So long as we have some way to separate the two topologies along the [C,D] link, so each topology appears to be its own "network," we can build two apparently independent topologies through which to carry traffic.

Further Thoughts on Using Virtual Topologies for Security

The preceding example provides simplistic reductions of the many uses cases for virtualized networks, even from a security point of view. One example that is used in the real world on a regular basis is separating publicly accessible servers and services (such as a public facing web server) from private backed servers (such as a database or business logic service). By breaking an application apart into multiple components, those parts which need to be publicly accessible can be addressed using public pools, and those parts that should not be publicly accessible can be addressed out of private pools. Taking this to maximum scale often results in the creation of microservices,[4] very small services, each with a focused purpose, that only communicate over the network; the interfaces for such services need to be protected not only from public access, but also from internal users. Carrying the concept of microservices into another realm, microsegmentation breaks a single network up into virtual topologies, and gives users and applications access to these topologies only when they need the services that reside there. Much like the example given in the text, this provides an alternate route to security that not only protects against unauthorized access, but also blocks any internal or external attacker's ability to even reach the processes that house critical services.

These sorts of design enable scaling, as well, by conserving address space, and breaking what could be a large failure domain up into potentially many different failure domains.

While this is a bit oversimplified, this is the essence of most virtualization deployments—the ability to create virtual topologies allows us to transfer the complexity of configuring a lot of filters into the complexity of an additional set of control plane and data plane primitives.

While there are many reasons to virtualize, they all come down to some form of multiplexing or another, whether between applications, groups of users, users, or some other dividing line. There are also many forms of virtualization, but they all come down to the same set of concepts—putting an out wrapper, tunnel header,

---

4. For an excellent introduction to microserves, see Sam Newman, *Building Microservices*, 1st edition. (O'Reilly Media, 2015).

or some other maker in the packet header to segregate one topology from another. Let's consider some of the tradeoffs of virtualization from this rather simplistic viewpoint.

Functional Separation

Virtualization allows the network operator to break a single problem into multiple parts, and then solve each one separately. An easy example—rather than managing the quality of service and interactions of hundreds of different flows from dozens of different applications, configurations can be molded around a small set of applications traveling along one virtual topology, and then manage inter-virtual topology configuration separately. This layering of functions is essentially what we see in building protocols, hierarchical network designs, and even the building and testing of software based on units, rather than as monoliths. Functional separation is a major simplification tool; virtualization is a good, time tested way to provide functional separation.

Separating layers and problems into multiple parts, however, can generate more complexity by increasing the number of surfaces which must interact. Each component created also creates a set of points of interaction between the new module and other existing modules. To return to the quality of service example, while there are fewer traffic flows and applications to manage—they're grouped off by virtualizing them—a number of new questions need to be answered, such as:

- Should each virtual topology be considered a single "class of service," or should there be multiple "buckets" or classes of service within each virtual topology?

- If there each virtual topology is going to have multiple classes of service, how should these classes of service be indicated? Is copying the quality of service information from the "inner" header to the "outer" header enough? Does there need to be some form of mapping between these two pieces of quality of service information?

- How should the different classes of service interact between the virtual topologies? Should all the "gold" service be lumped into a single class on the underlying transport network, or should one topology have priority over the others (and why)? This is specifically problematic when each topology represents a different customer. If two customers have both purchased a "gold" level of service, how should the network react when a link or path is congested enough that this level of service cannot be maintained for both customers? Should one customer "lose" to the other? Should both receive degraded service? Should there be different levels within the "gold" class based on the size or total worth of the customer? These are difficult questions to answer.

Forwarding Plane Complexity

The forwarding plane is simpler because each packet forwarding device in the network must only examine a small set of header bits, a label, or a tag, to determine which links a packet can be forwarded on or not. The alternative, of course, is to have a rather explicit set of filters, built on a per host basis, which forwarding devices must examine to make the same determination. Given the complexities of maintaining and search such a list, header bits or an outer header is a much simpler solution to the traffic separation problem.

On the other hand, the forwarding plane is more complex in some ways; traffic, on being accepted into the network, must have some set of bits, a label, or an outer header imposed on each packet. These same bits of information must be stripped as the packet passes out of the network.

Control Plane Complexity

Virtualizing simplifies the control plane by segmenting off reachability, topology, and policy information normally carried in a single control plane among several different control planes. Each individual control plane in a virtualized stack is therefore simpler—but what of the overall network complexity? Adding more control planes stacked on top of each other clearly increases complexity by the following:

- Increasing the amount of *state*. Link and node status impacting multiple topologies must be carried in multiple control planes.

- Increasing the *speed* of change. While the actual rate at which changes take place might remain the same, the speed at which these changes are reported (the velocity of information flow in the set of control planes) must increase.

- Increasing the interaction surfaces throughout the network. Multiple control planes, each operating with their own timing and convergence characteristics, must now operate over the same set of topology information. Solutions such as *wait for bgp* are designed to manage these intercontrol plane interactions—but these solutions inevitably add state complexity, as well.

Wait for BGP

Wait for BGP is a perfect example of the interaction between two control planes running on top of one another in one form of virtualization (BGP is used to carry global reachability, while IGPs are used to carry local reachability, making this a form of virtualization). Figure 5.14 illustrates the interaction between the IGP and BGP, and the solution wait for BGP provides.

In this example, we being with the best path between 2001:db8:0:2::/64 and 2001:db8:0:1::/64 passing through [A,B,C]. Note that in iBGP, from Router A's perspective, the next hop for 2001:db8:0:1::/64 is the interface on Router C facing the cloud, rather than someplace within or beyond the cloud, and the final router in the path (which directly connects to the destination). Note also that 2001:db8:0:1::/64 is not a reachable destination in the underlying IGP; the only path Routers A, B, and D have to this destination is through BGP.

If router B fails, then the IGP will quickly find a new route toward C through D. Router A's path to the next hop will now be [A,D,C], rather than [A,B,C]. As the BGP process on both B and D have reachability to 2001:db8:0:1::/64 through BGP, Router A switching it's path toward Router D, as the BGP next hop, has no effect on traffic forwarding.

When Router B comes back into service, however, there is a problem. The IGP will recalculate the path between Routers A and C quickly, switching traffic between these two routers back to the path through Router B. iBGP will not converge as quickly—it will take some time before Router B relearns the route toward 2001:db8:0:1::/64 through its iBGP peering session with Router C. During the period of time when Router A is using the path through Router B to reach its next hop toward 2001:db8:0:1::/64, and router B's iBGP table is reconverging, Router B will be receiving traffic it does not know how to forward—hence, this traffic will be dropped.

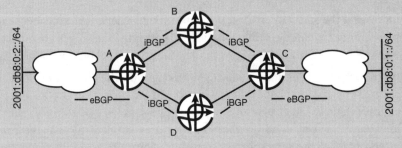

Figure 5.14 *Wait for BGP*

To resolve this, most major router vendors implement a feature that allows the IGP on Router B to wait in advertising reachability to Router C toward Router A until the local BGP process signals it has converged—wait for BGP. This feature slows down one of the two control planes in operation on the network to allow the second control plane to "catch up"—a solid idea that prevents a lot of dropped packets across BGP networks in operation.

Shared Fate Risk Groups

While Shared Risk Link Groups (SRLGs) are probably the most easily understood result of virtualization, they are often the most difficult to remember and account for in network design and implementation. Sometimes, in fact, they are impossible to discover until the common risk has reared its ugly head through a major outage. Essentially, an SRLG is formed whenever two virtual links share the same physical infrastructure. For instance:

- Two different circuits running over the same Frame Relay link/node.
- Two different VLANs running over the same physical Ethernet link, or across the same switch.
- Two different virtual processes running on the same physical compute and storage set.

Quite often, SFRGs are buried under layers of virtualization to the point that very few designers think about their existence or impact. In some cases, SRLGs can be buried under contracts and subcontracts—two major providers leasing redundant circuits to a single facility across a common fiber cable, or two hosting services providing redundant services out of a single data center. It's up to the network designer to find these sorts of overlapping service offerings—very few providers are going to be helpful in determining which facilities are shared, and which are not, for instance.

A Final Thought

Design complexity is not always obvious, and therefore not always completely considered or dealt with. In fact, the law of unintended consequences, a side effect of the impossibility of solving or removing complexity in the face of hard problems, makes many of these design problems the most haunting, and difficult to solve. In the next chapter, we're going to look at the tools network engineers have that can help balance complexity against the other factors.

Chapter 6

Managing Design Complexity

The last chapter examined the tradeoffs engineers and architects need to consider when designing the topology and control planes of a network. How can the network engineer manage these tradeoffs—state versus stretch, topology versus the speed of convergence, and virtualization versus design complexity? When should one (for instance, virtualization) be chosen over the other (for instance, fate sharing)? These are, in fact, some of the most difficult decisions to make in the field of network engineering, perhaps even more so because they rarely come to the surface as intentional decisions at all.

This chapter will consider a few ways engineers can manage these types of decisions, from the traditional to the not-so-traditional. Three specific areas considered are as follows:

- Modularity, which enables information hiding.

- Information hiding as a potential solution to managing control plane state.

- Models and visualization tools as a method to work with virtualization and fate sharing issues.

Modularity

Modularity is a longstanding, tried, and true method used in network design and engineering. Let's consider some examples of modular design, and then consider how modular design attacks the complexity problem.

Uniformity

Uniformity is a common mechanism used by network designers and engineers to reduce complexity within a network. The following sections discuss several of these techniques, and their tradeoffs.

Uniform Vendor

It's common for a company or network operations team to choose devices from the same vendor for use throughout their network to reduce the number of interfaces and implementations, thus reducing the amount of training and variety of skill sets required to configure new nodes as well as troubleshoot problems as they arise.

There are three tradeoffs when choosing this route to controlling complexity:

- **Vendor Lock-in**: If a single vendor's equipment is chosen throughout the network, then the vendor ends up driving the hardware and software life cycles. Barring a great deal of self-control, the vendor will also end up controlling the architecture of the network, whether or not that's best for the company.
- **Cost**: Using a single vendor will almost always drive up cost, as the vendor faces no competition.
- **Monoculture Failures**: A single vendor's equipment, running a single operating system, and a single set of applications, is a monoculture. A monoculture suffers from a shared set of failure modes across all the devices; if one device in the network reacts poorly to a specific set of circumstances, all the devices in the network will. Seemingly small problems can turn into major failures in a monoculture.

Uniform Hardware

Using the same physical switches throughout a single data center fabric is one approach to uniformity. Based on the principles laid out by Charles Clos in 1952, spine and leaf designs were originally created to build a large fabric based on minimal equally sized switches, as shown in Figure 6.1.

Assuming that there are only four connections from each leaf node shown in Figure 6.1 to some sort of load, each switch in the Clos fabric illustrated has the same number of interfaces—8. Using a single device type, each with 8 interfaces, a total of 32 devices can be interconnected (internally, or not connected to an outside network). In fact, the entire point of the original design was to allow the

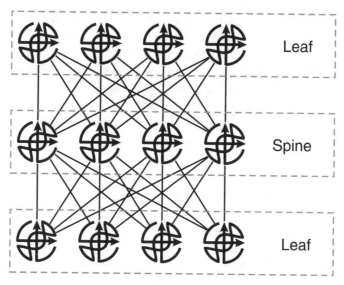

Figure 6.1 *A Clos, or Spine and Leaf, Topology*

interconnection of a large number of devices by combining the switching capabilities of small, equally sized switches. Using a single device type throughout an entire data center in this way allows the network operator to minimize the number of spares on hand, as well as minimize the configuration and management involved when swapping out a failed device or link hardware.

> **Note**
>
> The Clos fabric may appear similar to a traditional hierarchical Ethernet or IP network design, particularly when it is drawn with all the leaf nodes on one side (in the "folded" configuration). However, there are several crucial differences. For instance, in the spine and leaf topology (or fabric), there are no cross connections between any two leaf nodes, or any two spine nodes. This property means there are no topological loops in the fabric other than those passing through a leaf node. If the leaf nodes are configured so they cannot forward traffic received on an interface connected to a spine node back to another spine node, the spine and leaf design has no topological loops. This property simplifies the design of the network, allowing it to scale through the addition of more spine and leaf nodes, and reducing the work on the control plane.

Several realities make this attempt at reducing complexity more difficult than it might appear on the surface. For instance, device models change over time, which means serious thought needs to be put into controlling the life cycle of devices installed in the network. Theory aside, it's very difficult to use a single device in every location, even in a data center fabric; spine switches often need higher port count than top of rack devices, fat tree designs force the designer into choosing between multiple, less expensive, fixed configuration devices or more consistent usage of more expensive, blade- or slot-based devices, etc.

Uniform Control and Management

It is possible to purchase equipment from multiple vendors, and then rely on open standards implementations of control planes and management interfaces. For instance, a network operator may decide to standardize on IS-IS as a control plane throughout their network, and to standardize on open standards based YANG models, using a NETCONF or RESTCONF transport to manage all the devices.

There are, of course, several tradeoffs to consider when attempting to deploy this type of solution. For instance:

- Vendors are financially driven to support features, rather than management interfaces. This means management interfaces often lag far behind the implementation of new protocols or features on networking products.

- Vendors are, at least to some degree, driven away from supporting standardized interfaces. By supporting standardized interfaces, vendors are opening themselves up to being easily replaced in any deployment—in effect, standardized interfaces drive equipment into more of a commodity role.

- Standard bodies are often slow to produce new features or extensions to protocols. If a network operator waits until a new idea is fully standardized, or even looks like it will be standardized in a specific form, they could risk losing some advantage over their competitors.

It is often possible to cover up interface differences through a variety of tools, of course—network management systems and open source tools like Puppet can often work to find a common set of features through a *thunk or hardware abstraction layer*. However, keep the problem of leaky abstractions in mind when working with these sorts of tools.

The Law of Leaky Abstractions

What is a leaky abstraction? In 2002, Joel Spolsky coined the *law of leaky abstractions* on his blog, *Joel on Software*.[1] The law of leaky abstractions posits, "All non-trivial abstractions, to some degree, leak." Joel uses TCP as an example of such a leaky abstraction—TCP is, in effect, an abstraction of the underlying IP connectivity designed to emulate a connection oriented end-to-end link across an unreliable path. The problem is that TCP, as an abstraction, leaks.

There are two ways to see this leaking effect. The first is to realize that no matter how well TCP covers up the underlying network with an apparently connection oriented link, there are still artifacts of the underlying connectionless, unreliable link to deal with. When a piece of software using TCP to transfer data encounters jitter, for instance, it must decide what to do—whether to buffer the traffic so the user is presented with the experience they expect from an end-to-end lossless connection, to break the connection, and start over, or to deploy some other strategy. The specific strategy chosen is application dependent, of course, but the application cannot operate as if a TCP connection is truly an end-to-end connection between two hosts, or two devices. Thus the application developer must understand something of the IP network over which the TCP session runs—so the abstraction leaks.

The second way to see the leaky abstraction in TCP is to consider what happens when a TCP session actually does fail. If TCP were truly an end-to-end connection, an engineer troubleshooting the problem could confine themselves to TCP mechanisms—the timers, windows, data marshaling, and other techniques TCP uses to transfer information. In reality, however, engineers working on TCP problems must dive into the interaction between TCP and IP, IP itself, the interaction between IP and the lower physical layers, the queuing mechanisms used on the devices forwarding the IP traffic, the control plane that directs IP traffic, etc. The abstraction leaks—just because it looks like an end-to-end lossless connection doesn't mean you can actually treat it that way all the time. The key is to know when you can treat TCP as an end-to-end lossless connection, and when you can't, and to manage the exceptions.

The same problem crops up in network management, particularly at the device level. You can build an abstraction that will describe all the various configuration possibilities, all the various modes of operation, etc., for any

---

1. Joel Spolsky, "The Law of Leaky Abstractions," Blog, *Joel on Software*, n.p., last modified November 11, 2002, accessed January 19, 2015, http://www.joelonsoftware.com/articles/LeakyAbstractions.html.

given device. However, there are two problems that confront us. *First*, to build a complete list is to destroy the point of the abstraction itself. *Second*, no matter how complete such an abstraction might be, it will still be leaky. There will still be times when the engineer must work through the abstraction to understand what the real configuration on the real device is, and how to manipulate it to make the device do what the engineer needs it to do.

The problem with leaky abstractions is that the leakier the abstraction, the less useful the abstraction really is. At some point, for instance, it becomes harder to figure out how to configure the device through a device model (such as YANG) than to simply configure the device directly using native configuration commands. It's a matter of discipline, of course, to use the abstraction whenever possible, and to put the work into fixing the abstraction rather than simply going around it on a regular basis. In the end, though, there has to be some balance between the amount of time it takes to keep the abstraction "clean," and simply getting the work done. If the abstraction is so leaky that it requires a lot of time and effort to work within it, the end result might be more complexity rather than less.

Uniform Transport

One of the overlooked areas of network complexity is the wide array of transport systems deployed in the real world. Remember the old IP focused model, with one transport over a variety of circuits, and a lot of different applications running on top? The reality today is a spaghetti of overlays, tunnel types, and transports scattered throughout the network, as Figure 6.2 (partially) illustrates.

The spaghetti transport system has several interesting (and difficult to manage) features, including:

- Several upper layer protocols are heavily reliant on information contained in and state generated by lower layer protocols. For instance, many upper layer applications actually rely on the IP address as a sort of identifier for a particular system connected to the network, although the IP address is actually a locator.

- Several upper layer protocols can carry lower layer protocols, creating a complex and overlapping stack. Although Virtual Extensible Local Area Network (VXLAN) tunnels rely on IP, it actually carries Ethernet frames; IPv4, IPv6, and Generic Routing Encapsulation (GRE) tunnels (including MPLS carried inside a GRE tunnel) are regularly carried on top of VXLAN.

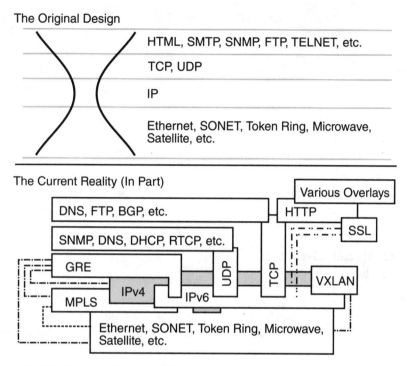

Figure 6.2 *The Spaghetti Transport System*

- IPv4 and IPv6 can run as parallel network protocols, either with their own control plane or separate control planes.

Each of these protocols is a leaky abstraction; laying them one on top of another in this way, especially when protocols are designed and deployed in "stacking loops," such as Ethernet over VXLAN over IP over Ethernet, causes the leaks in each abstraction to mingle, making a complete mess in terms of management and troubleshooting. Each pair of protocols in this illustration represent another interaction surface in the overall system, as well.

What can be done to alleviate this spaghetti transport system? Reducing the number of transports running in any given network to the minimum possible. Designers should try and choose the minimal number of protocols, both overlays and underlays, which will support all the applications and all the requirements. This will necessarily involve tradeoffs in support for specific applications or systems, but the gain in reduced complexity is well worth it, as it will reduce the MTTR, control plane state, and many other factors. Using MPLS as an example—a single MPLS deployment can support Ethernet, IPv4, and IPv6 virtual links with full virtualization across a very minimal transport system. Deploying dual-stack IPv4/IPv6 and VXLAN for Layer 2 virtualization (with IP on top for Layer 3 virtualization) is a much more complex solution to the same set of problems.

Remember that just because another protocol is available, it doesn't mean you have to deploy it in your network—just because you can doesn't mean you should.

The one downside to standardizing on just a few transports can be illustrated by returning to MPLS. It's much harder (or rather more expensive) to obtain MPLS support in enterprise or data center class equipment, as MPLS is seen as a "transit service provider solution." Sometimes our own preconceptions can cause us to choose solutions based on what they're "meant for," rather than what they're really useful for; in the end, this can make our networks more, rather than less, complex.

Interchangeable Modules

At the device level, using a single vendor's products, or in a more complete way, the same model of device (see the previous example on data center fabrics), can reduce complexity through uniformity. The same principle can be applied at the network level, as well, by cataloging each of the different types of modules in the network, and then building each one to be as similar as possible. For instance, you might be able to divide a network into a small set of topologies:

- Campus
- Data Center
- Point of Presence
- Core

For each one of these "places," determine a set of roles and the requirements that go with that role. For each role in each pin, deploy a single network topology and configuration that will support the range of requirements. So long as discipline is maintained in:

- Keeping the configurations and deployments of every instance of a single "place" the same across time and location.
- Keeping the number of "places" and roles to the minimum possible.

The amount of work required to design, deploy, manage, and troubleshoot these modules is greatly diminished.

Within the data center, this type of thinking is often used of "pods," or "modules," as well. Each set of racks within a data center can be considered a modular unit, where the data center grows in units (rather than devices), and units are upgraded or replaced, rather than individual devices. There are, as usual, a number of problems that come along with interchangeable modules.

First, interchangeable parts often aren't. In spite of all the work network managers do to make each module identical, local conditions, spread across time, work against consistency. As manufacturers replace lines of equipment, or replace one device with another, it quickly becomes difficult to ensure consistency across a large number of identical modules. This is also a problem when interconnecting different Places In the Network (PINs). As an example, if you decide to upgrade the connection speed between PINs, you will need to modify every PIN in the entire network. Modularity is often difficult to maintain in the face of such problems.

Second, a problem often hidden behind interchangeable modules is the "places in the network" syndrome, where the modules become the focus of all network design and operations, leaving the network as a whole, or as a system, off the table as something to be considered. It's a bit like building a house by choosing a lot of different rooms you think you want, and then choosing a hallway to connect them all. It might be really nice from the perspective of the person living in the house, but the builder is going to face some real trouble in trying to build what the customer wants—and maintenance is going to be a disaster.

> **Note**
>
> See the section on "Places in the Network" later in this chapter for a more complete description of PINs.

How Modularity Attacks the Complexity Problem

Network engineers often equate modularity with hierarchical network design and aggregation, but these two are not precisely the same thing. Hierarchical network design is a discipline that uses modularity as one of its principles, but not all hierarchical network designs are modular, nor are all modular network designs hierarchical. In the same way, aggregation often depends on modularity, but you can build a very modular network that doesn't aggregate any information at all. So, if aggregation and hierarchy are not the point, how does modularity, and the examples given here—uniform hardware, uniform management, uniform transport, and interchangeable modules—really impact the complexity of a network's design?

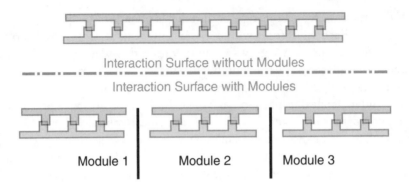

Figure 6.3 *Modularization and Interaction Surfaces*

While a truly modular design often leads to the ability to reduce state, modular designs, themselves, don't actually reduce state. The same can be said for *speed,* as well—building a modular design might provide opportunities to reduce the speed at which information is spread through the control plane, it doesn't directly impact the *speed* at which the network operates.

Surface, then, is the primary means through which modularity reduces complexity in network design. By breaking the network up into multiple smaller pieces, modularity reduces the size of interaction surfaces in the network, as illustrated in Figure 6.3.

Information Hiding

Modularization, on its own, provides some reduction in network complexity, both from a management and a control plane perspective, by reducing the size of the interaction surfaces. But, as above, modularization doesn't really attack the *state* or *speed* aspects of network complexity. Modularity does, however, enable information hiding—and information hiding directly attacks state and speed. Let's look at two forms of information hiding commonly used in network design: aggregation and virtualization.

Aggregation

Aggregation is, by far, the most common form of information hiding in networks. There are actually two types of aggregation in use in network design, although they are often conflated into the same thing: hiding topology information and summarizing reachability information. The easiest way to understand the difference between the two is by examining aggregation in a link state protocol, such as IS-IS. Figure 6.4 will be used to illustrate the difference.

Given the network as illustrated, with no configurations beyond placing Routers A and B in a single level 2 flooding domain, and Routers B, C, D, and E in a separate level 1 flooding domain, what would Router B see in its level 1 IS-IS topology database versus what Router A sees in it level 2 topology database?

Router B:

- 2001:db8:0:1::/64 connected to D
- 2001:db8:0:2::/64 connected to E
- Router B => Router D
- Router D => Router B
- Router E => Router D
- Router D => Router E
- Router E => Router C
- Router C => Router E

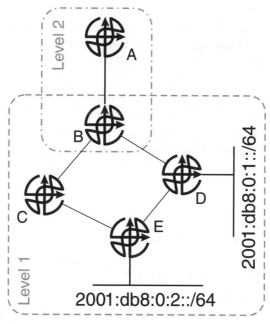

Figure 6.4 *Aggregation*

- Router C => Router B
- Router B => Router C
- Router B connected to a level 2 routing domain (the connected bit set in Router B's LSP)

Router A:

- 2001:db8:0:1::/64 reachable through Router B
- 2001:db8:0:2::/64 reachable through Router B
- Router A => Router B
- Router B => Router A

Examining these two lists, the big differences are as follows:

- The connection points for the two reachable subnets are attached to Router B's routing information, rather than Routers D and E.
- The links between Routers B, C, D, and E are all removed from the topology database.

By attaching all the reachable destinations within the level 1 flooding domain to the level 1/level 2 flooding domain border, Router A doesn't need to know the internal details of the level 1 topology. The point of creating multiple flooding domains in a link state protocol like IS-IS is, in fact, to block the topology information from "outlying" flooding domains into the "core" flooding domain—from the level 1 flooding domains into the level 2 flooding domain. Router B, then, is aggregating the topology information, carrying just the reachable destinations and the cost to reach them, rather than passing the link state between each pair of routers within the level 1 flooding domain to Router A. What does aggregating this topology information accomplish? Two things:

- Aggregation of topology information decreases the *state* carried in the control plane by removing the link information carried in the level 1 flooding domain from the level 2 flooding domain, hence reducing the size of the topology database and the size of the tree the SPF algorithm must calculate across.
- Aggregation of topology information decreases the *speed* of the information flowing through the control plane by removing information about the state of the links within the level 1 flooding domain from the level 2 database; it

doesn't matter to Router A what the state of the link between Routers D and E are, for instance, so long as the reachable destinations remain constant from the perspective of Router B. By blocking topology information from flowing into the level 2 link state topology database, aggregation slows down the pace of updates, and hence the pace at which Router A must react to those updates.

Aggregation can be taken one step further by configuring Router B to aggregate the reachability information in the level 1 flooding domain to which it's attached. In this case, the two routes, 2001:db8:0:1::/64 and 2001:db8:0:2::/64, can be aggregated to a single shorter prefix route, 2001:db8::0/61. If you examined Router A's level 2 topology database after this aggregation is configured, you'd find it is now slightly smaller.

- 2001:db8::0/64 reachable through Router B
- Router A connected to Router B
- Router B connected to Router A

Once again, examining this from the perspective of state and speed:

- Aggregation of reachability information decreases the *state* carried in the control plane by reducing the two reachable destinations to a single reachable destination.
- Aggregation of topology information decreases the *speed* of the information flowing through the control plane by removing information about the state of the two individual reachable destinations within the level 1 flooding domain. No matter what the state of either 2001:db8:0:1::/64 or 2001:db8:0:2::/64 are, the state of 2001:db8::0/61 remains constant.

Aggregation, like all abstractions, has a set of tradeoffs (as always, there is no such thing as a free lunch). The last chapter spent a good deal of time discussing the impact of aggregation on stretch—that discussion won't be repeated here, but it's important to bear in mind. Beyond stretch, however, network engineers should remember that aggregation is also subject to the law of leaky abstractions, explained in a sidebar above. How do aggregates leak? Figure 6.5 illustrates aggregation as a leaky abstraction.

Router B is configured to aggregate 2001:db8:0:1::/64 and 2001:db8:0:2::/64 to 2001:db8::/61 using the lowest metric from the two component routes. In this case, the metric would be chosen from the [B,D] path, so the aggregate would be

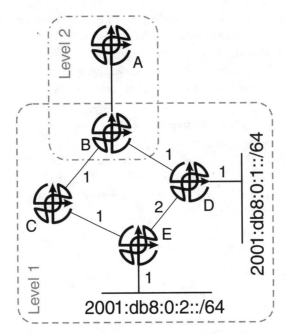

Figure 6.5 *Aggregation as a Leaky Abstraction*

advertised with a metric of 2. If the link between Router B and D fails, however, the lowest metric among the components would be the path [B,C,E], with a total metric of 3. When this link fails, the aggregate route will change metric from a cost of 2 to a cost of 3—hence the abstraction has leaked information about the topology through the aggregation. It is possible, of course to plug this leak; however, it's important to remember that any solution used here will have its own set of tradeoffs to consider.

Failure Domains and Information Hiding

No discussion of information hiding would be complete without some examination of failure domains. Both aggregation and virtualization are used to limit the size of a failure domain—but what is a failure domain, and how does it relate to complexity? To begin, let's define what a failure domain is, then let's look at the relationship between failure domains and network complexity. Figure 6.6 illustrates failure domains.

Router B in this IS-IS network is configured to aggregate 2001:db8:0:1::/64 and 2001:db8:0:2::/64 into a single route, 2001:db8::/61, which is then advertised into the level 2 flooding domain (toward Router C). 2001:db8:0:8::/64 does not fall within this aggregate, so it is advertised "as is" into the level two

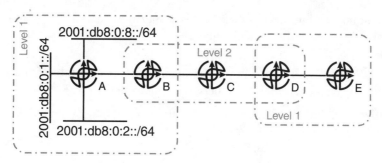

Figure 6.6 *Failure Domains*

flooding domain. Using this configuration, you can build a high-level overview of what the database for a selection of routers in the network will look like in relation to these three routes.

- **Router B, Level 1 Database:**
- Router B is connected to Router A.
- Router B is connected to a level 2 flooding domain.
- Router A is connected to Router B.
- Router A is connected to 2001:db8::0/64.
- Router A is connected to 2001:db8:0:2::/64.
- Router A is connected to 2001:db8:0:8::/64.

- **Routers B, C, & D, Level 2 Database:**
- Router B is connected to Router C.
- Router C is connected to Router B.
- Router C is connected to Router D.
- Router D is connected to Router C.
- Router B is connected to 2001:db8::/61.
- Router B is connected to 2001:db8:0:8::/64.

- **Router E:**
- Router D is connected to Router E.
- Router E is connected to Router D.
- Router D is connected to a level 2 flooding domain.

Examining this high-level view of the link state databases at various places in the network would show the following:

- If 2001:db8:0:1::/64 or 2001:db8:0:2::/64 are disconnected from Router A, only Routers A and B will need to recalculate their SPT.

- If 2001:db8:0:8::/64 is disconnected from Router A, Routers B, C, and D will need to recalculate their SPT.

Hiding information, then, reduces the number of routers that must recalculate their SPT in reaction to a change in the network topology. This is, in fact, as good a definition of a failure domain as you are likely to find:

A failure domain is the set of devices that must interact with the control plane when network topology or reachability changes.

Given this definition, if 2001:db8:0:2::/64 is disconnected from Router A, the failure domain contains only Routers A and B. Routers C through E are not included in the failure domain in this case, because the information in their control planes doesn't change. So by hiding information through aggregation, the size of the failure domain has been reduced. This reduces the scope of the interaction surfaces within the control plane, as well as reducing the speed at which the control plane receives new information.

Another point to note from this example is that the failure domain is not a "solid line" you can paint around any particular part of the network. Some information (such as the example of the aggregate's metric changing given above) will always leak through any point where information is being hidden in the network (see the previous sidebar on *The Law of Leaky Abstractions*), so there are actually many different overlapping failure domains in any given network.

Final Thoughts on Information Hiding

Information hiding in one form or another is one of the best tools the network designer has to deal with complexity. By hiding information between modules:

- The amount of *state* carried in the control plane is reduced. Aggregation removes reachability and topology information, reducing the total amount of information carried in the control plane. Virtualization (discussed in the last chapter) breaks the topology and reachability information up among multiple control planes, so that each control plane only manages a subset of the total network state.

- The *speed* of the control plane is reduced. Aggregation, for instance, reduces the speed at which the information the control plane is carrying by either removing state entirely (topology) or replacing more volatile state with less volatile state (summarization of reachability information). Virtualization reduces the speed of changes in the control plane by spreading the changes across multiple control planes (it's important to remember that virtualization impacts the speed of control plane operations less than aggregation does).

- The interaction *surfaces* are contained in aggregation primarily through modularization, and the creation of "choke points" in the network limiting the places where various pieces of the control plane interact. Virtualization reduces the size of the interaction surfaces by tying specific applications or customer to specific logical topologies, thus allowing each set of applications to be treated as a case that's independent of the rest of the applications running on the network. Of course, virtualization isn't quite as straight forward as aggregation, because the virtual topologies themselves must interact, creating another interaction surface in the network.

Models

Models aren't an "on network" tool to deal with complexity, but rather a way of categorizing and abstracting out what is happening in the network. Most network engineers are generally familiar with the seven and four layer models—and these are good models for abstracting the operation of protocols. What about useful models for understanding the deployment and operation of the network as a whole, or the operation of the network and applications? Three different models are presented in this section, and finally a modeling language.

Waterfall

The waterfall model isn't a model of network operation, but rather a model of traffic flows. This model is based on the basic insight that all routing and switching protocols essentially build a tree sourced at the destination, and spread out to each available source. Figure 6.7 shows the waterfall model.

The waterfall model shows how data flow splits in a network at every network device so that a single stream becomes a set of streams. Once any network data stream has split, there is no way to rejoin the streams back into a single

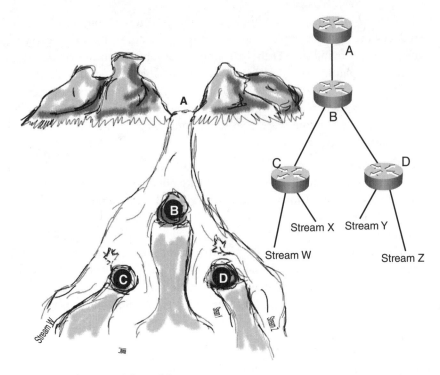

Figure 6.7 *The Waterfall Model*

stream of data without risking loops in the network topology. To understand how this relates to modeling a network, consider the difference between spanning tree and routing operation in a waterfall model.

Spanning tree builds one large tree which is shared by every source and destination pair. This single tree means that all traffic must "leap up the waterfall" to the head end, where it can then follow the flow of water back toward its real destination. For instance, a packet flowing along Stream W toward the end of Stream Z must follow the stream to its source at A, and then follow the path for Stream Z.

For a routed control plane, each edge device builds its own tree, so each device is at the head end of a waterfall, or a spanning tree. Rather than "leaping up" the waterfall to reach the top, and then flowing back down, each traffic stream follows its own set of streams down. In the example given here, if traffic were flowing from an entrance point at Stream W to an endpoint at Stream Z, it would follow a different tree originating at Router C. This is why a routing protocol is more efficient than spanning tree; traffic doesn't need to "leap up" the tree to reach its destination.

Places in the Network

PINs are a way to divide a network along functional, rather than topological links. Figure 6.8 illustrates a PINs view of a network.

Each functional section of the network is separated into a different component, such as the two data centers and the two campuses, and they are connected using interconnection points (marked IC in the illustration). Splitting the network up in this way emphasizes the function of each piece of the network. Different design paradigms can be used in each section, to match the specific purpose of the PIN being designed. For instance, a large-scale hub and spoke topology might dominate the retail environment, while the first data center might be designed using a traditional switched Ethernet topology, and the second as a Clos topology.

Security, management mechanisms, and other aspects of each PIN can also be different; Data Center 1 might have an open security policy within the data center itself, and strong restrictions on outside access, while Data Center 2 might have no entrance policies, but strong per server/application security mechanisms. Every PIN is completely opaque to every other PIN in the network. Data Center 1 is simply a traffic sink for Data Center 2, and the WAN PIN is simply a transport mechanism to reach the other PINs in the network. This is a form of strictly typed modularity.

Connecting these different PINs is a series of interconnects, shown as light gray circles in Figure 6.8. Some PINs might connect directly to each other as well as to the Wide Area Network (WAN), or Core PIN, as illustrated with the DMZ

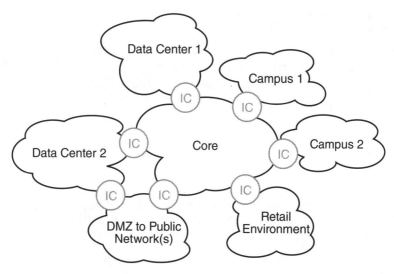

Figure 6.8 *Places in the Network*

and Data Center 2 PINs. Others might connect only to the Core. Each PIN's internal structure is completely different from every other PIN's. For instance, Data Center 1 might have core, distribution, and access layers, and Data Center 2 might have only a core and aggregation layers. These layers are completely independent of the overall network design.

PINs are useful for understanding a network design from an operational perspective, because they provide a strong functional view based on business use for each PIN. This allows each business problem to be approached independently, which can often clarify the problems involved. Vendor sales folks tend to work within PINs almost exclusively, because it helps to narrow the solution to a particular environment, helping to drive requirements.

As a model, PINs fail in one particular regard—they focus the network architecture on a bottom up view of functionality. This does allow the network to more closely mimic the functionality required; it pushes the overall architecture out of sight. This can result in a systemic architecture that "just grows organically," rather than producing a well thought out overall plan and architecture.

> **Note**
>
> Several other positive and negative aspects of PINs are similar to the positive and negative aspects of interchangeable modules discussed earlier in this chapter.

Hierarchical

Hierarchical network models, grounded in scale free networks, are as old as networks themselves. Hierarchical design is, in essence, taking the rules of modularity, combining them with a waterfall model of traffic flow, and finally combining these two with aggregation for information hiding, and building a set of "rules of thumb" that generally work for just about any network design project. Figure 6.9 illustrates a basic hierarchical design.

> **Note**
>
> Hierarchical network design is covered in detail in the Cisco Press book, *Optimal Routing Design.*[2] Many networks are now two layer designs, rather than three, with "layers within layers" to build out to scale.

---

2. Russ White, Alvaro Retana, and Don Slice, *Optimal Routing Design* (Cisco Press, 2005).

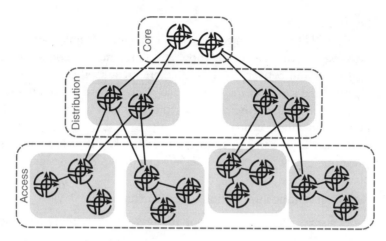

Figure 6.9 *A Basic Hierarchical Design*

Consider some of the "rules of thumb" for hierarchical network design in network complexity terms.

Focused Layered Functionality

Each of the three layers in the hierarchical design—access, distribution, and core—should be focused on a small set of functions or purposes. For instance, the network core should be focused on forwarding traffic between the distribution layer modules, rather than implementation of policy, or even connectivity to outside networks. For instance, the Internet and outside partner networks should not be connected to the network core, but rather to an access layer module parallel to the other access layer modules.

Focusing functionality within each layer helps manage complexity by controlling the interaction surfaces within and between the network modules. By focusing on forwarding between distribution layer modules, for instance, the configuration of the network core devices can be greatly simplified—admittance policy and per user or device security can be left off these devices, as those functions are handled someplace else in the network. Restricting the location of any particular function also simplifies equipment choices, and allows the modules within the layer to be more similar. As an example, if high-speed forwarding over a long distance dark fiber interface is a function consistently pushed to the network core devices, then distribution layer devices can be chosen without reference to the types of interfaces required to support this capability.

Focused Policy Points

The hierarchical design pattern also provides convenient "choke points" in the network topology. At the edge of the topology, along the user connection point to the access layer, and between each layer, there are a smaller number of connections that pull the topology together. These places, where the amount of connectivity is more limited by the design of the network, are perfect places to implement policy in a more centralized way.

By way of illustration, consider aggregation as a policy. It makes sense to configure aggregation on the links between layers in a hierarchical design, as this:

- Provides full routing information within each module.
- Provides a small set of places to look for aggregation within each module.
- Provides a small set of places to look for suboptimal traffic distribution between the modules.
- Provides a separation point between the control plane state between modules.

Providing "choke points," in the topology allows for controlled interaction surfaces between the network modules, points at which to reduce the control plane state being carried between modules, and, in turn, a way to control the speed at which the control plane must manage network changes.

> **Note**
>
> The tradeoffs around aggregation are discussed in the Information Hiding section earlier in this chapter and Chapter 5, "Design Complexity." The tradeoffs around policy placement are discussed in Chapter 5, "Design Complexity."

UML

The Unified Modeling Language (UML) might seem out of place here, because it's a modeling tool, rather than a model or a system. However, the network engineering world tends to "fly by the seat of its pants," rather than intentionally think through the way the network interacts with applications and policies. A process focused modeling language can be really helpful in understanding how an application works in some detail, which can then be directly mapped to policies and packet flows in the network. This is particularly true in large-scale data center and cloud deployments. Although large-scale cloud and data center deployments are designed to be "application agnostic," there often comes a point in troubleshooting an application running on a data center fabric when understanding the packet flow, and where policies are put in place, is really helpful in determining where the problem lies.

Figure 6.10 illustrates a UML model for a web application.

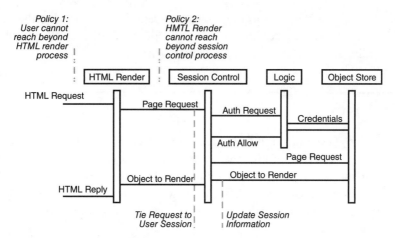

Figure 6.10 *Example of a Simple Web Application Modeled Using UML*

While the diagram shown in Figure 6.10 focuses on the interaction between the different processes which make up the web application, the interactions between the applications all happen across the network—as such, each interaction represents a flow of packets that must be planned for. Examining this diagram, a network engineering might ask questions like:

- What type of connectivity is used between each of these processes? If it's Layer 2 connectivity, then the processes must be placed into a single Layer 2 domain, or the traffic must otherwise be handled so the processes believe they are connected over a Layer 2 link.

- What protocol is used at each connection? For instance, TCP might be used between the Hypertext Markup Language (HTML) Render component and session control, but User Datagram Protocol (UDP) might be used between session control and the logic components. This information will play a large role in determining where and what types of quality of service need to be deployed.

- Where and how is policy implemented? There are only two policies noted on the diagram (this is rather simple compared to most real-world application deployments)—are these policies implemented by the network, the application, or both? How are they to be implemented?

Beyond these questions, getting a solid estimate of the sizes of each traffic flow could be very helpful in building a picture of the way the application uses network resources. If you have this type of information for each application, it is possible to roll this information up into an overall picture of what the traffic should look like on the network—but even at the individual application level, understanding these sorts of traffic flows can be useful.

A Final Thought

Network designers and architects face very uncertain environments from a complexity perspective. While the tools are "out there," they aren't often widely understood in terms of managing complexity, nor are they always well developed. Instead, most network designers work from "rules of thumb," based on "seat of the pants flying," based on long years of experience with what *doesn't* work.

By examining the "rules of thumb" from a complexity perspective, you can begin to put some reasoning behind them—why they work, where they work, and when they won't work. Examining the problems of network design from a complexity perspective helps to untangle some of the mysteries, and to point the way toward better network design through a deeper understanding of what the tradeoffs really are, and how the techniques and models really work.

Chapter 7

<hr style="width:30%;height:6px;background:black;border:none" />

Protocol Complexity

Who cares about protocol complexity? It's a topic reserved for the geeks with their heads in radix trees and deep math, right?

Wrong.

The protocols deployed on a network, whether used in the control plane or to carry data through the network, are actually systems in their own right—often complex systems—that interact with the other systems in the network along the same sorts of interaction surfaces discussed at the network and design levels. Because of these design surfaces, network engineers working "down in the protocols" need to know network design just as much as network architecture folks need to know protocol design.

This chapter aims to bring the complexity tradeoffs discussion to the world of protocol design, so network engineers can understand why one protocol might work better in one situation, and others in another. There are two opposite trends in the network engineering world to guard against:

- Trying to solve every problem with a single protocol; this is most pronounced in the drive with the BGP (at presstime). While a single control plane for everything (and one ring to rule them all) can greatly simplify the job of the network designer, it can also push suboptimal designs.

- Solving every problem with its own protocol suite.

The tradeoffs here aren't always obvious, but there clearly needs to be a balance between deploying a point solution for every problem and deploying a single solution for all problems. This is where layering in a network design (virtualizing topologies so different control and data planes see different views of the network) can be very useful.

This chapter begins with a section considering the tradeoff between flexibility and complexity, using OSPF versus IS-IS as the "classic" example of how different complexity tradeoffs lead to completely different protocols, each with their own set of tradeoffs. The second section considers layering versus complexity, specifically in light of John Day's iterative model of network transport. The third section considers protocol complexity against design complexity using two examples; the first is a return to the concepts of microloops and fast convergence in link state protocols, and the second considers the perception of EIGRP in the "early years" against the reality, and changes made to the protocol over the years to contain complexity in network design.

Flexibility versus Complexity: OSPF versus IS-IS

Perhaps the classic example of complexity versus flexibility in the world of protocol design is the original contrasting designs of OSPF and IS-IS. A little bit of history is required to understand the original context of the discussion and decisions that were made in relation to the two protocols.

> **Note**
>
> IS-IS is a link state protocol widely deployed in large-scale service provider networks. The standards specification for the protocol is contained in the ISO 10589.[1]

IS-IS was originally designed to support the Open Systems Interconnect (OSI) protocol stack (the original seven-layer stack), which was designed around End Systems (ES) and Intermediate Systems (IS). Each ES was assigned an address based on the Layer 2 address of the device that was then advertised by the connected IS throughout the network—essentially host routing was the normal mode of operation for OSI-based networks, with aggregation only taking place at the flooding domain boundary. The actual systems involved were heavier weight computers (for that time), and hence had a good deal of processing performance

---

1. For more information on IS-IS, see Russ White and Alvaro Retana, *IS-IS: Deployment in IP Networks*, 1st edition. (Boston: Addison-Wesley, 2003).

and available memory, so the original designers of IS-IS were more concerned about designing a protocol that was flexible and extensible to new address types (in case the OSI networking protocols ever took on a new type of end host to route for, or Layer 2 addressing changed, etc.), as well as the ability to handle level 1 and level 2 flooding domains with a minimal number of packet types.

This general outlook led to a protocol that was focused on carrying information in TLVs; to add new information, a new TLV to carry the information could easily be added to the protocol. At the same time, all the information originated by a single device was carried in a single, corresponding, Link State Packet (LSP), which could be fragmented if the size of packet became larger than the Maximum Transmission Unit (MTU) of the network.

OSPF, on the other hand, was designed with a slightly different set of goals in mind. In the time during which OSPF was designed, routers (in particular) had what would today be considered very low performance processors. As special purpose devices, routers simply were not equipped with the processing performance or the memory that any given ES might have—so while IS-IS counted on a relatively high-performance device handling forwarding, OSPF was developed around the concept of a relatively low-performance device handling forwarding.

To meet these goals, three specific points came to the forefront in OSPF's design:

- Fixed length encoding. Rather than using TLVs to encode and carry information, OSPF focused on using fixed length encoding, which requires less resources both on the wire (the TLV header can be dispensed with) and in processing (fixed blocks of code can be used to process specific packet formats, rather than the longer, more complex blocks of code required to dynamically read and react to various TLVs carried within a single stream).

- Fixed packet types of a smaller size. Rather than each router originating a single "packet" that is fragmented, and the numerous headaches around synchronizing these fragments, OSPF focused on shorter packets that would (in theory) fit in a single MTU packet on the network. This made flooding and synchronization simpler.

- Aggregated reachability. In IP, Layer 3 addressing is untied from Layer 2 addressing, which means (in practice) that reachability is aggregated from the first hop. IP routers advertise subnets, which are an aggregate of a set of hosts, rather than each individual host. This means OSPF needed to handle multiaccess links and aggregation in a way that was more IP centric than IS-IS in the initial phases of the design.

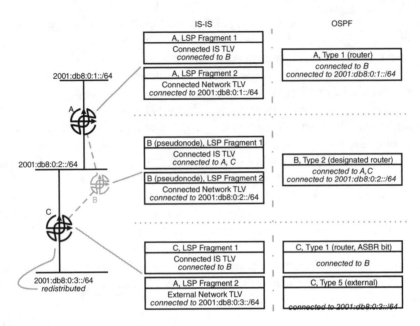

Figure 7.1 *OSPF versus IS-IS*

As a result of these goals, OSPF was designed with a number of different LSA types, each one having a fixed format, and each one carrying a different type of information. Figure 7.1 illustrates the difference.

The network illustrated in Figure 7.1 consists of only two routers, each connected to a stub link, and both connected to a common broadcast (multipoint) link. Both OSPF and IS-IS elect a pseudonode (though it's called a *Designated Router* [DR] in OSPF) to represent the broadcast link to reduce the number of adjacencies and routing protocol traffic flowing across the link; this is represented by Router B, which is smaller and gray. Treating each IS-IS TLV as a separate packet (or fragment of a single LSP), the two sets of packets generated by each protocol are set side-by-side. If you understand the concept of link state routing, the result isn't very surprising—the same information must somehow be carried in both protocols. The main difference is in how the two protocols encode the information. IS-IS encodes the information in TLVs within fragments, while OSPF encodes the information in different types of packets. If each TLV in IS-IS represents a single LSA type in OSPF, the correlation is almost one-to-one.

OSPF traded off complexity in coding and transport against fixed length packets. This leads to the question—what advantage does using TLVs give IS-IS?

The cost of the TLV is a larger packet size and more complex processing; how does IS-IS gain against OSPF for increasing the packet formatting complexity in this way?

The most obvious answer is in the ability to quickly and easily add new types of information to IS-IS. For instance, when IPv6 was developed, both of these link state protocols needed to support the new IP format. IS-IS simply added a new set of TLVs, while OSPF required an entirely new protocol—OSPFv3. The downside of fixed length formats is immediately obvious. In general, IS-IS proliferates TLV types, while OSPF proliferates packet types.

> **Note**
>
> This is a bit simplified to illustrate a specific point; the TLV formatting is not the only reason why OSPFv3 was created rather than simply adding IPv6 to OSPFv2. For instance, OSPFv2 builds adjacencies, and carries LSAs, across layer IPv4, so the next hops in OPSFv2 are IPv4 addresses—which would cause some headaches when trying to deploy IPv6, which should naturally use IPv6 next hops. OSPF is more intimately tied to the underlying Layer 3 transport than IS-IS, which peers directly at Layer 2.

Is OSPF better, or IS-IS? There's no clear cut answer to this question—a lot depends on the use to which the protocol is being put, the skills of the network operators, and the individual implementations. In the real world, the tradeoffs made years ago based on the different environments each protocol was designed for have been overcome by events; that the details hardly matter is apparent in the level of detail any debate about the two protocols must reach to actually find a difference worth mentioning.

Layering versus Protocol Complexity

Figure 7.2 illustrates two protocol stacks; which one is simpler?

If you're like most network engineers, you're likely to have one of two reactions to this illustration:

- The XYZ protocol, because there's only one protocol in the stack—and one protocol is always simpler than many protocols interacting.
- The XYZ protocol stack, because layering is good. Aren't transport protocols (such as TCP and IP) layered like this?

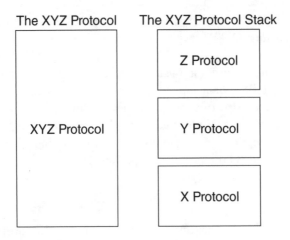

Figure 7.2 *Protocol Stacks*

Either you believe that layers are good because they've been drilled into the head of every network engineer because of their first console experience, or layers are a necessary evil that make it hard to remember when you're sitting down to take a certification test or college exam. Which is it?

It's neither.

Which one is more complex actually depends on several factors, including:

- What the total functionality of the stack of protocols is. Changing the context of the illustration changes the perception of the problem; if someone said, "the XYZ protocol stack is a replacement for the IP component in the current transport stack, increasing the layers in that stack from four to six," you'd immediately think "too complex." If someone said, "the XYZ protocol replaces three layers of tunnels currently running in the network with a single tunneled protocol," you'd probably immediately yell, "hurrah!"

- How well defined the interaction surfaces are between the protocols in the stack. Protocol stacks with well-defined layers make for well-defined interaction surfaces. Well-defined interaction surfaces are still leaky abstractions, but better definition tends to reduce the leaks. Well-defined interactions surfaces are still interaction surfaces that add complexity, but well-defined depth and scope both contribute to less cross-layer abstraction leaks, and make it easier to understand the interactions for modifications and troubleshooting.

Layering, then, can either be a good thing or a bad thing from a complexity standpoint. It all depends on how the layering impacts the following:

- **State:** Does the addition of a layer actually divide state in some meaningful way? Or are the additional layers simply spreading out state that often "acts together" across the layering boundary, making the interaction surface more complex?

- **Speed:** Does the additional layer reduce the speed at which one layer must operate, or separate two processes with completely different "operation tempos"?

- **Surface:** Does the additional layer produce a set of clean interaction points and minimize leaky abstractions? Are there just a few places where unintended consequences can come into play, or many?

> **Note**
>
> The concept of unintended consequences is closely tied to the concept of subsidiarity, which is covered in more detail in Chapter 10, "Programmable Network Complexity."

One of the ways network engineers have dealt with the questions raised above about layering in protocol stacks is by building protocol stacks according to models. Two common models are the four-layer *DoD model,* and the seven-layer *OSI model.* While most network engineers are familiar with at least one of these models, a quick review might be in order.

The Seven-Layer Model

Virtually anyone who has ever been through a networking class or studied for a network engineering certification is familiar with using the seven-layer model to describe the way network's work. Connectionless Networking Protocol (CLNP) and a routing protocol, IS-IS, were designed by the ISO to meet the requirements given within the seven-layer model. These protocols are still in wide use, particularly IS-IS, which has been modified to support routing in IP networks. Figure 7. 3 illustrates the seven-layer model.

Each pair of layers, moving vertically through the model, interacts through an API. So to connect to a particular physical port, a piece of code at the data link layer would connect to the socket for that port. This allows the interaction between the various layers to be abstracted and standardized. A piece of

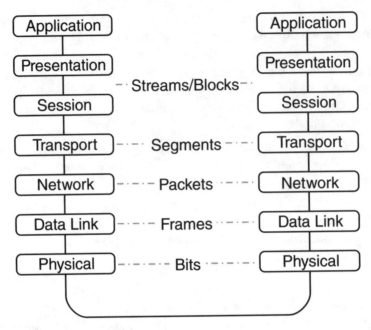

Figure 7.3 *Seven-Layer Model*

software at the network layer doesn't need to know how to deal with various sorts of physical interfaces, only how to get data to the data link layer software on the same system.

Each layer has a specific set of functions to perform:

- The physical layer (Layer 1) is responsible for getting the 0s and 1s modulated, or serialized, onto the physical link. Each link type has a different format for signaling a 0 or 1; the physical layer is responsible for translating 0s and 1s into these physical signals.

- The data link layer is responsible for making certain that transmitted information is sent to the right computer on the other side of the link. Each device has a different data link (Layer 2) address that can be used to send traffic to that specific device. The data link layer assumes that each frame within a flow of information is separate from all other packets within that same flow and only provides communication for devices that are connected through a single physical link.

- The network layer is responsible for transporting data between systems that are not connected through a single physical link. The network layer, then, provides network-wide (or Layer 3) addresses, rather than link local addresses, and also provides some means for discovering the set of devices and links that must be crossed to reach these destinations.

- The transport layer (Layer 4) is responsible for the transparent transfer of data between different devices. Transport layer protocols can either be "reliable," which means the transport layer will retransmit data lost at some lower layer, or "unreliable," which means that data lost at lower layers must be retransmitted by some higher-layer application.

- The session layer (Layer 5) doesn't really transport data, but manages the connections between applications running on two different computers. The session layer makes certain that the type of data, the form of the data, and the reliability of the data stream are all exposed and accounted for.

- The presentation layer (Layer 6) formats data in a way that the application running on the two devices can understand and process. Encryption, flow control, and any other manipulation of data required to provide an interface between the application and the network happen here. Applications interact with the presentation layer through sockets.

- The application layer (Layer 7) provides the interface between the user and the application, which in turn interacts with the network through the presentation layer.

Each layer in the model provides the information the layer below it is carrying; for instance, Layer 3 provides the bits Layer 2 encapsulates and transmits using Layer 1. This leads to the following observation: not only can the interaction between the layers be described in precise terms within the seven-layer model, the interaction between parallel layers on multiple computers can be described precisely. The physical layer on the first device can be said to communicate with the physical layer on the second device, the data link layer on the first device with the data link layer on the second device, and so on. Just as interactions between two layers on a device are handled through sockets, interactions between parallel layers on different devices are handled through network protocols:

- Ethernet describes the signaling of 0s and 1s onto a physical piece of wire, a format for starting and stopping a frame of data, and a means of addressing a single device among all the devices connected to a single wire. Ethernet, then, falls within both Layer 1 and Layer 2 in the OSI model.

- IP describes the formatting of data into packets, and the addressing and other means necessary to send packets across multiple Layer 2 links to reach a device that is several hops away. IP, then, falls within Layer 3 of the OSI model.

- TCP describes session setup and maintenance, data retransmission, and interaction with applications. TCP, then, falls within the transport and session layers of the OSI model.

This was illustrated in Figure 7.3, where each "layer-wise" interaction is labeled using the name used to describe the blocks of information transferred. For instance, segments are transferred from the transport layer on one device to another, while packets are transferred from the network layer on one device to another.

The Four-Layer Model

One of the reasons why engineers have so much difficulty fitting the IP transport stack into the seven-layer model is that it was developed with a different model of network communications in mind. Instead of a seven-layer model, the IP transport stack was designed around a four-layer model, roughly described in RFC 1122 and illustrated in Figure 7.4.

In this model:

- The link layer is roughly responsible for the same functions as the physical and data link layers in the OSI model—controlling the use of physical links, link-local addressing, and carrying frames as individual bits across an individual physical link.

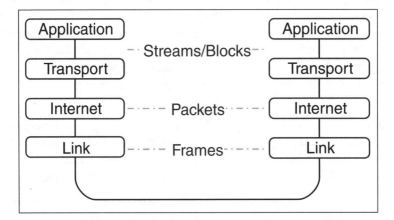

Figure 7.4 *Four-Layer Model*

- The Internet layer is roughly responsible for the same things as the Network layer in the OSI model—providing addressing and reachability across multiple physical links and providing a single packet format and interface regardless of the actual physical link type.

- The transport layer is responsible for building and maintaining sessions between communicating devices and providing a common transparent data transmission mechanism for streams or blocks of data. Flow control and reliable transport may also be implemented in this layer, as in the case of TCP.

- The application layer is the interface between the user and the network resources, or specific applications that use and provide data to other devices attached to the network.

In this model, Ethernet fits wholly within the link layer; IP and all routing protocols fit in the Internet layer; and TCP and UDP fit within the transport layer. Because of this neatness, this is a cleaner model for understanding IP as its deployed today, although it doesn't provide the detailed structure of splitting up the various levels of signaling that might be useful in a more research-oriented environment.

The Iterative Model

The seven- and four-layer models rely on the concept that as you move up the stack from the physical to the application, each layer adds some specific function, or a set of related functions. This functionality is generally tied to a component of the network, such as a single link, an end-to-end path, or application to application communication. By grouping functionality into layers, the complexity of each protocol in the stack can be minimized, and the interaction surface between each protocol or each layer of protocols within the stack can be defined and managed.

To understand these concepts a little more fully, it's useful to look at one final model for protocol stacks in networks. While this model isn't as popular or used as widely as the seven-and four-layer models, it more clearly illustrates the tradeoff between complexity and layering.

If you examine the actual function of each layer in the protocol stacks above, you'll find many similarities between them. For instance, the Ethernet data link layer provides transport and multiplexing across a single link, and IP provides transport and multiplexing across a multihop path. This leads to the following observation: *There are really only four functions that any data carrying protocol can serve: transport, multiplexing, error correction, and flow control.*[2] There are two natural groupings within these four functions: transport and multiplexing, error and flow control. So most protocols fall into doing one of two things:

- The protocol provides transport, including some form of translation from one data format to another, and multiplexing, the ability of the protocol to keep data from different hosts and applications separate.

- The protocol provides error control, either through the capability to correct small errors or to retransmit lost or corrupted data, and flow control, which prevents undue data loss because of a mismatch between the network's capability to deliver data and the application's capability to generate data.

From this perspective, Ethernet provides transport services and flow control, so it is a mixed bag concentrated on a single link, port to port (or tunnel endpoint to tunnel endpoint) within a network. IP is a multihop protocol (a protocol that spans more than one physical link) providing transport services, whereas TCP is a multihop protocol that uses IP's transport mechanisms and provides error correction and flow control. Figure 7.5 illustrates the iterative model.

Each layer in this model groups the information required to manage a single set of parameters within a given scope into a single protocol.

Protocol Stacks and Design

What does this little excursion into protocol design and layering tell us about network complexity, particularly in the area of design? First, layering is a time tested, proven way to separate complexity from complexity by dividing functions

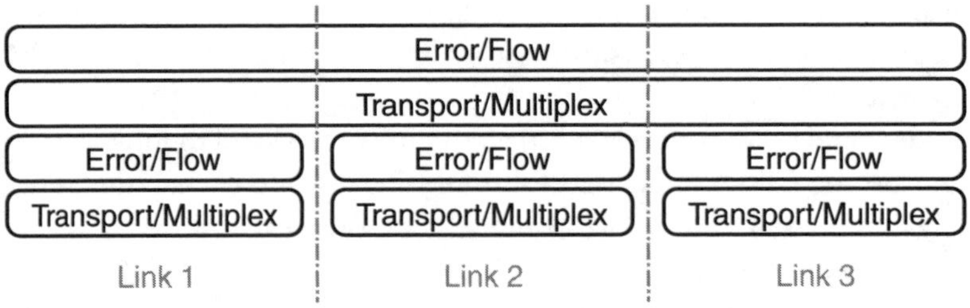

Figure 7.5 *Iterative Model of Network Protocols*

2. John Day, *Patterns in Network Architecture: A Return to Fundamentals* (Upper Saddle River, N.J.; London: Prentice Hall, 2008).

across an API boundary. Second, the comparison of the three models shows that matching the layers to what they do, rather than where they are, provides a cleaner and easier to handle model of operations. While the four- and seven-layer models work, they neither really describe what the protocols at each layer are doing, nor do they really suggest a way to insert new protocols into the stack in the future. The iterative model, on the other hand, provides both of these.

Protocol Complexity versus Design Complexity

Protocols stacks aren't just self-contained systems, however, they interact with the larger network environment through application performance, manageability, and design. This section focuses on the tradeoff between network design and protocol complexity a little more deeply, to give network engineers a better feel for the tradeoffs in these areas. Specifically, how does protocol complexity tradeoff against design complexity?

As the protocol takes on more complexity, some elements of design become less complex. On the other hand, as the protocol becomes more complex, troubleshooting and managing the protocol becomes more complex as well. Each action has an equal and opposite reaction, creating a chain of action and reaction as the complexity levels of each component in the overall system rise and fall. Engineers need to be aware that the complexity doesn't just "go away," once they've "thrown it over the cubicle wall." Some other system must pick that complexity up and manage it.

Microloops and Fast Reroute

The first example of this tradeoff between protocol complexity and network complexity is a concept that's already been discussed in Chapter 5, "Design Complexity." This section will dig a little deeper in the protocol complexity pieces of fast reroute. Figure 7.6 will be used as an illustration here.

Assume that this network starts with the state:

- Router B's shortest path to 2001:db8:0:1::/64 is through A.
- Router C's shortest path to 2001:db8:0:1::/64 is through B.
- Router D's shortest path to 2001:db8:0:1::/64 is through C.
- Router E's shortest path to 2001:db8:0:1::/64 is through A.
- All routers are running a link state routing protocol (either OSPF or IS-IS).

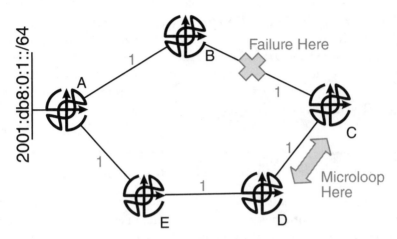

Figure 7.6 *Microloops in a Link State Control Plane*

When the [B,C] link fails, what will be the result? To answer this, consider:

- Routers B and C will be notified of the link failure immediately, and local processes will remove the impacted destinations from the local routing table.

- Routers B and C, because they've been notified of the failure first, will calculate a new tree and switch to the new routes first.

- Routers D and A will be notified of the failure second, calculate a new tree, and switch to the new routes.

- Router E will be notified of the failure last, and hence will calculate and install any new necessary routing information last.

> **Note**
> In link state protocols, flooding is a separate process from calculating the SPT; for convenience, the description above considers them both at the same time.

Combining the original state of the network with the order of convergence when the [B,C] link fails, it's obvious where the microloop occurs. When Router C discovers the failure, it quickly recomputes the SPT and discovers that the path through Router D is the new shortest (loop free) path. While Router C is forwarding through Router D, Router D is still discovering the failure and recalculating a new shortest path three. During the differential in time between

Router C's recalculation and Router D's, traffic destined to 2001:db8:0:1::/64 will be looped between the two routers.

Why not set a timer so Router C waits until Router D has recalculated to install the new routes? This simply won't work. Every router in the network must react the same way to received information; the entire point of a link state protocol is to ensure that every device participating in the control plane has a single view of the state of the network, and acts in the same way. This is one of the foundations of the determinism of link state control planes like OSPF and IS-IS. Setting up a timer during which Router C must wait to converge means setting the same timer on Router D; all this solution does is to slow the total network convergence down, rather than actually resolving the microloop.

> **Note**
>
> It is possible to force the routers in a link state control plane to order the installation of the prefixes to prevent microloops; however, it's not as simple as using timers. Instead, each router must calculate its distance from the network change, and calculate the amount of time it must wait before it can safely install new shortest paths to each destination in the local routing table. This process does prevent microloops, but at a cost in terms of convergence speed. RFC6976 describes the ordered Forwarding Information Base (FIB) solution, and a message of completion system that can alleviate some of the convergence speed impact.

Why not just force all the routers in a link state network to recalculate at the same time? Surely there must be a way to synchronize all the clocks across all the devices participating in the control plane so they all begin calculating at the same time, or they all install their routes at the same time. But how closely can you get all the timers on all the devices across thousands of distributed nodes synchronized? The answer is: not down to the microseconds. Even if you could synchronize all the clocks to this level of precision, it would be almost impossible to ensure every router installs the route at the same time after the calculation. Some routers have distributed forwarding planes, while others unify forwarding with route calculation. Among routers that have distributed forwarding planes, each one is going to have different paths between the control plane and the forwarding hardware, and each of those paths are going to take a different amount of time to install the route. Even among routers with identical distributed systems, the processor load on each router will vary moment to moment, which again impacts the amount of time it takes to install a route once it's been calculated.

Several answers to this problem are considered in the following sections.

Loop Free Alternate

Loop Free Alternates (LFAs) were probably first outlined academically in a paper by J. J. Garcia—the paper that became the foundation for Cisco's EIGRP.[3] The concept of an LFA relies on simple geometry, as shown in Figure 7.7.

In the network illustrated in Figure 7.7, there are three paths between Router A and 2001:db8:0:1::/64:

- [A,B,E] with a metric of 4
- [A,C,E] with a metric of 5
- [A,D,E] with a metric of 6

To understand LFAs, three more metrics need to be noted:

- [B,E] with a metric of 2
- [C,E] with a metric of 3
- [D,E] with a metric of 4

The concept of a LFA comes from this simple observation: the cost of any path that loops "through me" cannot be less than "my cost" to reach that same

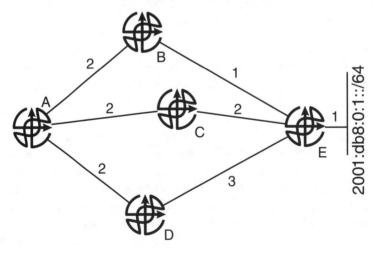

Figure 7.7 *Loop Free Alternates*

3. J. J. Garcia-Lunes-Aceves, "Loop-Free Routing Using Diffusing Computations," *IEEE/ACM Transactions on Networking* 1, no. 1 (February 1993): 130–141.

destination. To put this in other terms—if a path is a loop "through me," the cost of the neighbor advertising the route must be more than or equal to the local best path to reach that same destination.

In terms of Figure 7.7, from the perspective of Router A:

- If the cost of a path to reach 2001:db8:0:1::/64 from Router A is greater than 4, then it might be a loop.

- If the cost of a path to reach 2001:db8:0:1::/64 is less than 4, then it cannot be a loop passing back through Router A itself.

With this information in hand, Router A can now examine the cost to reach 2001:db8:0:1::/64 from the perspective of each of its connected neighbors to determine if their path to reach this destination is a loop back through Router A itself or not. Examining each of the paths available:

- (A,B,E): This is the best (lowest cost) path, so it does not need to be examined.

- (A,C,E): The cost at Router C (Router A's neighbor) is 3, and the best path at Router A is 4. Because Router C's cost is less than Router A's cost, this path cannot loop back through Router A itself. Hence, this path is loop free (from Router A's perspective), and is therefore a valid loop free alternate path.

- (A,D,E): The cost at Router D is 4, and the best path at Router A is 4. Because these two costs are equal, it is possible/probable that traffic forwarded to 2001:db8:0:1::/64 could be forwarded back to Router A during certain topology change events (this is another instance of a microloop). Because of this, EIGRP would declare this path as being a looped path, while link state protocols (OSPF and IS-IS) would determine this is a viable loop free alternate path to the destination.

> **Note**
>
> Just to be complete, the metric of the best path at Router A is called the Feasible Distance in EIGRP, and the metric at Routers B, C, and D is called the Reported Distance at Router A—because this is the cost (or distance or metric) they've reported to Router A.

What are the tradeoffs, in terms of complexity, when using LFAs to provide fast reroute, from a protocol perspective?

- **State (carried):** There is no additional state carried in the control plane protocol itself to provide the loop free alternate. For link state protocols, the cost to reach a destination at a neighbor can be computed from the link state database by simply running SPF from the neighbor's perspective. For EIGRP, the cost at the neighbor is simply the metric contained in the original route advertisement (without the cost of the connected links added in).

- **State (local):** There is some additional state within each router, or each device participating in the control plane. For a link state protocol, SPF must be run not only for a local view of the network, but also once for each neighbor, to obtain each neighbor's cost to any given destination. The backup path must also be somehow stored once calculated, so the forwarding plane can quickly switch over to it if the primary path fails.

- **Speed:** In theory, fast reroute mechanisms reduce the global speed at which the control plane must react to changes in the topology by increasing the speed at which they can react locally.

- **Surface:** As there are no changes to the protocol "on the wire," there is little change in the surface between the control plane and any other system when using LFAs for fast reroute.

From a protocol perspective, the negative results of the tradeoff in complexity are minimal, while the positive results are fairly large. From a design perspective (covered more fully in Chapter 6, "Managing Design Complexity"), LFAs don't provide coverage for many commonly used topologies. For the network engineer determining whether to deploy LFAs or not, two things must be considered:

- Which parts of the network will LFAs cover, and which will they not cover?

- Is it worth the additional complexity of deploying LFAs to cover the parts of the network they will cover? A specific point that needs to be considered here is that if there are parts of the network that will not be covered, deploying LFAs may not increase the delay/jitter characteristics of the end-to-end path in a measurable way (or rather, deploying LFAs won't allow the operator to claim a fixed, high-speed convergence time).

The crucial point is to consider the tradeoff between business requirements for fast convergence, network coverage, and the added complexity at a protocol, configuration, troubleshooting, and management perspectives.

NotVia

The primary topology LFAs cannot provide fast reroute for is a ring, as illustrated in Figure 7.8.

In this network, Router A has two loop free paths to 2001:db8:0:1::/64, but it will mark the path through Router B as a potential loop when considering LFAs. How can Router A use the path [A,B,F,E]? The problem is that during transitions in the network topology, any traffic Router A sends to Router B, destined to a host on 2001:db8:0:1::/64, might be looped back by Router B (see Chapter 5, "Design Complexity," for more details). How can this problem be solved? If Router A can figure out how to tunnel the traffic to a router that always points to Router E to reach 2001:db8:0:1::/64, then it can forward traffic over this tunnel during topology changes and still be certain the traffic will not loop (will reach the correct destination).

How can Router A find out about potential tunnel endpoints that meet this criteria? NotVia is one solution. Assume that the network administrator determines the link [D,E] needs to be protected from failure. In a rather simplified form:

- Router E is configured with a special IP address. This address is called *E notvia D* for reference throughout this explanation.

- *E notvia D* is advertised by Router E to every other neighbor than Router D. In this case, *E notvia D* is advertised only to Router F.

- Router A receives this advertisement only from Router B, giving it a route to Router E no matter what the state of the [A,D,E] path is.

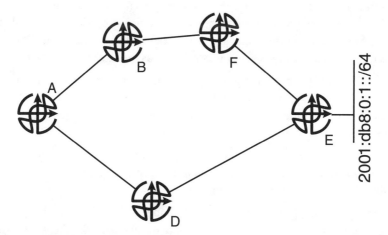

Figure 7.8 *A Ring Topology for Fast Reroute*

- When Router A calculates the path to 2001:db8:0:1::/64, it first finds the best (lowest cost) path along [A,D,E], and installs this in the local table.

- Router A then searches for an alternate path to this destination. Finding Router B is in the path, and there is, in fact, a route *E notvia D,* it installs the *notvia* route as a backup tunnel path to the destination.

- If the path [A,D,E] fails, Router A switches traffic destined to 2001:db8:0:1::/64 to the tunneled path. Traffic is encapsulated in a header that follows [A,B,F,E]. Router E removes this outer header and forwards based on the information inside the packet. Because the inner header in the tunneled packet is destined to a host on 2001:db8:0:1::/64, the packet is forwarded out the directly connected interface.

> **Note**
>
> This sequence assumes that the best path to Router E from Router A is along [A,B,F,E]. Because this may not be the case, NotVia would calculate to Router F instead. How this is done is beyond the scope of this simple explanation of the concept.

How does NotVia fare from a complexity perspective?

- **State (carried):** NotVia requires an additional IP address for each protected link or node in the network. This may (depending on how many links or devices are protected) be a large number of additional IP addresses injected into the control plane—and these addresses must be somehow marked in the protocol as *notvia* addresses, so they're not used for normal forwarding. State is, therefore, increased with NotVia. In fact, this additional state is the primary reason NotVia was rejected as an Internet Standard.

- **State (local):** Each device participating in the control plane will need to keep the additional *notvia* addresses, and calculate their local SPT with these links included to discover alternate routes. The calculation time is likely minimal, but there is some additional state.

- **Speed:** In theory, fast reroute mechanisms reduce the global speed at which the control plane must react to changes in the topology by increasing the speed at which they can react locally.

- **Surface:** Although there are protocol changes, there is little change in the interaction surfaces between the control plane and the other network systems it interacts with. NotVia does deepen the interaction surfaces between routers, however, in two ways. First, there is additional state that must be carried, computed, and relied on in the control plane. Second, there is the addition of an "open tunnel" on any device in the control plane hosting a *NotVia* address.

NotVia does add some state to the control plane, and hence does increase control plane complexity.

Remote Loop Free Alternate

An alternative to NotVia is for Router A, in Figure 7.8, to use some other mechanism to calculate a remote next hop that will reach 2001:db8:0:1::/64 even if its primary path through Router D has failed, and find some alternate way to tunnel packets to this intermediate router. Remote LFAs provide just such a solution. To calculate a remote LFA:

- Router A calculates a SPT from its neighbor's *neighbor's* perspective. In this case, Router A would calculate the best path to 2001:db8:0:1::/64 from the perspective of Router F.

- Finding Router F does, in fact, have a loop free path to the destination, Router A can then build a tunnel to Router F, and install this tunnel as a backup to the primary route through Router D.

The main question, in this solution, is what form of tunneling should be used to build these alternate paths. The most common answer to this question is MPLS, as it is lightweight, and has all the signaling necessary to dynamically build tunnels. Given MPLS signaling of some type is already running in the network for other reasons, adding Remote LFAs is a fairly trivial exercise from a network management perspective. Dynamically created tunnels can add some excitement to the troubleshooting process, of course; it can take some time and careful work to sort out why specific flows are traveling over specific links in the network with dynamic tunnels, because there's no connection between the configurations on individual devices and the actual tunnels created.

Again, it's worth examining how Remote LFAs compare to the complexity model used here.

- **State (carried):** Remote LFAs don't add any new information to the routing protocol specifically, but they do require some way to build backup tunnels through the network. If some form of dynamical tunneling system is already running on the network (for instance, to support MPLS virtual private networks or traffic engineering/MPLS-TE), then this additional state is very small. If some form of dynamic tunneling signaling must be deployed to support Remote LFAs, then the additional control plane state—and increase in complexity—could be daunting.

- **State (local):** Each device participating in the control plane will need to perform an additional set of SPF calculations, and to store information about a backup tunnel. Of course, the state of the backup tunnel must be maintained, as well, so this could well be a large amount of state (and hence, a large amount of complexity).

- **Speed:** In theory, fast reroute mechanisms reduce the global speed at which the control plane must react to changes in the topology by increasing the speed at which they can react locally.

- **Surface:** Remote LFAs add at least one new system to the network, some mechanism to dynamically build and manage an overlay of alternate path tunnels. This adds several new interaction surfaces, such as the interface between the control plane and the tunnel signaling system, and the physical topology and the tunneled overlay. If a dynamic tunneling mechanism has been deployed for some other reason, then these additional interaction surfaces are already in place, and complexity isn't increased in the network. If dynamic tunneling is being deployed to support Remote LFAs, however, their deployment will increase the number of interaction surfaces in the network.

> **Note**
>
> This list of tradeoffs assumes that Label Distribution Protocol (LDP) is, in fact, running on all the nodes required to build backup tunnels, so the cost to add Remote LFAs is primarily in the amount of state carried in the network, as well as additional tunnels, endpoints, etc. In fact, if deploying Remote LFAs requires deploying LDP to a wider set of nodes in the network—a distinct possibility in most network designs—the increased network performance would need to be greater, or the business drivers more insistent, to justify deploying LDP on the additional nodes. The cost of deploying protocols and solutions onto additional nodes in the network should always be included when considering the complexity tradeoffs.

EIGRP and the Design Conundrum

Early in the era of large-scale networking, EIGRP gained a reputation as being a routing protocol you could "throw onto any topology, without a lot of design effort, and will just work." There is, in fact, a good deal of truth to this belief—in fact, there's a bit too much truth to this statement. Soon enough, very large unplanned networks began failing in a big way while running EIGRP—leading to the opposite conclusion, that EIGRP is a really horrible control plane. In a way, EIGRP is a victim of its own early success in supporting large complex networks with little thought to actual design.

Why did EIGRP hold up so well in large-scale networks with little design effort? A short review of EIGRP operation might be helpful in explaining, using the topology in Figure 7.9.

If Router A loses its link to 2001:db8:0:1::/64, what happens?

1. Router A will first examine its local information to determine if there is an LFA (a *FS* in EIGRP) for this destination.

2. Finding none, it will mark the route *active* (which means EIGRP is actively looking for an alternate route to this destination), and send a *query* to each of its neighbors, in this case Router D.

3. Router D, on receiving this query, will examine its local tables and discover Router A is the only path available to 2001:db8:0:1::/64. Router D will mark this route *active,* and send a *query* to Router E.

4. Router E will follow Router D's example, sending a *query* to Router F.

5. Router F will follow Router E's example, sending a *query* to Router G.

6. Router G will find it has no neighbors to query, so it will mark 2001:db8:0:1::/64 *unreachable,* and send a *reply* to Router F stating it has no alternate path to the destination.

7. Router F, on receiving this *reply,* will mark the route *unreachable,* and send a *reply* to Router E stating it has no alternate path to this destination.

8. This chain of *replies* will continue until Router A receives a reply from Router D. At this point, the route is removed from Router A's routing table, and Router A sends a *following update* with an unreachable metric for 2001:db8:0:1::/64. This removes the destination from the other router's tables.

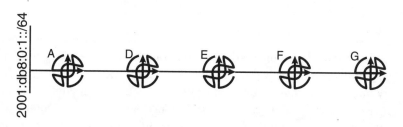

Figure 7. 9 *EIGRP Operation Overview*

Note

In simple networks like the one shown in Figure 7.9, this entire query process seems redundant—and even "not very useful." In reality, the entire query mechanism in EIGRP is designed to find alternate paths previously marked as loops, or not reported because of split horizon. As such, the query process in EIGRP acts much like the mechanisms used in a link state protocol to discover a remote LFA—only it's built into the protocol as a part of normal convergence, rather than added on as a fast reroute mechanism.

There are several interesting points about this process worth noting:

- The amount of state being carried through this process is minimal. As EIGRP is a distance vector protocol, no topology information is carried, only reachability information.

- Through this diffusing update process, EIGRP spreads the load of finding any available alternate paths to every router within the failure domain. This load spreading mechanism makes EIGRP extremely robust to large-scale environments (half a million routes or more is possible, with hundreds of neighbors, especially in hub-and-spoke topologies).

- The process of discovering any alternate routes is similar to running SPF on the tree itself, in real time. Because this is performed in a serialized way, no microloops are ever formed in EIGRP. Packets will be dropped during convergence, but never looped.

So why does EIGRP scale so well in relatively design free networks? Because the state carried in the control plane is minimal compared to most other protocols, and because the Diffusing Update Algorithm (DUAL) does such a good job at spreading the convergence load through the network.

Why, then, do EIGRP networks fail? EIGRP can encounter several specific network situations that will cause a convergence failure of some type, including:

- Extremely long "query tails." An EIGRP query stops wherever there is no local knowledge of the destination contained in the query itself—this generally means "the edge of the network," or someplace where reachability information is aggregated. If there is no aggregation configured in the network, each and every query will be processed by every router in the network. If a single link fails that causes thousands of destinations to be dropped off the network, the distributed convergence process that makes EIGRP robust actually works against the protocol, causing a lot more work than is necessary to bring the network to convergence.

- High numbers of parallel paths. Because each EIGRP router sends a query to each of its neighbors, a high number of parallel paths cause a large number of queries to be transmitted through the network. This works the EIGRP state machine very hard, again causing DUAL to work against its better attributes.

- Network devices with low amounts of memory or processing performance paired with devices that have big processors and lots of memory. A mismatched set of devices in the network means one router can quickly send thousands of queries to a neighbor that simply cannot handle the processing load. Again, the DUAL process begins to work against itself in these types of situations.

The most obvious result of any of these situations is a *stuck in active* route. As each router in the EIGRP network transmits a query, it sets a timer; the router expects to receive an answer for this query within this period of time. If no reply is received within this time period, the route is declared *stuck in active*, and the adjacency with the neighbor for which no reply was forthcoming will be reset.

As you can imagine, the last thing you want to do when the protocol is already under the stress of a large-scale convergence event is to reset the neighbor adjacencies, causing another round of queries, and hence more stress in the network. Why was the protocol designed to work this way? Because, in effect, once the timer has fired the control plane has *stepped outside the finite state machine defined by DUAL*. There is no real way to resolve the problem other than to reset the state machine.

For years, many engineers simply increased the *stuck in active* timer when they would see *stuck in active routes* in their network. This is, however, precisely the wrong solution to the problem. If you view the *stuck in active* timer as the amount of time you're willing to allow the network to remain unconverged (and hence dropping packets to a destination that should, actually, be reachable), you can immediately see the bad side effects of increasing this timer. Instead, the network and protocol both need to work to resolve this situation.

Real field experience with the protocol in large-scale environments revealed these problems. In response, two lines of action were taken:

- The perception of EIGRP as a protocol that would run over just about anything you could configure it on was changed to a more balanced view. EIGRP will, in fact, tolerate a wide variety of topologies and network conditions. However, there still needs to be thought put into some specific design parameters, such as the size of a failure domain, the quality of the equipment deployed, and other factors. In the realm of complexity, this is effectively throwing some of the complexity being handled by the protocol "back over the cubicle wall," to be handled by the network designer. There is an important lesson in balancing the location of complexity here.

- EIGRP's *stuck in active* process was modified to allow the protocol to more gracefully remain inside the DUAL state machine for longer while decreasing the impact on the actual network operation. Specifically, the expiration of the *stuck in active* timer caused a new query to be transmitted through the query chain, rather than resetting the neighbor adjacency. This allowed routers with smaller processors and memory pools the time they needed to process large groups of queries, or a local adjacency problem to be sorted out without impacting the network as a whole. In complexity terms, this added set of packets and timers increased the complexity of the protocol to resolve some of the problems being seen in actual deployments. Here, complexity in deployment was traded off against protocol complexity, as the protocol complexity didn't appear to be as difficult to manage as redesigning every EIGRP network in the world wholesale.

The development, and modification, of EIGRP through years of experience shows how complexity tradeoffs must be handled in the real world. Sometimes it's best to move the complexity someplace else, sometimes it's best to keep the complexity in the protocol. It all depends on the specific situation the engineer faces.

A Final Thought

The intersection of protocol, design, and system complexity is itself a complex topic. This chapter really only scratches the surface of this broad and interesting area of investigation. However, the examples and outlined thoughts here should provide you with a solid core of working knowledge, a set of tools that will help you at least recognize the tradeoffs in any given situation, and to think twice about "tossing complexity over the cubicle wall."

Chapter 8

How Complex Systems Fail

Every happy family is happy in much the same way, but every unhappy one is miserable in completely unique ways.

To apply this to the network world with just a slight change—"every network that succeeds does so in much the same way as every other network in the world, but every network that fails does so in a completely unique way." Turning this around, this means one of the best ways to learn network design is to work on failures. Every failed network design an engineer touches teaches some lesson in design, as well.

But to really learn network engineering, a little theory of failure is called for—an understanding of what might be called "failure theory" provides a context, or a framework, into which an engineer cannot only place failures, but also new ideas. New (and old) ideas in protocols, network devices, and networks as a system can be effectively evaluated for potential failures by knowing what sorts of failure modes to look for—and then actually looking. What tends to happen in network engineering is finding a problem that needs to be solved, and then solving it—without thought for the complexity tradeoffs, and without considering the failure modes that might result up in the protocol or network.

This entire concept of potential failure modes works alongside the concept of unintended consequences, and the unreachable space at the bottom left corner of the complexity curve (or the unfillable triangle of the CAP theorem, discussed way back in Chapter 1, "Defining Complexity").

This chapter will discuss two major reasons why networks fail from a theoretical perspective:

- Positive feedback loops
- Shared fate

These categories might seem broad, but this chapter will flesh them out with a number of examples that should help you understand what to look for in each case. These failure modes will also be examined to see how they interact with other commonly asserted causes of network failure, such as the speed of a finely tuned control plane, or redistribution.

Feedback Loops

Feedback loops are useful for a lot of different things—for instance, in a *phase locked loop,* the feedback of the circuit is carefully controlled to produce a constant frequency waveform or *carrier*. Phased locked loops form the foundation, in fact, of almost all modern radio systems. Another example of a feedback loop is the various types of mechanisms controlling the air and fuel flow into internal combustion and jet propulsion engines. Without these feedback loops, these types of engines can only run at a very minimal level, and at a somewhat low efficiency.

There are two kinds of feedback: negative and positive. Figure 8.1 illustrates a negative feedback loop using a very simple oscillating signal style of explanation.

In this figure, there are two devices; you don't need to understand how the components illustrated here actually work to understand the concept of a feedback loop:

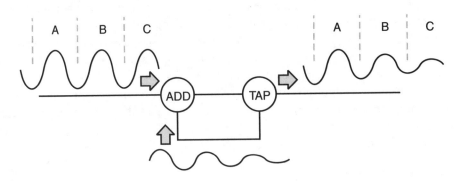

Figure 8.1 *A Negative Feedback Loop*

- **Add**: This device simply takes the two input signals and combines them to create a single-output signal.

- **Tap**: This device simply replicates the signal presented to one input, does any programmed modification, and outputs the result on its second output interface.

In this case, the TAP device is configured to invert the signal and reduce its strength (amplitude in more precise terms) a bit. What happens in this illustration is this:

1. The section of the wave marked A passed through the ADD device.

2. At first, there is no signal on the second input, so the wave passes through the ADD device without change.

3. The wave continues on and passes into the TAP device.

4. At the TAP device, a small replica of the wave is made and inverted (so the positive peaks are reversed with the negative peaks), and this little replica of the signal is passed back along the path to the second input of the ADD device.

5. This signal, being fed back from the TAP device, is added to the original signal by the ADD device.

6. Because this signal is inverted, the addition of the two waves has the effect of reducing the strength of the output of the ADD device. This process is much like taking a large number, multiplying it by some very small number (say 0.01), inverting the number (changing it from a positive sign to a negative), and adding it back to the original number.

7. This has the effect of causing the output level of the ADD device to decrease.

8. This decreased signal is then fed back into the TAP device, which takes the same proportion of the received signal, inverting it, and feeding it back to the ADD device.

The result, as you can see from the output signal on the right side of the illustration, is a signal that is constantly decreasing in strength. It's tempting to think this situation will stabilize, but it never really will—leave the circuit running long enough, and the signal exiting the TAP device will eventually be reduced to the point that it cannot be measured. An alternative way to envision

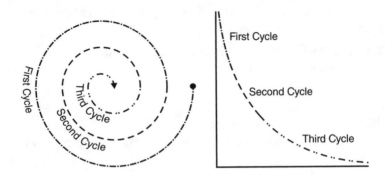

Figure 8.2 *Negative Feedback Loop Alternate Conceptions*

this negative feedback loop is as a spiral, with the strength of the signal repre-sented as a spiral and a graph to show the decreasing signal on the output over time as shown in Figure 8.2.

The spiral chart, on the left in Figure 8.2, shows the input and output of the circuit as a set of cycles, with each cycle moving closer to the null point in the middle of the spiral, or the point where the signal becomes unmeasurable. The curve version, on the right in Figure 8.2, shows the constantly reducing signal strength against a graph, with the same cycles marked out for reference.

To illustrate a positive feedback look, reverse the action of the TAP device shown in Figure 8.1; Figure 8.3 illustrates the result.

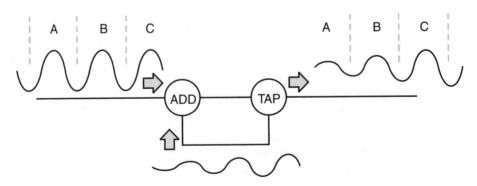

Figure 8.3 *A Positive Feedback Loop*

In this case, the TAP device is configured to leave the signal in phase with the original and reduce its strength (amplitude in more precise terms) a bit. What happens in this illustration is this:

1. The section of the wave marked A passed through the ADD device.

2. At first, there is no signal on the second input, so the wave passes through the ADD device without change.

3. The wave continues on and passes into the TAP device.

4. At the TAP device, a small replica of the wave is made, and this little replica of the signal is passed back along the path to the second input of the ADD device.

5. This signal, being fed back from the TAP device, is added to the original signal by the ADD device.

6. Because this signal is not inverted, the addition of the two waves has the effect of increasing the strength of the output of the ADD device.

7. This process is much like taking a large number, multiplying it by some very small number (say 0.01), and adding it back to the original number.

8. This has the effect of causing the output level of the ADD device to increase.

9. This increased signal is then fed back into the TAP device, which takes the same proportion of the received signal and feeding it back to the ADD device.

Once again, it is sometimes useful to illustrate the same concept in a different way, as shown in Figure 8.4.

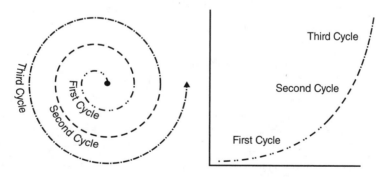

Figure 8.4 *An Alternate Illustration of a Positive Feedback Loop*

Looking at these two illustrations (Figures 8.3 and 8.4), it should be obvious why positive feedback loops are dangerous. *First,* unless there is something that limits the amplitude of the resulting signal, there is no end to the loop. In fact, most positive feedback loops do occur in systems with a limiter of some type; most of the time the limiter is some physical property of the system itself. As an example, consider feedback in an audio system—that loud screeching noise you hear sometimes when a microphone is placed too close to a speaker. Feedback of this type is caused by any noise in the amplification and speaker system (and there will always be some) being picked up by a microphone (TAP in the diagrams above), then fed back into the amplification system (ADD in the illustrations above), to create a higher volume noise, which is then picked up by the microphone as a louder noise, and hence amplified to a higher level, and then played by the speakers. The limiting factor in the audio example is the upper limit on the speaker's volume, combined with the physical properties of the microphone.

Second, once the system reaches the limiter, it will stay there permanently. And reduction in the rate or strength of change is immediately overcome by the action of the TAP/ADD feedback, which adds in whatever level of signal is needed (over time) to bring the system back to the limiting point. This is called *saturation* in the field of control systems and electronics.

> **Note**
>
> The illustrations here indicate that a positive feedback loop will always result in an increasing level of output, as the input and some part of the output are added in the processing. However, many positive feedback loops simply achieve stability, and hence are called self-reinforcing, or stable, feedback loops. In this case, the loop doesn't add to the point of increasing output, but simply keeps the output stable at an elevated level. The result is a constant amplification of the input to the output, rather than an ever increasing output. To simplify the discussion, these cases are still treated as positive feedback loops in this text.
>
> The difference between a positive feedback loop and a negative feedback loop is the sign of the number fed back into the ADD in these illustrations. If the ADD is fed a negative number, the feedback loop will be negative. If it's fed a positive number, the feedback loop will be positive. The steepness of the feedback, the rate at which it impacts the output signal, is impacted by the percentage of the original signal that's taken off at the TAP and fed back to the ADD. The higher the percentage, the greater the speed at which the output increases or decreases.

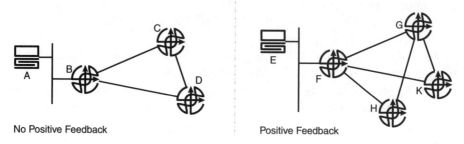

No Positive Feedback   Positive Feedback

Figure 8.5 *Packet Loop Examples*

Positive Feedback Loops in Network Engineering

How do feedback loops—positive feedback loops in particular—relate to network engineering? Returning to the original model of network complexity described in Chapter 2, "Components of Complexity," feedback loops interact with all three pieces of the complexity model: *state*, *speed*, and *surface*. Working through some examples is going to be the best way to understand how feedback loops relate to complexity; this section will consider a packet duplication loop, a redistribution loop, and a link flap control plane failure loop.

Packet Loop

Packet loops are more common than might be initially supposed in any given network—but they don't always form feedback loops, and hence aren't always related to a network failure. Figure 8.5 illustrates a typical packet loop.

The left half of Figure 8.5 illustrates a loop in which packet replication does not take place—so there is no immediately obvious positive feedback loop. Packets transmitted by Host A are forwarded by Router B to Router C, which are then forwarded to Router D, then back to Router B, where they are again forwarded to Router C. There is, however, a self-sustaining loop, or enough positive feedback to sustain the increased traffic levels across the links in the network. This self-sustaining loop can still cause the amount of traffic that can reach the limiter, or saturation point, for the loop, if Host A is transmitting enough traffic.

To understand why, consider that the only way to prevent traffic from passing along this loop eternally is to put a maximum number of hops in the packet itself—a time to live. If the time to live is set very high, to allow for a wide diameter network (a network with a lot of hops), then each packet Host A transmits will increase the load on the network while older packets are still counting down to their time to live. If the time to live is set to 16, Host A can consume up to 16 times the bandwidth available along the link from itself to Router B along other links in the network. If the Host A → Router B link is 1g, then Host A can consume up to 16g across the [B,C], [C,D], and [D,B] links (combined, or one third of 16g on each of the three links).

The right side of Figure 8.5 illustrates a forwarding loop with positive feedback characteristics. Here a packet transmitted by Router E to Router F is forwarded by Router G to both Routers H and K, each of which replicates the packet and transmits it back to Router F. Each time the single packet traverses the loop, it doubles; in the first round, then, the single packet transmitted by Host E becomes two, in the second round it becomes four, in the third round it becomes eight, and so on. It should also be obvious this is only a problem in the case of multicast or broadcast traffic; unicast traffic wouldn't normally be duplicated at Router F.

What would the limiter be for either of these forwarding loops? Limiters would include:

- The speed at which any device in the forwarding path can forward the traffic.

- The bandwidth of the links connecting the devices.

- The time to live of the packets being transmitted into the forwarding loop. This generally isn't going to be much of a limiter, as any time to live is normally set high enough to ensure transport across a large diameter network, which is almost always too high to prevent collateral damage from a forwarding loop.

- The viability of the control plane state passing over the links through which the forwarding loop passes.

While most of these are fairly obvious, the last limiter might not be—what precisely does the viability of the control plane mean? If the traffic along the links involved in the loop becomes large enough to cause packet drops, the control plane will not be able to maintain state. When the control plane state fails, the reachability information that formed the link will (likely) be removed from the table, causing the loop to "unwind." If the loop is stable, it will be re-formed when the control plane relearns reachability information across the links in the loop.

Packet Loops in the Control Plane

How do forwarding loops that lead to feedback loops form in a network? Generally the problem begins someplace in the control plane. Generally speaking, control planes will form forwarding loops when the actual state of the network

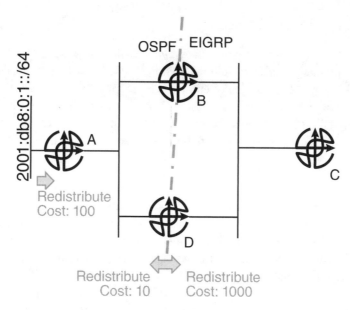

Figure 8.6 *Redistribution Control Plane Loop*

doesn't match the control plane's view of the network. Some examples might be helpful in understand how and when this happens.

Mutual Redistribution

Figure 8.6 illustrates a network with mutual redistribution between two routing protocols.

In this network, Router A is redistributing 2001:db8:0:1::/64 into OSPF v3 toward Routers B and D with a cost of 100. To simplify the explanation, take one side of the loop; Router B redistributes this destination into EIGRP with a metric of 1000. 2001:db8:0:1::/64 is then picked up as an EIGRP external route by Router D, and redistributed back into OSPF with a cost of 10. Router D then advertises this route back to Router B along the broadcast link shared by Routers A, B, and D; the route reaches Router B as an external OSPF route with a cost of 10. Because the cost through Router D—10 plus the cost of the [B,D] link—is less than the cost of the route through Router A—100 plus the cost of the [B,D] link—Router B will choose the path through Router D to reach this destination. This type of routing loop can time itself out through the increasing costs each time the destination is redistributed between the two protocols, but it will quickly be rebuilt once the first cycle of redistribution is completed. This type of routing loop can also remain stable, depending on the way the redistribution metrics are chosen.

> **Note**
>
> The reason this works is the original route is redistributed into OSPF, rather than simply being advertised into OSPF. 2001:db8:0:1::/64 must be an external route at both points of entry to create the loop; otherwise Routers B and D will have one internal OSPF route and one external OSPF route, and they will always prefer the internal route over the external, breaking the loop. Multiple points of redistribution are required to cause this type of loop.

It's tempting to say the problem here is that information passing from one routing domain is being leaked, or redistributed, into another routing domain, and then it's being redistributed back again—that the mutual redistribution is actually the root of the problem. But while removing the mutual redistribution, or blocking redistributed routes from being redistributed again (though filters, tags, communities, or other mechanisms) will resolve the problem, mutual redistribution is not the root cause.

The root cause is actually *the removal of information about the state of the network in the redistribution process itself.* Reaching back to routing fundamentals, you might recall that routing protocols determine whether a particular path to a destination is a loop by examining the metrics. Because the metrics of any two protocols use cannot be directly compared, the metric assigned to a redistributed route must simply be configured or calculated in some way— no matter how this configuration or calculation is done, information about the state of the network (the cost of the path to the destination in this case) will likely be lost when redistributing routes.

Hence, when routing information is redistributed between two different routing protocols, a mismatch between the actual state of the network and what the control plane believes to be the state of the network occurs. Any time such a mismatch occurs, there is the possibility of a routing loop, which then causes a (potentially permanent) forwarding loop in the network.

Microloops

Chapter 7, "Protocol Complexity," spent a good deal of time examining microloops and various solutions, specifically in terms of increasing protocol complexity in an attempt to reach the "corner" of the Turing Curve (see Chapter 1, "Defining Complexity"). A quick revisit here in the context of forwarding loops will be useful, using Figure 8.7.

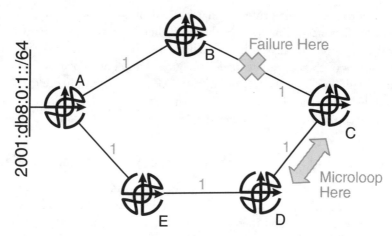

Figure 8.7 *A Microloop in the Control Plane*

Given this network is running a link state protocol, and Router D's best path to 2001:db8:0:1::/64 is through Router C, a failure at [B,C] will cause a loop to form between Routers C and D during the time after Router C has converged and before Router D has converged. Chapter 7, "Protocol Complexity," discussed a number of solutions for this problem—but what, really, is the root cause?

While the most obvious problem is the two routers should recalculate at the same time, the actual root cause is the mismatch between the network topology as it exists and the network topology as Router D believes it to be. This reinforces the point that any time there is a mismatch between the topology as it exists and the control plane's view of the topology, bad things happen.

Seen from this angle, it becomes obvious why the problem is so difficult to solve. The CAP theorem states that you can design a database that is consistent, available, and exhibits tolerance for partitions (perhaps it should be the CAT theorem, named in honor of that inexplicable creature, the cat?)—you must choose two of the three. If the control plane is simply treated as a distributed real time database, the routing protocol must give up something—which one should it be?

Tolerance for partitioning is certainly not something a distributed routing protocol can give up; that would destroy the very essence of its distributed nature. Accessibility is another area that simply isn't in doubt; a routing protocol database that isn't accessible by every device participating in the control plane all the time really isn't much use for packet forwarding duty. Consistency, then, is the point that must give way in a distributed control plane—and as Chapter 7's exploration of the problem of microloops illustrates, there's no simple way to resolve the problems that come from an inconsistent view of the network (in fact, according to CAP theorem, there's no way to actually resolve the problem entirely, no matter how much complexity is thrown at the problem).

Another set of choices can be made, of course—the control plane database can be centralized, removing the "P" out of the CAP theorem, and hence making the "A" and "C" theoretically possible. It doesn't always work out this in real life, however, as you'll discover in Chapter 10, "Programmable Network Complexity."

Speed, State, and Surface: Stability in the Network Control Plane

With this understanding of feedback loops in the background, it's time to move back into the world of complexity. This section will begin with another example of a control plane loop, and then continue with a discussion of the speed, state, and surface of complexity in relation to network engineering.

A Spanning Tree Failure Case Study

Spanning Tree is famous—perhaps infamous is a better term—for cascading control plane failures. Figure 8.8 illustrates a small network over which it is possible to trace such a failure.

This network begins with Switch A as the root bridge, and the path [B,D] blocked by the Spanning Tree Protocol. Assume that two things occur at the same time:

- An outsized unidirectional flow is passing through the switched network, using a large amount of the available bandwidth, from Switch A through Switches B and C, to Switch E (and someplace beyond Switch E).

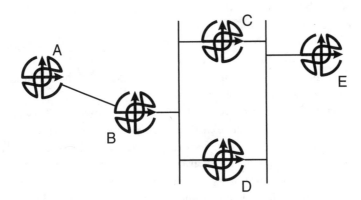

Figure 8.8 *Spanning Tree Failure Example*

- Some process on Switch B misbehaves, causing the Bridge Protocol Data Unit (BPDU) process to fail in sending regular hello packets.

If the spanning tree process fails to send regular BPDUs at Switch B, Switches C and D will begin to elect a new root bridge, and hence to determine the shortest set of paths through the network without reference to the current state of Switch A as the root bridge, or the existence of Switch B. This will result in the [B,D] link being unblocked for traffic, so:

- The large flow originating at A will be transmitted across the broadcast link [B,C,D].
- The large flow will be transmitted by both Switches C and D onto the broadcast link [C,D,E].
- Switch D will receive the same large flow at its [C,D,E] interface and retransmit it back onto the [B,C,D] broadcast link, setting up the forwarding loop.

Once the forwarding loop is started, the only limiting factor will be the saturation point for the links, interfaces, and forwarding devices in the network. As the traffic on the wire builds, the BPDUs that Spanning Tree counts on to form a shortest path tree along the network topology will be dropped, causing the network to further fragment into independent switches each electing their own root bridge. Once the network reaches this point there is no way to recover other than the failure of one (or more) of the switches, causing the traffic to stop being forwarded, and giving Spanning Tree the chance to re-establish loop free paths through the network.

Riding the See-Saw

There are several points to be considered in the examples given thus far; the state/speed/surface model will be used here to put these points into complexity terms.

State: In each of these cases, control plane state plays a role in starting or maintaining the feedback loop. The problem is a lack of information about the true state of the network topology. Any time there is a mismatch between what the control plane believes about the network topology, and the actual network topology as it exists in the real world, there will be some forwarding issue. The examples above used a packet loop to remove topology information through packet loss (spanning tree failure), and the removal of control plane state describing the actual network topology (redistribution) to illustrate this mismatch between state and reality.

Speed: The loss of information in the control plane, resulting in a mismatch between the network and the control plane's view of the network, is the primary cause for each of the examples given here. However, it is important to note the role speed plays in each situation, as well. In the case of microloops, the control plane isn't fast enough to keep up with changes in the network topology. Speeding the control plane up, however, simply causes other complexity issues to surface—there is no such thing as a free lunch in the world of complexity (or, rather, you can't beat the complexity demon as easily as just setting a timer to make things go faster).

An alternative way to look at this is as a see-saw: the fast the network reacts to topology changes, the more likely you are to find situations where the control plane forms a positive feedback loop. Speed is good, but speed is also bad. It's far too easy to push to one side of the see-saw without thinking through what's going to happen when the weight shifts, and your side starts heading toward the ground. What is it you'll face when you "saw" rather than "see"? A nasty bump on the bottom, or something worse?

Surface: Two of the examples just discussed illustrate the problem with broad, deep surfaces connecting two different systems. In the redistribution example, the surface between the two routing protocols can be said not to be deep enough. Because information isn't fully exchanged between the protocols, the interaction surface is inefficient. Further, the interaction surface in this case is too broad; redistribution doesn't need to take place at more than a minimal number of places in the network. Reducing the points at which redistribution does take place can potentially reduce the efficiency of traffic flow through the network, but this is a common tradeoff against control plane state.

In the case of the spanning tree failure, the interaction surface in view is between the control plane and the traffic flowing through the network, or the data plane. This isn't normally an interaction surface network engineers think about, but because the control plane rides on the same links as the data plane (the control plane is *in band*), there is a definite interaction surface that needs to be considered.

The third example, microloops, illustrates the surface problem in another way. The control plane can be said to be one system, while the network topology can be said to be a separate system. The detection of the topology state by the control plane is therefore an interaction surface. In this case, the interaction surface can be said to be too shallow, in that the control plane cannot always react to changes in the topology as quickly as those changes actually occur. This is another way of looking at the problem described as a state and speed issue in the paragraphs above.

Shared Fate

Feedback loops between systems or within a system are interesting, but they are often easy to spot once you know what you're looking for. Shared fate, however, is often very difficult to see in any given network—most often because shared fate situations are intentionally buried under layers of abstraction designed to reduce the apparent complexity of the network. What is a shared fate problem, and how does it impact network failure in the real world? The best way to understand this type of problem is through examples. Once these examples have been considered, shared fate problems will be related back into the complexity model used throughout this book—speed, state, and surface.

Virtual Circuits

Virtual circuits aren't new—in fact, the use of tagged packet header to put several different "circuits" onto a single physical wire have been common from almost the very beginning in networks. Starting with multiplexed T1's, working through Frame Relay, and the more modern 802.1Q and 802.1ad headers placed on an Ethernet frame to break a single Ethernet link into multiple virtual topologies, virtualization has been the rule, rather than the exception, in data link protocols. Today, engineers can choose from VXLAN, MPLS, and many other technologies to virtualize their links.

Virtualization provides many benefits, such as:

- The capability to hide one virtual topology from another; a form of information hiding that reduces the state carried in the overlay control plane, and the speed at which the control plane must react to changes in the topology.

- The capability to abstract the physical topology into multiple logical topologies, each with their own characteristics, such as per hop behaviors.

- The capability to carry traffic across a longer than shortest path (to increase the stretch of a specific path) to meet specific business or operational goals.

There is a downside to virtualization, however—the SRLG. Figure 8.9 illustrates shared risk link groups.

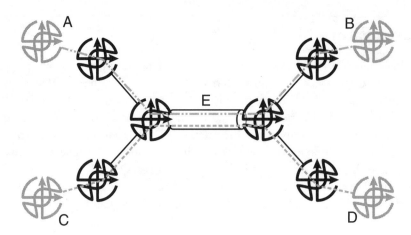

Figure 8.9 *Shared Risk Link Groups*

Assume the following:

- Routers A and B are both demarcation (or handoff) points for Provider X, which is selling a high-speed link between two cities.
- Routers C and D are both demarcation (or handoff) points for Provider Y, which is selling a high-speed link between two cities.

A customer purchases a virtual circuit from Provider X, and a backup link from Provider Y, to connect their facilities in the two cities that both providers interconnect. A backhoe operator then proceeds to fade the network at Link E (perhaps they are cleaning out a drainage ditch someplace alongside a road).

This will cause both of the virtual circuits to fail, as they share a single physical link.

How can the customer avoid this situation? Neither provider is likely to explain exactly how their virtual circuit is provisioned, hop-by-hop—this would be giving out competitive information that could negatively impact the provider's business. From the customer's perspective, the virtualization of the single link, E, has created an SRLG that is not visible because of the magic of abstraction—and there's little the customer can do about the situation other than use a single provider and demand this type of situation doesn't arise in the network.

The virtualization abstraction can be said to leak; state at a lower logical layers leaks into higher logical layers in the form of shared risk groups, where a single failure translates into a number of different outages.

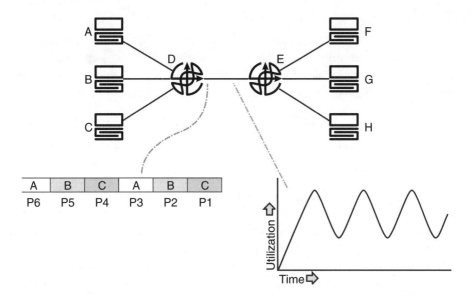

Figure 8.10 *TCP Synchronization*

TCP Synchronization as a Shared Fate Problem

Shared fate problems don't just ride atop virtualized links, however; any time virtualization is used, there is the possibility of a shared fate situation developing. The behavior of multiple TCP flows passing through a single set of buffers or queues in a network is an unexpected variant of a shared fate problem. Figure 8.10 illustrates the behavior of several TCP flows passing through a network.

In this diagram, three hosts, A, B, and C, are sending three different TCP streams to three other hosts that are only reachable across the single [D,E] link. Examining the output queue at D, there are six packets waiting to be transmitted; one from each of the three streams. If this output queue can only hold three packets, then three of the packets placed in the queue will be dropped. If a tail drop mechanism is used, the three newest packets in the queue will be dropped, which means P4, P5, and P6.

Note that these three packets represent one packet from each stream, so each of the three TCP sessions will go into slow start mode *at the same time*. Whether or not the three TCP sessions are using the same timers to rebuild to a larger window, the same situation will arise when the [D,E] link reaches some percentage of its maximum capacity, causing the cycle to restart. The result is the sawtooth utilization chart on the bottom right of the figure—clearly a suboptimal use of the link capacity. There are several ways to look at this problem.

First, this can be modeled as a case of a leaky abstraction. Each TCP session sees the path from host to host as an exclusive channel, but it's not—the channel is being shared with other TCP sessions. The single link, then, is abstracted into three links, each appearing to be an exclusive link. The underlying reality leaks through in the single output queue at Router D, forcing the upper layers to interact with the underlying reality.

Second, this problem can be seen as a case of interacting surfaces—the "other side" of the leaky abstraction explanation. Within the model of complexity theory used throughout this book, speed, state, and surface are the key points. Here the problem is caused by the interaction between the underlying transport system (the physical and data link on the [D,E] link) and the overlay transport system (IP and TCP). At the intersection of these two systems there is a surface along which they interact—specifically the output queue at Router D. Within the model of network complexity used here, then, this problem can be solved by either removing the interaction surface (making the three links three actual links, rather than one shared link), or by adding more depth and complexity to resolve the nuances of the interaction. Of course there will be tradeoffs in adding this depth to the interaction surface.

Weighted Random Early Detection (WRED) is one mechanism used to resolve this problem. By randomly dropping packets off the queue, rather than always dropping the last set of packets added to the queue, the impact of TCP going into slow start is spread across time on different sessions, preventing the original synchronization of the various streams. However, WRED can have side effects on a single stream running across such a queue, and it's often difficult to precisely tune WRED to manage both tiny (mouse) flows that only last a few seconds alongside larger, long lived (elephant) flows along the same link. It's often useful to move mouse and elephant flows onto different links in a network just to mitigate the effects of TCP synchronization and quality of service buffer issues. So in an attempt to resolve one problem in a specific interaction surface, complexity ripples outward like the little wavelets expanding from a stone thrown in the water. Okay, that was very philosophical, but you get the point.

Finally, to return to the theme of this section, this problem can be seen as a shared fate issue. In this case, you can model the three TCP streams as virtual circuits running across a common physical infrastructure. The output queue at Router D is a shared resource through which all three streams must pass, and the fate of that queue is shared by all three flows.

This specific example is useful because it's relatively easy to see all three perspectives—leaky abstractions, interaction surfaces, and shared fate—as different ways to model the same underlying problem. Each of these three models can suggest a different set of solutions, or even point you to problems with any given solution.

A Final Thought

This chapter has covered two broad areas of the interaction between complexity and failure: feedback loops and shared fate. Both of these situations can be mapped to the complexity model first described in Chapter 1, "Defining Complexity," and used throughout the book:

- **State:** The mismatch between the actual state of the network and the state as viewed by the control plane is the ultimate cause of microloops formed through the control plane, while the removal of state about the actual topology through a variety of means is often the ultimate cause of more permanent forwarding loops formed in the control plane. In the case of shared fate, the state of a single shared resource leaks through the abstraction created by upper layers in the protocol stack to impact the operation of the upper layer protocol.

- **Speed:** The speed of change in the actual state of the network can overwhelm the control plane, or happen quickly enough that the control plane cannot react in real time. In reality, all control planes are *near real time,* rather than real time, to provide enough "buffer" to prevent a control plane failure in the case of rapid changes.

- **Surface:** The interaction surface between the topology and the control plane plays a large role in positive feedback loops and in many shared fate problems, such as TCP synchronization.

Thoughts on Root Cause Analysis

This chapter has discussed root causes for failures, but this is a concept engineers need to be cautious with. Complex systems, particularly highly redundant and available ones, are always in a pseudo-failure mode. There is always something wrong someplace in any truly complex system. The techniques used to manage and control the impacts of failures are generally sufficient to prevent a total system failure, so the overall system is not impacted. As a result (or corollary) of this, when a major, or systemic, failure occurs, it usually has more than one cause. A common situation is the combination of some set of pseudo-failures with a single shift in the topology, control plane, or forwarding plane that acts as a catalyst, resulting in a systemic failure.

This implies that the search for a single root cause is generally counterproductive in managing or doing postmortems of systemic failures in large complex systems. What postmortems should do, instead, is attempt to find the original conditions, the catalyst, and the feedback loops and interaction surfaces that led from the one change to the final failure. In a complex system, a failure isn't a single thing—it's a complex system in and of itself.

There is a human side to consider, as well. A well thought out expression of this human side is given by Robert Cook:

> *The evaluations based on such reasoning as 'root cause' do not reflect a technical understanding of the nature of failure but rather the social, cultural need to blame specific, localized forces or events for outcomes. . . . This means that ex post facto accident analysis of human performance is inaccurate.*[1]

Instead of just seeking out a root cause and then fixing the blame, organizations that build and manage large complex systems need to focus on finding and fixing the problem—including reaching back into the business drivers that drove the creation of complexity in the first place. One possible solution to constant failure through complexity is to remember that complexity arises as side effect of solving hard problems. Sometimes the only real solution, the only way to truly reduce complexity, is to reduce the hardness of the problems.

Engineering Skills and Failure Management

For the individual engineer, what skills are best for managing failure in a large complex system? There are three answers to this question:

- The ability to see where and how feedback loops can form in any particular design or deployment. Positive feedback loops are probably the most destructive force in the world of control plane failures; in many years as a network engineer, I can almost always point to a positive feedback loop as part of the root cause—or the primary root cause—in virtually every control plane failure.

- The ability to "reach through" abstractions, and to "see" the interaction surfaces, as they exist in the real world. Being able to model these interaction surfaces in a number of different ways can help the engineer to really understand the problem at hand, and to find a good solution within the realm of complexity tradeoffs. Or to simply ignore the problem on determining the tradeoffs given will simply overwhelm any possible solution.

---

1. Richard I. Cook, *How Complex Systems Fail* (Cognitive Technologies Laboratory, 2000).

- Gaining experience with failure. Many skills, like riding a bicycle, must be learned through physical experience. Managing failure on large complex systems is one of those skills—and like riding a bike, it's also a skill not easily forgotten once well learned. There is no simple way to develop these sorts of skills in the real world other than putting new engineers on smaller failures, teaching them the thinking and engineering sense needed to develop failure management skills, and then letting them practice. This is a hard lesson for those who depend on large complex systems to learn, but it's a necessary one.

Why not just solve these problems? Because complexity doesn't allow for a "silver bullet." The Turing Curve always catches up with any proposed solution, no matter how well thought out. Unintended consequences and leaky abstractions will always find a way to sneak through even the most tightly woven net.

Chapter 9

Programmable Networks

In a sense, networks have been programmable from the beginning. BGP communities, originally outlined on two napkins drawn at a Washington DC bar by Tony Li and Yakov Rekhter, enshrined carrying complex policy within a routed control plane. While the tagging capability in many routing protocols, including OSPF, IS-IS, and EIGRP were useful for simple tasks, the ability to attach a full policy set to a single prefix added an entire range of capabilities. What else can policy-based routing and traffic engineering be considered other than programming the network? What's different with the modern drive to make networks programmable (at press time—networking technology changes almost as quickly as the width of men's ties and the length of hemlines)? How are DevOps and software-defined networks (SDNs) different, and what's driving this movement toward a programmable network? There are several possible answers to this question:

- The specific mechanism used to interact with the control and forwarding systems.

- The rate of business change.

- The changing perceived business value of technology.

- The perceived complexity of distributed control planes.

This chapter provides the groundwork for Chapter 10, "Programmable Network Complexity." It begins with the drivers and a definition, as these underlie the tradeoffs network engineers make when considering how and where to deploy network programmability. The second section considers use cases for network programmability to put a little flesh on the bones of the business drivers and definition. The third section then considers the SDN landscape by examining several proposed interfaces.

Drivers and Definition

A number of years ago, an international service provider suffered a large-scale network outage. In response, the provider's management demanded that 16 well-known network design and escalation engineers—distinguished engineers and engineers from the global escalation team—gather in a single office and work "as long as it took," to redesign their network so it would never fail again. As one of the engineers involved remarked: "It's going to take a long time to come up with such a perfect design. What we're going to have is one person writing on the white board, and fifteen erasing." This story transfers directly to defining the programmable network—if you put sixteen engineers in a room and ask them to define "the programmable network," you'll end up with one writing and fifteen erasing.

Because you can't erase the pages of this book, however, this section will attempt to answer the question, what is a programmable network?—though you might be tempted to use correction tape on your computer screen before this section is done. The easiest path to a definition is through the drivers for programmable networks. Two subsets of drivers will be discussed here:

- Business drivers
- The ebb and flow of centralization

Business Drivers

Every business is an information business.

It doesn't matter if most businesses believe they're not in the information business—they are. In fact, business has always been about information, though the focus of the information has shifted over the years. First, there was information about technique (craftsmanship), then about who could be trusted where for trade (mercantile systems), then there was a return to technique (manufacturing systems), and so on. In today's world, the information that rises to the top of everyone's mind is about the customer—who are they, what do they want, and how do I "talk" to them in a way that will get their attention?

A key difference between the old information economy and the new is the speed at which the things business leaders want to know is changing.

Manufacturing systems, techniques, formulas, processes, and trading partners change more slowly than the latest fad; customer desires change direction like the wind in a storm. As the information driving the business increases in speed, it's only natural for business leaders to look for ways to manage that information. As Jill Dyche points out: "With the advent of trends like big data, businesspeople are more apt to see connection through the lens of information, consolidating key data in an effort to reach a single view of the business."[1] Handling and producing information on a fairly static set of systems (including the network) is very difficult.

Virtual topologies can be built quickly and efficiently on top of a physical underlay in a much faster way to respond to new applications and requirements. While the underlay can remain fairly constant in design and scope (generally achieved by using a scale out paradigm allowing new capacity to be added fairly quickly), new virtual topologies can be spun up and managed for different applications or business groups to meet short or long term needs as they arise.

Spinning up such overlays on a regular basis is difficult with traditional distributed control planes. Programmable networks allow overlays to be built and managed more quickly, providing the ability to manage information at the speed of business.

Driving the top line up—increasing revenues—is only one side of the equation for programmable networks, however. Manually provisioning networks requires a lot of time, effort, and expertise—and can often lead to a lot of mistakes just through human error. Repeating the same configuration across a large number of devices manually will inevitably result in some mistake being made someplace. Large-scale repetition of common tasks is, however, ripe for automation, saving time, and making the network more available by reducing the MTBM. Automating these tasks can drive the bottom line down by reducing the OPEX required to run the network.

Another way programmable networks can drive the bottom line down is by increasing the overall utilization of the network. For instance, traffic often follows daily, hourly, weekly, and seasonal patterns. Because of the difficulty of rapidly moving traffic around to lower utilized links, network operators often overbuild their networks. Bandwidth is chosen to support the highest traffic across a single link. During non-peak times, this bandwidth is not used, and is therefore a cost that has no return on investment. If the network is programmable, however, traffic can be engineered in near real time to adjust to increasing load on the network—or the network can signal some applications (such as a

---

1. Jill Dyche, *The New IT: How Technology Leaders Are Enabling Business Strategy in the Digital Age* (McGraw-Hill, 2015), n.p.

backup job) to wait until another time to send any traffic at all. Planning bandwidth usage in advance in this way is called *bandwidth calendaring*. While calendaring cannot replace the need for effective bandwidth planning, it can move the emphasis away from building for peak load and toward building for a number closer to the average load across longer time periods.

Finally, many network operators see programmable networks as a way to separate their hardware investment from their software, or systems, investment. In traditional networking, the control plane—and therefore the basic architecture of the network—is intimately tied to the hardware. Purchasing a particular vendor's equipment ties the operator to a particular feature set. Vendors have often made a fine art out of being "just standard enough" to claim interoperability, while including features that produce the highest degree of lock in possible. From the vendor's perspective, these "lock in features" are actually examples of innovation and added value.

Programmable networks are seen, by many operators, as a way out of this back and forth with vendors. A programmable network might often be able to provide the same level of service as vendor-specific "lock in features," while avoiding the actual vendor lock in. This could, in turn, drive down Capital Expenditures (CAPEX), and vendors are forced to compete on hardware and software features separately.

The Ebb and Flow of Centralization

Part of the rush to programmability is, of course, part of the normal ebb and flow of centralization versus decentralization in the world of information technology. The first desktop computers were stuffed into closets, hidden from the IT department. Data was first pulled off mainframes into Lotus 123 and other software packages through screen scrapers on desktop computers connected to the mainframe through terminal emulation cards. As data was distributed through the organization, IT tried to regain control through minis, Structured Query Language (SQL), and middleware. At press time, centralization is the rage again, this time with cloud computing. What drives these cycles? Table 9.1 discusses a few.

The ebb and flow of centralization and decentralization is obvious enough for general computing, but what about network control planes? Looking back across the history of networks, the same sort of cycle can be observed. Telephone networks were the "original" networks, operated by a small army of people who understood how to wire cables for manual cross connects, and to manage central offices with rotary relays that would make connections based on sequential circuit interruptions. These centralized management systems were automated over time, resulting in large-scale Private Branch Exchange systems.

Table 9.1 *Centralized versus Decentralized for General Processing*

	Centralized	Decentralized
Data Ownership	Information scattered across a large number of devices is difficult to manage, protect, and pull together to mine for insights. Centralization helps bring data into a centralized repository, where it can be effectively shared and protected, as well as used to improve the business.	Information in a centralized repository is often inaccessible to individual departments and employees without "jumping through the hoops" of information management. Projects using that data can take years to develop, costing the department (and company) revenue and savings opportunities. Often data pushed into a central repository feels like it has passed through the outer ring of a black hole, never to be seen again.
Network, Storage, And Compute Costs	If the network is cheap, it's relatively easy to build a system where anyone can access the information they need without actually storing it locally on some device. In fact, it's possible that the strong network capacity build out in the late 1990s, during the ".com bubble," could have made networks so inexpensive in the ensuing years that it was one of the drivers of cloud computing.	If network access is expensive relative to processing power and storage, there is a strong case to be made for keeping information local. Untying data from centralized processes allows individual pieces of the business to move a lot more quickly in collecting and mining information available locally.

	Centralized	Decentralized
Mobility	If data can only be accessed from one location, or from a specific set of devices, there is a drive to decentralize the data to make it more accessible.	If mobility reigns, there is a requirement to make data available from any device, anywhere (really an extension of the drive to make information more accessible). In the case of mobile devices, however, that may well have less processing and memory available than a larger resource, this drives data into centralized repositories. Once information is centralized, anyone can access the data itself, and any attendant processing capabilities, from the lowest powered device.

The public telephone network eventually fell into competition with packet switched networks, adapting principles of the distributed control planes used in IP and other packet switched networks in Signaling System 7. Distributed networks eventually took over the role of the telephone network, with most voice carried on top of IP, facilitated by distributed control planes. The drive toward programmable networks can also be seen as a drive toward centralized control once again.

Table 9.1 considered some of the reasons for the ebb and flow of information between central repositories and decentralized compute and storage devices. What drives the ebb and flow of centralization and decentralization in the control plane? Perhaps the strongest driver is perceived complexity.

When distributed systems are the norm, network engineers develop a close and personal relationship with the complexity inherent in those distributed systems. Because there is little experience abroad with centralized systems, theories around how to build a simpler system through centralization grow like mushrooms, and there's a move toward centralization to simplify networks. In periods where centralization is the rule, and decentralization the exception, the opposite occurs—decentralization appears much simpler than the centralized mess currently in use, and so the market moves toward the perceived simplicity of a decentralized system.

Complexity isn't always just perceived, of course—to build the large networks required to support the centralization of data and processing, some form of network programmability is required. The sheer scale of such large networks requires automated processes to configure and manage thousands of physical devices and their connectivity, along with the virtual machines and virtual network overlays required to support a large number of customers or applications running on a single infrastructure.

Defining Network Programmability

These, then, are the drivers for network programmability:

- Increasing the ability of the network to change to business requirements, which are, in turn, changing more quickly in a consumer-driven world.

- Decreasing the OPEX required to manage large-scale networks by automating many processes that would otherwise require talent and time.

- Decreasing the CAPEX required to purchase and build large-scale networks by separating software from hardware. This allows the architecture of the network to be separated from vendor-driven architectures, or rather the appliance model of hardware explicitly tied to a particular piece of sheet metal. This has two effects; the first is simply to put hardware in competition with hardware and software in competition with software, reducing what is normally seen as a system into separate pieces that compete independently. The second is to allow the hardware and software to be managed as separate systems, each with their own lifecycles. Replacing hardware, in this model, doesn't necessitate a new design or architectural conception of the way the network operates.

- The ebb of data from distributed computers and into more centralized compute and storage resources.

- The belief that the grass is greener on the other side of the centralized/decentralized fence.

- The belief that if I "invent it here," it must be better often plays into the equation in some way, as well. The desire to be a "special snowflake," or to build a unicorn, often drives engineers to change things around "just to be different," in some number of cases.

Based on the drivers reviewed up to this point, how can network programmability be defined? While there is no perfect definition, a good working definition might be:

A network is programmable when the control and data planes provide an interface that allows the state of the network to be modified and monitored through a machine readable data-driven API.

The scope of this definition is wide, encompassing almost any mechanism that allows the monitoring and modification of state across an array of network devices. Several points should be noted:

- Command-line interfaces (CLIs), Graphical User Interfaces, and other interfaces designed for interaction with humans would not be included in this definition.

- Standardization is not included; while standardization is important, a single vendor network with a single set of interfaces would still qualify. This type of solution might not be ideal (or even acceptable) from the network design and management perspective. Vendor neutrality might be achieved through programmable networks, but it's not a certain outcome. On the other hand, vendor neutrality is going to be almost impossible to achieve without programmable interfaces on networking devices.

- The state is both the control and the data plane. An entire taxonomy can be built around what the programmable API changes (for such a taxonomy, see Chapter 17, "Software Defined Networks," in *The Art of Network Architecture, Cisco Press, 2013*).

- There needs to be some differentiation between *managing* a network and *programming* a network. The speed at which information flows into and out of the control and data planes isn't a reliable measure of which category any particular action belongs on. The definition used here is that management relates to devices, network programmability relates to the control or data plane. This isn't a perfect split, but it's useful for the discussions that follow.

Note

There is bound to be some question about the inclusion of screen scraping mechanisms off of a CLI in the definitions here. Two points should be noted about CLIs. First, the complexity of a screen scraping application is much greater than the complexity of a true machine interface. Screen scrapers must keep up with each possible change in the output and input formats of each device; dealing with the raw data models of each device, even if they are all different, and can potentially all change on a regular basis, removes one step out of the processing. It can be argued moving from screen scraping to a true programmable interface removes the most complex and difficult to maintain pieces of the process. Second, screen scraping is an imperfect adaption that works over small-scale problems, but doesn't really provide a holistic view of the network, nor is it scalable in the same way. Screen scraping is not included here as a programmable interface for these reasons—it will be mentioned here and there, but it's not considered a future looking well thought out solution for the network programmability problem.

Use Cases for Programmable Networks

One good way to understand a technology is to think through the problems it's designed to solve. Examining use cases not only helps engineers to understand how the technology works, but also to understand why it works the way it does. Two use cases are presented here: bandwidth calendaring and software-defined perimeter.

Bandwidth Calendaring

Each network has a normal "pattern of usage" across time. There are times when the network is oversubscribed, and dropping packets, and other times when the network is undersubscribed, with bandwidth available that's not being used. Figure 9.1 illustrates somewhat typical bandwidth utilization for a corporate network.

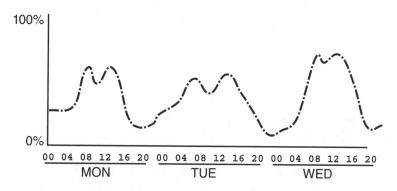

Figure 9.1 *Bandwidth Utilization across Time*

What should be immediately obvious are the times during which the network (or link, or fabric, or some other point at which this utilization is being measured) is very low. It's intuitive to try and put applications that use a lot of bandwidth into these lower utilization periods. The solutions in this space range from the simple to the complex. For instance:

- How much of the network is utilized? Measuring the utilization of a single link is different than measuring the utilization of a set of links across the network, especially when any application could use any particular path, and the path might actually change over time (given equal cost load sharing, topology changes, etc.).

- The time at which the application kicks off large-scale transfers must be manually managed. If network utilization changes, then the times must be changed, as well. While this manual process can be automated through screen scraping and other means, no such process is going to be ideal.

- If the gaps in the network's utilization are too short in duration, the application might not be able to finish its work within the available gap in utilization. In this case, should the application somehow be paused—and how should that "pausing" take place? What is the impact of such a pause on data consistency and application usage? The obvious solution is some sort of interface into the network, including a feedback loop that allows the application to see the impact of changes in the data flow in network conditions in near real time.

- There may be situations where the applications traffic can be placed on a specific set of links, allowing the remainder of the network to be unaffected by the application's traffic. This type of traffic engineering solution is tangential to bandwidth calendaring—the two solutions can interact and overlap in a single network—but also to elephant and mouse flows across a single fabric.

These challenges can be met—with a lot of fingers on keyboards across many people-years of time—through manual configuration. A definite improvement can be made in the process through more advanced screen scraping types of automation, given the user interfaces of each device doesn't change too often. To truly make the interaction between the network and application to work well, however, the network needs a programmable interface through which the application and the network can communicate. Figure 9.2 illustrates the use case.

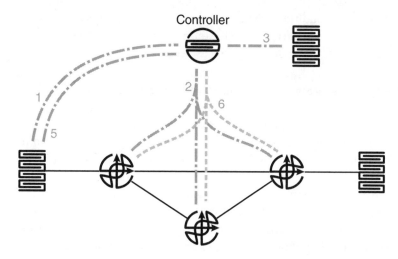

Figure 9.2 *Bandwidth Calendaring*

The process shown in Figure 9.2:

1. The application sends a notification to the controller about an upcoming flow. This could include information about the size and rate of the flow, the time by which the flow must be completed, the ability of the flow to be paused, and whether the flow is near real time (streaming information) or fairly static data (block storage).

2. The forwarding devices in the network provide information on the current utilization, queue sizes, and other network state information.

3. The controller interacts with a data store that contains historical information about the state of the network, including bandwidth utilization, queue depths, jitter and delay across each link, and so on.

4. The controller determines when the application should start to finish within the time required with minimal impact on the other applications running on the network.

5. The controller signals the application when it should kick the flow off.

6. If necessary, the controller will configure—Quality of Service (QoS), reserve links, move traffic off of links, and so on, to make the application's transfer successfully.

7. If network conditions change on the fly, the controller can recalculate the time required to carry the application's flow across the network, signaling the application to pause the flow as needed.

This type of process requires a solid set of interfaces between the forwarding devices, the application, and a controller. This is all arguably possible without such a set of interfaces, but it would be difficult to achieve on a large scale.

To carry this one step further, any such interface should be open, in the sense that any application, either built in house or commercial, should be able to communicate with any controller, and the controller should be able to communicate with any set of network devices, regardless of the vendor. Whether this last implication applies only to the hardware—any vendor's hardware with a single vendor's software—or across both software and hardware is a matter of further discussion (actually political maneuvers and loud boisterous arguments) within the computer networking world.

Software-Defined Perimeter

Network security is often defined like a castle; there is an inside and an outside, as illustrated in Figure 9.3.

In Figure 9.3, there is a portion of a castle wall defense system.

- The end towers, A and E, provide coverage for the wall and gate. Defenders can shoot into the flank of any attackers from these points, discouraging attacks on the walls and gate system.

- The outer gate, B is not the bulwark you might think—though they tend to look impressive in movies. In reality, the gate of a walled city was normally a

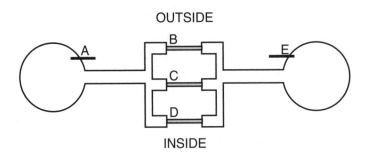

Figure 9.3 *Castle Security as an Example*

system, rather than a single gate. In ancient Israel, the system has six chambers with seven gates, with the innermost gate being the most formidable. Gate B is a formidable gate, of course, but its primary purpose is to filter, rather than to completely block. If attackers can get past this gate, it is designed with a secondary gate that will drop from above—a portcullis—trapping attackers inside the first chamber, where they can be destroyed from the protection of the surrounding walls and ceilings. Breaking your enemy up into smaller groups (divide and conquer) was much of the strategy of wall systems.

- C and D are inner gates. Each chamber is a complete defense system, designed as a fall back in case the previous gate fails—the first stage of defense in depth. In a sense, gate C is only there to protect gate D from attack (to protect the integrity of the inner gate).

If an invader made it inside the outer wall, there was often an inner wall with gates, and so on, and finally a keep, or some form of temple that would serve as a complete fortress within a fortress. Such wall systems were effective in their time; 250 defenders could hold a walled city against armies of incredible sizes, necessitating long sieges to starve the defenders out. The most effective attack against a walled city was an *insider attack*—bribing someone in the city to leave a smaller side gate open. In the modern world, these systems seem impressive but ineffectual. Why?

- Artillery made breaching the walls much easier.
- Tunneling mechanisms allowed breaching the walls from underneath.
- Airplanes made it possible to just fly over the walls, dropping stuff from above.

Network security perimeters are built much like a walled city, as shown in Figure 9.4:

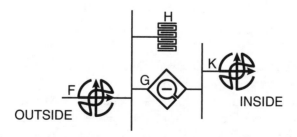

Figure 9.4 *A Network Demilitarized Zone (DMZ)*

- Router F is configured primarily to do some basic filtering. This isn't really to block most attacks, but rather to protect G, a firewall, from attack from the outside through methods designed to overflow the link, G's input interface, or other means. This is the equivalent of gate B on the walled defense system; this outer layer takes care of some simple attacks quickly without using a lot of network resources.

- Host H may host "sacrificial" services, but it also serves as a honeypot. Any attacks against this server can be measured and quantified, which helps build better filters on Router F and better stateful inspection rules on G. Information gathered here can also indicate which internal services attackers are trying to reach, and so on. This is the equivalent of the chamber between Gates B and C in the walled defense system. Note this host can be used as a base of attack by an intruder if it is taken over, much as the chamber between the gates in a walled city. Such a host needs to be well controlled with tight local security.

- The security appliance, G, may include stateless filters, stateful packet filters, and network address translation. This is the "primary gate," similar to gate C in the walled defense system. Network address translation at this point provides a "fail closed" safeguard; software errors result in a loss of connectivity, rather than open access.

What are the weaknesses of the traditional DMZ system? Pretty much the same as a walled city:

- Denial of Service (DoS) attacks can throw artillery at the DMZ, breaking or breaching the network gate system.

- Tunnels to the outside world provide an entry point through which attackers can reach through the wall without passing through the gates.

- Direct to server attacks (such as scripting attacks against HTTP servers) provide a way to "fly over" the defense system.

- And, of course, there's always the ever present insider attack.

As it turns out, things haven't changed much since the Middle Ages. As the tools for attacking the network's walls become more advanced, network security needs to move from building walls to building fluid mobile forces that can defend specific spots against a variety of attacks—just like the modern fluid mechanized force. To put it in less military terms, the network needs to move from being crunchy on the outside and chewy in the middle to being crunchy through and through.

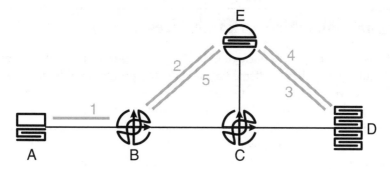

Figure 9.5 *Software-Defined Perimeter Example*

But how do networks make the transition? One possibility is to enlist the tools available in the programmable network. Figure 9.5 illustrates.

In this network:

1. Host A sends a packet toward a service, located on Server D. For this example, assume this packet is initiating a session with the service, and the packet contains some form of login credentials to the service.

2. Router B, rather than simply forwarding this packet, notes the service has been marked secure, so it redirects the packet toward a controller.

3. The controller, E, examines the packet and determines which service the packet is destined toward. The controller then contacts the service itself (shown here), or some centralized identity service (such as a Keystone service instance in OpenStack), to verify the user's ability to access the service.

4. The target service, or the identity service, returns a denial for the request to access the service for this particular user.

5. The controller uses this information to set up a filter blocking the user from accessing the server, D, on which the service resides, and replies to the original packet with a denial or login failed.

While this is more of an Authentication, Authorization, Access (AAA) example, the same principle holds for stateful filtering and other security measures. Programmable networks can push security policy to the edge of the network, providing a software-defined perimeter on a per service or per network topology element basis.

Programmable Network Interfaces

Interfaces are a key point in bridging the gap between traditional control planes, applications and policy implementation, and the programmable network. The interface between the network (or network devices) and applications or systems programming the network is broken into two different pieces.

The *northbound interface* is information individual network devices provide to controllers; this information would normally be rolled up into a larger view of the network as a whole. This interface contains three specific kinds of information:

- **Capabilities:** Provides information what can be programmed or controlled. This included metadata, or rather information about how the control structures are organized, and how information is presented by network devices to the controller.

- **Inventory:** Provides information about what devices are installed where in the network, potentially including any information about physical connections.

- **Topology:** Provides information about the state of links connecting network devices. This may include things like the native bandwidth.

- **Telemetry:** Includes operational state, counters, and other information about the current network state. This includes things like the available bandwidth, queue depths, delay, and jitter.

The southbound interface is desired state pushed from the controller into the network (or network devices). There are at least three specific interfaces here:

- **Forwarding Information Base (FIB):** A direct interface into the actual tables used to forward packets through the switching device. This interface bypasses and internal control plane processes, statically configured forwarding information, and so on.

- **Routing Information Base (RIB):** A direct interface into the tables used to build the FIB. Information injected into this interface is mixed with forwarding information installed by other control plane process, static forwarding information, and so on. This could include interfaces into protocol specific tables, such as an internal RIB or topology table—the problem with such interfaces, however, is they interfere directly with the operation of distributed protocols that have very specific rules designed to prevent loops in the calculation of best paths. Interfacing with these tables can have much larger

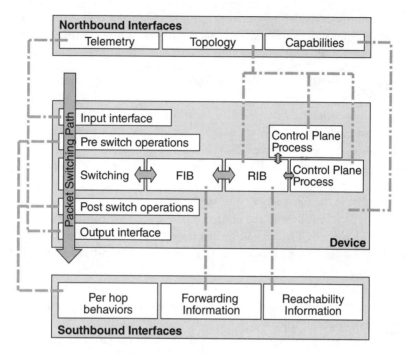

Figure 9.6 *Programmable Network Interfaces*

side effects than a single device failure or a local routing loop by injecting information that causes the protocol to fail to converge.

- **Switching Path**: An interface into forwarding parameters that don't relate to the forwarding tables, but directly impact packet handling, such as QoS.

None of these interfaces encompass what might traditionally be considered network management. They all three relate directly to how packets are handled as they pass through the device, and not to things like the power level, the temperature of any installed processors, memory utilization, and so on. Figure 9.6 illustrates these interfaces.

The Programmable Network Landscape

What technologies are being developed to address the use cases described so far? This section provides an overview of four very different types of technology developed (or being developed) in the programmable network space. This overview doesn't offer a complete picture, because the focus here is to provide a solid background for considering network programmability and complexity. The technologies that will be considered are OpenFlow, YANG, Path Computation Element Protocol (PCEP), and the Interface to the Routing System (I2RS).

OpenFlow

OpenFlow was originally designed to facilitate the study of new control plane protocols and systems in an experimental setting. As most high speed forwarding hardware is tied to a specific vendor's equipment, there is little room to develop and implement a new control plane to see if more efficient systems of managing the advertisement of reachability can be found. OpenFlow was developed at a time in the networking industry when large chassis-type switches were common; in a chassis switch the control plane runs on a route processor, while the actual high-speed forwarding hardware is installed and configured on line cards. This separation of functionality provides a natural point at which an external device can be connected; separating the route processor from the line cards in most chassis-based routers allows the control plane processes running on the route processor to be replaced by a different control plane deployed on an external device, a controller.

Within Figure 9.6, then, OpenFlow is a southbound interface providing forwarding information to the FIB.

Figure 9.7 illustrates the operation of OpenFlow.

In this figure:

1. Host A transmits a packet toward Server D.

2. This packet is received by Router B, which examines its local forwarding table, and discovers it doesn't have forwarding information for this

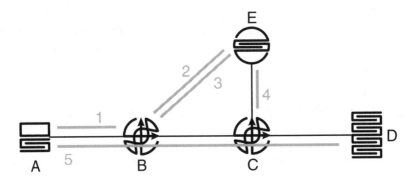

Figure 9.7 *OpenFlow Operation*

destination. As there is no local forwarding information, Router B forwards the packet to the Controller, E, for processing.

3. The Controller, E, examines the packet it has received from Router B. The controller determines the correct routing information (the process by which this information is discovered is left up to the controller, but it could be something as simple as connecting the controller to every router in the network, so it has full visibility for every destination—or the controller could run a distributed routing protocol to exchange reachability information with other controllers). Once this information is determined, including a next hop rewrite, the correct outbound interface, and so on, a flow entry is installed into Router B's forwarding table. This creates the state necessary for Router B to forward packets in this flow.

4. The Controller, E, can also determine this traffic flow must pass through Router C, so it installs the calculated outbound interface and other information into Router C's forwarding table, as well.

5. Some future packet Host A sends toward Server D will now be forwarded through Routers B and C based on this cached flow label information.

> **Note**
>
> This packet processing process should sound familiar to long time network engineers. It is almost identical to the "fast cache" processing of older Cisco routers, for instance; see *Inside Cisco IOS Software Architecture* for more information.

A key point to remember about OpenFlow is it was originally designed to carry flow entries with full information from the header of the forwarded packet, including the source IP address, the destination IP address, the IP protocol number, the source port, and the destination port. Flow labels can contain specific information that will implement forwarding for each specific flow, or they can contain information for a group of flows through wildcards. For instance, a standard IP route can be emulated using flow entries with just the destination IP address information.

OpenFlow has been implemented, in varying degrees, by a wide array of vendors.

> **Note**
>
> See *Foundations of Modern Networking: SDN, NFV, QoS, IoT, and Cloud* by William Stallings (Addison-Wesley Professional, 2015) for a more complete description of OpenFlow.

YANG

In most protocols, the data model is bound into the protocol itself. For instance, the IS-IS protocol carries reachability information in a set of Type-Length-Vectors, bound within a specific packet format any IS-IS process running on any device can understand. Hence, the format of the information carried within the protocol and the transportation mechanism for the information are combined into one object, or one thing. YANG is different in that it is actually a modeling language designed to describe the forwarding and other state in network devices.

> **Note**
>
> Data models and information models are closely related but different things. An information model describes the flow of information as well as the structure of the information and the interaction between the different processes that handle the information. A data model is focused on the structure of the information itself, including the relationships between different structures that hold information. YANG, as a modeling language, is a data model rather than an information model, as it focuses on the structure of information. An information model based on YANG could potentially include the transport of data structured using a YANG model, as well as information about how the data is used to achieve specific states in the network.

> **Note**
>
> The YANG specification is published as RFC6020[2] by the Internet Engineering Task Force (IETF).

---

2. M. Bjorklund, ed., "YANG - A Data Modeling Language for the Network Configuration Protocol (NETCONF)" (IETF, October 2010), accessed September 24, 2015, https://datatracker.ietf.org/doc/rfc6020/.

YANG is a modular language expressed as an eXtensible Markup Language (XML) tree structure—a more familiar subset of XML is the HTML, used to carry the instructions browsers render as web pages. As a language, YANG doesn't really specify any information about network devices; it just provides a framework for expressing information about network devices, much like a set of grammar rules for any natural language.

> **Note**
>
> While HTML is a rough subset of XML, HTML was actually developed before XML. The success of HTML in the field led to the development of a superset markup system that could be used for a wider array of uses than HTML, including the general structuring of information such as YANG. In a sense, HTML is the "father" of XML, which, in turn, has spawned a number of peers to HTML. YANG can be considered a peer of YANG in this sense, as it's a subset or more specific definition of YANG used for a specific case.

A number of YANG models are being developed for network protocols and devices at the time of this writing. For instance, a snippet of a model for structuring the notification of a link failure follows.[3]

```
notification link-failure {
    description "A link failure has been detected";
    leaf if-name {
        type leafref {
            path "/interface/name";
        }
    }
    leaf if-admin-status {
        type admin-status;
    }
    leaf if-oper-status {
        type oper-status;
    }
}
```

---

3. M Bjorklund, "YANG-A Data Modeling Language for the Network Configuration Protocol (NETCONF)," *YANG Central*, n.p., last modified October 2010, accessed June 14, 2015, http://www.yang-central.org/twiki/pub/Main/YangDocuments/rfc6020.html#rfc.section.4.2.2.5.

```
<notification
    xmlns="urn:ietf:params:netconf:capability:notification:1.0">
  <eventTime>2007-09-01T10:00:00Z</eventTime>
  <link-failure xmlns="http://acme.example.com/system">
    <if-name>so-1/2/3.0</if-name>
    <if-admin-status>up</if-admin-status>
    <if-oper-status>down</if-oper-status>
  </link-failure>
</notification>
```

This first code snippet shows the information in the model as a set of declarations (such as might be appropriate for building a piece of software around handling this information). The second shows the same information expressed in XML, with markups to indicate what type of information is contained in each section. Most user interfaces will show models in the XML format for human readability, though they can also retrieve the declaration type representation.

> **Note**
>
> For more complete examples of YANG models, see RFC6241.[4]

If every vendor implements interfaces that can express the state of each network element in terms of a standard YANG model, then every device in the network could be programmed through a single interface. This is a "unicorn dream," of course, but the IETF and other open standards organizations are working toward this goal by creating models for all open standards based protocols, and common models for generic network devices.

With the modeling language and actual models in place, the next question that must be answered is—how is this information carried through the network? While there are a variety of ways, two are of special note, as they are being defined specifically to carry YANG information.

- NETCONF is a Remote Procedure Call-based protocol designed specifically to carry YANG encoded information in an XML format. NETCONF allows an application to retrieve, manipulate, and update device configuration. An access control YANG model is also provided with NETCONF.

---

4. R. Enns, "Network Configuration Protocol (NETCONF)" (IETF, June 2011), accessed September 24, 2015, https://www.rfc-editor.org/rfc/rfc6241.txt.

- RESTCONF is a variation on NETCONF. It is still specifically designed to carry YANG encoded information in an XML format, but it only provides a REpresentational State Transfer (REST) interface. A REST interface, in this case, means there is no state held on the router, such as what the external application has asked for in the past, the previous command issued by the external application, and so on. A REST interface transfers the complexity of managing current state out of the device being controlled and into the controlling application, making it easier to implement a REST interface on the controlled device; this can be ideal for many types of network devices and applications.

YANG, NETCONF, and RESTCONF were originally developed to provide northbound and southbound interfaces into device capabilities and management, and to provide a northbound interface for telemetry and topology.

> **Note**
> YANG is designed to be transport independent; YANG models are not supposed to rely on the formatting or capabilities of either NETCONF or RESTCONF. Conversely, NETCONF and RESTCONF could, in theory, carry information modeled using some other language than YANG. While it's probable, however, that YANG will be widely used outside RESTCONF or NETCONF, it's not likely that the two transport protocols will ever be used for anything other than transporting YANG formatted information.

Path Computation Element Protocol

PCEP was originally developed to connect:

- A Path Computation Element (PCE), which can calculate paths through the network based on specific constraints, such as available bandwidth, to a —
- A Path Computation Client (PCC), which can receive the paths computed by a PCE and forward traffic based on them

PCEP was originally designed to support traffic engineering for flows that cross Service Provider (SP) boundaries (called Inter-AS traffic flows). Documented in IETF RFC 4655, the general idea was to allow one SP to set specific parameters for flows being passed to another SP so the second SP could calculate an optimal path for the traffic without allowing the first SP to actually control their network's forwarding policies. Figure 9.8 illustrates this.

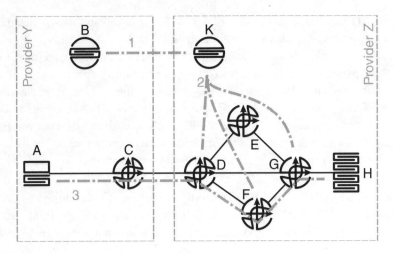

Figure 9.8 *PCEP Operation by Design*

In this illustration:

1. Provider Y's controller (B) sends information about the quality of service requirements for a customer's virtual topology to Provider Z's controller (K). This information may be manually configured, automatically configured as part of a provisioning system, or signaled in some other way. Assume, for this example, that the customer's traffic, originating from Host A, will require a minimum amount of bandwidth.

2. Provider Z's controller (K), will compute a path through the network that will meet the constraints required by the policy for this specific traffic or tunnel. This computation would normally involve running a constrained SPF computation, but it may be calculated using any method—this is an implementation detail within the controller software from the protocol's point of view. Provider Z's controller will then use PCEP to configure Routers D, F, and G with the correct information to ensure the flow passes along a path with the required qualities.

3. Traffic transmitted by Host A will be carried along the indicated path to Server H.

How is the traffic forwarded through the path requested (the path through [D,F,G]) rather than along what appears to be the shortest path (the path through [D,G])? By building an MPLS tunnel through the network—in fact, PCEP is just installing labels along the path to make certain that the traffic inserted into the tunnel headend at Router D is carried through the tunnel through Routers F and G to Server H.

> **Note**
>
> This example assumes one way of setting up the MPLS tunnels to carry the traffic along the engineered path. There are many others—the tunnel may begin in one provider's network and terminate in the other, or the labels required to tunnel traffic from Router D to G might already exist, so Controller K only needs to single Router D at the headend to effect the policy required. In fact, there is probably an almost infinite number of ways to set these tunnels up, depending on how the provider has configured their network, the relationship between the two providers, and other issues.

If you think OpenFlow and PCEP are similar in operation and intent, you're right. They're both southbound interfaces that transmit forwarding information from an external controller to the forwarding plane. Some differences between the two technologies, however, include:

- OpenFlow signals an entire 5 or 7 tuple to build the flow table on the forwarding devices, and anticipates that forwarding will take place based on the packet header as it's transmitted by the originating host or device.
- PCEP signals an MPLS label stack, and anticipates forwarding will take place based on the MPLS label stack.
- OpenFlow is designed to replace the entire control plane, or rather to allow the controller to operate like a route processor in a large chassis-based system.
- PCEP is designed to augment the existing distributed control plane.

While OpenFlow and PCEP are similar in where they interface with forwarding devices, they are different in their original intent and what they signal. The operation of PCEP—signaling MPLS label stacks to direct traffic along specific paths in the network—means it can be used as a more generic southbound interface. PCEP can be an effective tool to control the flow of traffic through a network with MPLS transport for any reason, rather than just for interdomain traffic engineering. That PCEP is widely deployed, augments the existing distributed routing system (rather than replacing it), and works with a widely available and understood tunneling mechanism (MPLS) means PCEP is a good candidate for a general purpose southbound interface in many networks.

PCEP, however, can only install MPLS labels, and not layer 2 forwarding information. In this sense, OpenFlow is more flexible than PCEP, in that it can be used to install either MPLS labels or layer 2 forwarding information. Of the choice between the two is going to be dependent on what is already deployed, what the operations staff are more comfortable with, future architectural plans, and what the already installed equipment offers the best support for.

Interface to the Routing System

The I2RS charter on the IETF website says:

> *I2RS facilitates real-time or event-driven interaction with the routing system through a collection of protocol-based control or management interfaces. These allow information, policies, and operational parameters to be injected into and retrieved (as read or by notification) from the routing system while retaining data consistency and coherency across the routers and routing infrastructure, and among multiple interactions with the routing system. The I2RS interfaces will co-exist with existing configuration and management systems and interfaces.*[5]

I2RS was not started to compete with OpenFlow, PCEP, and other southbound interfaces. Rather, it was originally started to complement those efforts by providing:

- A Layer 3 southbound interface into the RIB that would overlay and support existing distributed routing protocols
- A Layer 3 northbound interface into the RIB and routing processes that would make the topology, telemetry, inventory, and other information about the network already known by existing distributed routing protocols accessible

Figure 9.9 illustrates one way to model I2RS.

Applications may either communicate with devices—or rather, the network—through I2RS clients, which provide a common library of device capability, data marshaling, discovery, transport, and other services. An I2RS client, for instance, might gather information from the routing processes across multiple devices, and provide an interface into a unified topological view of the network. I2RS clients can also provide a unified data model for devices that hold specific pieces of data,

---

5. "Interface to the Routing System," *IETF,* n.p., accessed June 15, 2015, https://datatracker.ietf.org/wg/i2rs/charter/.

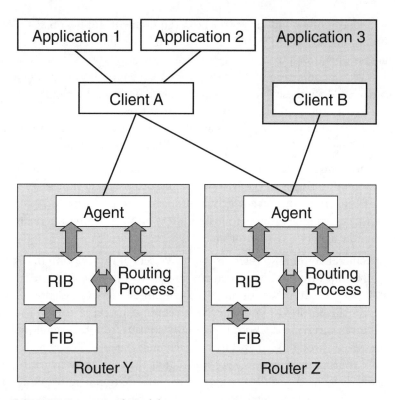

Figure 9.9 *I2RS Operational Model*

such as a RIB entry or a BGP table entry, in different ways. Ultimately, the goal of I2RS is to have all devices use a common set of data models, but in the real world this might not ever be possible; the client provides a point at which information can be transformed between data models without impacting application design.

A useful way to think of I2RS within a more traditional context is to consider Application 3 in Figure 9.9 "just another routing process" that happens to run on generic compute and storage off Router Z. This might be a route server, or a process running in a standard container or virtual machine in a data center. Either way, the interface between the on box routing processes and the RIB can be used by an off box routing process to interact with the other routing protocols and routing information sources on a router to appear to be on box.

Some key points of the I2RS architecture, as described in *An Architecture for the Interface to the Routing System* (draft-ietf-i2rs-architecture) are:

- **Multiple Simultaneous Asynchronous Operations**: Multiple clients should be able to query and set routes and other information without interfering with one another. This drives the I2RS requirements for near real-time event processing and REST-based operations. If state must be held by the agent across operations from multiple clients (the agent process in Router Z in Figure 9.8 could receive alternating events from two different clients), the order in which these operations are received *must not* be important. Different event orders, in other words, should not result in different state in the local RIB of any device. This is important to preserve the loop free nature of routing.

- **Asynchronous, Filtered Events**: Clients should be able to receive information about changes in the RIB or routing processes in managed devices in near real time. To prevent driving unneeded information across the network, clients must be able to install filters on the information being driven from the agents it is monitoring.

- **Ephemeral State**: I2RS interacts with two sets of information that are normally built through distributed routing protocols—the RIB, internal BGP, IS-IS, OSPF, and other routing protocol tables. Network engineers do not expect this information to survive a reboot—in fact, a route in the routing table surviving a reboot is generally considered a bad thing (unless it's preserved through some protocol mechanism such as graceful restart), as stale routing information may not match the current network topology. I2RS, then, never installs any permanent information in network devices. If state must persist through a device reboot, the process of reinstalling must be managed by an I2RS agent. This rules out using I2RS for configuring a device, or managing the configuration of a device.

While the decision isn't final at the time of this writing, it appears I2RS will resolve to using YANG models for the state of the RIB and routing protocol tables, combined with a RESTCONF interface into that information. The models are still in development, and it's uncertain that RESTCONF will be able to support the near real-time requirements of I2RS.

A Final Thought

The concept and use cases driving the programmable network aren't really new in any meaningful sense, but the current open API, open protocol, data model focused idea of a network API is breathing fresh air into the world of network engineering. Moving from manual configuration to expressing a policy that is then managed and implemented through a series of machine to machine interfaces is a complete revolution in the way network control planes are perceived and understood.

How does this world fare against complexity? The simplest answer is that because complexity is apparently buried under a layer of APIs, simple interfaces, and new ways of looking at expressing policy and state, networks will become dramatically simpler. This doesn't match the experience or theory of complexity in the real world, however—complexity can be moved, but it can't be eliminated. The next chapter will examine these questions in more detail.

Chapter 10

Programmable Network Complexity

The allure of the programmable network, as outlined in Chapter 9, "Programmable Networks," is two-fold: the reduction in complexity enabled by centralized routing decisions, and the ability to allow applications and orchestration to interact with the control plane. How do these promises pan out when considered in light of systemic network complexity? This chapter examines programmable networks in terms of network complexity—where does network programmability really decrease complexity, and where does it add complexity? The primary goal of this chapter is to consider a set of tradeoffs that will help guide the questions to ask when considering deploying programmable network technologies.

A short overview of the subsidiarity principle will frame the following discussion; while this principle is actually a governance construct, it is echoed in many principles and concepts used in the world of network engineering. Following this, four specific areas will be examined to consider the tradeoffs programmable networks bring to each one: policy management, control plane failure domains, the separation of the control and data planes, and the impact of application-based control on the concept of interaction surfaces. These four do not represent every possible area of investigation, and every one of these is not applicable to every type of network programmability, but they do provide a broad cross section of thought around tradeoffs in the realm of complexity.

Each of these will be considered in light of the model developed early in this book, and used throughout—what is the impact on the state, the speed, and the surfaces? And what is the tradeoff for any given solution in terms of optimal forwarding and use of network resources?

The Subsidiarity Principle

Virtually every network engineer working in the area of protocol design imple-mentation has heard of the end-to-end principle. Saltzer first articulated this principle in a paper published in 1984:

> *In a system that includes communications, one usually draws a modular boundary around the communication subsystem and defines a firm interface between it and the rest of the system. When doing so, it becomes apparent that there is a list of functions each of which might be implemented in any of several ways: by the communication subsystem, by its client, as a joint ven-ture, or perhaps redundantly, each doing its own version. In reasoning about this choice, the requirements of the application provide the basis for the fol-lowing class of arguments: The function in question can completely and cor-rectly be implemented only with the knowledge and help of the application standing at the endpoints of the communication system. Therefore, providing that questioned function as a feature of the communication system itself is not possible, and moreover, produces a performance penalty for all clients of the communication system. (Sometimes an incomplete version of the func-tion provided by the communication system may be useful as a performance enhancement.) We call this line of reasoning against low-level function imple-mentation the end-to-end argument.*[1]

The end-to-end principle might appear unique to the computer network world, but it's actually a domain specific restatement of a larger principle. In social and governmental circles, the same concept is called *subsidiarity*, which means to solve local problems with local control where possible—or to move the control and decision point as close to the problem as possible. The general idea is that the line of communication between the problem and the controller is a naturally congested space that lends itself to aggregation, but the more aggre-gated information is, the less effective any give solution will be in solving the problem at hand. This might be called "local information, local control."

Within the context of "local information, local control," when considering how and where to place to control over a specific process, engineers should ask:

- What device on the network has the most accurate information about the state of the process?

---

1. J. H. Saltzer, D. P. Reed, and D. D. Clark, "End-to-End Arguments in System Design," *ACM Trans-actions on Computer Systems* 2, no. 4 (1984): 277–278.

- What information must be transported, at what frequency, and how, if control of the process is moved off the device with the state?

Considering this from the perspective of the end-to-end principle—in terms of error and flow control, which device(s) in the network have the most accurate and up-to-date view of the state of any specific stream of data flowing through the network? The transmitting and receiving host. Hence, the hosts actually transmitting and receiving any given data stream should have the most control over retransmitting and controlling the flow of traffic. While routers, switches, and middle boxes can try to infer information from the flow state as it passes through, there is no certain way for such devices to know all of the state for any particular flow.

This same principle applies in the control plane as well—devices that are directly connected to the links making up the network topology (including the reachable destination) are more likely to know about, and react to, changes in that state more quickly.

While this does tend to push intelligence to the edge of the network, it doesn't necessarily mean every piece of state needs to be distributed as much as possible. Rather, it means each piece of state needs to be carefully examined to put the control of that state in the most logical place—and the most logical place is often going to be where the information originates and is the most complete. By reframing the end-to-end principle in terms of keeping state close to the origin of the state itself, or rather keeping control close to the most complete state available, the end-to-end principle can be applied across the system in both protocol and network design.

Policy Management

Policy is probably one of the most difficult issues to manage in network engineering. Before diving into a long discussion over the tradeoffs between complexity and policy, however, one question needs to be answered: *what is policy?* Perhaps the best way to address this question is by looking at some examples, starting from business requirements and moving through to the practical impact on the network design.

- **Flexible Design:** Businesses want a network design that will "roll with the punches." If the business expands, contracts, or changes direction, they don't want to perform a forklift upgrade across their systems. How is this accomplished at a design level? Using scale out design principles—modularized networks and workloads that can be expanded as needed and can redeploy resources without a major redesign. One common solution for building a flexible network is through modularity, which in turn means well-defined, interchangeable modules within the network. A second solution is to pull the intelligence out of the network as much as possible, so the network becomes useful for a wide array of tasks, rather than being narrowly focused on a small set of problems.

- **High Return on Investment:** This overlaps somewhat with flexible design, but it also stands as a separate concept in many network designs. For instance, there is little point in purchasing a new set of links between two locations in the network if there is excess capacity available, just not along the shortest path. To improve network utilization, many operators use various forms of traffic engineering, placing traffic on less than optimal paths from a shortest path perspective to achieve higher overall network utilization. ROI involves equipment cost, as well. Is it better to purchase smaller devices (such as a set of 1RU switches) that can be easily replaced, or a larger multiblade chassis system?

- **Business Continuity:** Businesses cannot withstand downtime—time, in the business application world, is definitely money. How is this accomplished at the design level? Modularizing the network to divide complexity from complexity, to break up failure domains, is the primary mechanism used to provide business continuity. Defense against Denial of Service (DoS) attacks also plays a major role in business continuity, again requiring points where traffic can be measured, and policies instituted.

- **Secure Information:** Businesses rely on secure information for operations, strategic advantage, and to protect their trust relationship with their customers. How does information security translate into network design? Primarily through containing data through virtualization, access policy, and other techniques that allow administrators to manage who and what can access specific information.

- **Application Support:** Many applications have specific requirements around jitter, delay, and bandwidth in the underlying transport. To achieve these goals, many networks deploy a combination of undersubscription (overbuilding the available bandwidth), traffic engineering (moving traffic from heavily to lightly used links), and quality of service (modifying the way packets are queued, queues scheduled, and congestion managed).

What are the common elements in these examples? In the data plane, permitting packets to pass through the network, and the handling of those packets passing through the network, are the two common elements. In the data plane, then, most (or all) policy resolves to the per hop handling, or the per hop behaviors, of actually forwarding traffic.

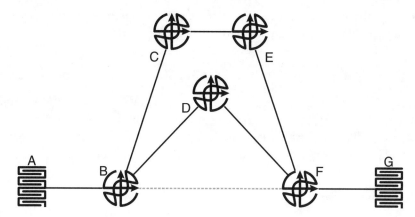

Figure 10.1 *Control Plane Policy Example*

The control plane is a bit more interesting. What is common between modular design, breaking up failure domains, traffic engineering, and controlling data access? In all these cases, traffic is potentially moved from the shortest path between two points in the network to some longer path to meet some policy goal. Figure 10.1 illustrates this concept.

- The path [B,F] would be the shortest path (based on the hop count alone, assumed throughout this example) between the two servers A and G, but it was not installed to create a module boundary, breaking a single network topology into two failure domains, and creating two separate network modules.

- The path [B,D,F] is the shortest path actually available, but it is overloaded, or close to its maximum utilization.

- The path [B,C,E,F] is the actual path used to carry traffic between the two servers A and G. This path is one hop longer than the actual shortest path, and two hops longer than the shortest potential path.

In this illustration, optimal traffic flow has been traded off to implement policy, which then supports some specific business requirement.

A simple rule of thumb is: any time policy is configured in a network, there is a high likelihood that traffic will take a less than optimal path between some pair of destinations. Reversing this, policy can be described as:

- Any mechanism that moves (or potentially moves) traffic off the lowest cost path in the network to meet some goal deemed more important than simply following the lowest cost path.

- Any mechanism that prevents traffic from entering the network, or blocks a particular flow from passing through the network.

> **Note**
>
> The Control Plane State versus Stretch section in Chapter 6, "Managing Design Complexity," provides more illustrations of policy versus the optimal path, as well as discussing the relationship between modularity, aggregation, and other design elements in relation to control plane complexity.

Policy Dispersion

Chapter 4, "Operational Complexity," poses a problem about policy dispersion versus network complexity in the section, "Policy Dispersion versus Optimal Traffic Handling." That section noted that the closer policy is deployed to the edge of the network (or rather, the source of a set of flow to which the policy must be applied), more optimal the use of network resources, and more protection against security breaches and various types of attacks, will be achieved.

The solution proposed to this problem was automated deployment of the policy through the network. Several points were noted in relation to this proposed solution, including *brittleness*.

Machine-based systems can react more consistently, but their consistency is a bad thing as well as good. Two events that appear to be the same from one set of measurements might actually be far different, for instance; attackers can learn the pattern of reaction, and change their attacks to take advantage of them. An unforeseen combination of reactions to multiple events occurring at the same time can cause failure modes software cannot resolve.

Programmable networks can provide a more complete solution to these problems by continuously monitoring multiple interlocking systems and encompassing more complex and nuanced reactions. For instance, a programmable network may be able to modify an application's behavior in response to network conditions, rather than just modifying the configuration of the network, or some set of links or forwarding devices. Through an application level interface, a programmable network can also discover exactly what a particular application would like to do, rather than embedding heuristics into the network that attempt to discover this information.

Programmable networks can also provide a larger amount of continuous state than a traditional management system through their closer to real-time interfaces into the state of the forwarding plane. By interfacing either at the routing table or forwarding table, controllers in a programmable network can

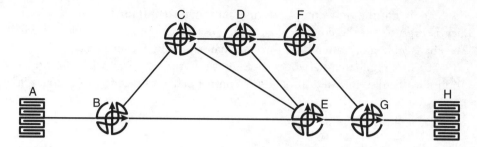

Figure 10.2 *Programmable Network State*

recognize and adapt to network conditions more quickly, and with less complexity, than a management system that primarily relies on interface and device level state.

There are tradeoffs, of course. The more finely controlled the network is managed to achieve optimal control on a near real-time basis, the more *state* the network must manage. Figure 10.2 illustrates the programmable network state.

Assume traffic originating from Server A and destined to Server H—for some policy reason—should flow along the path [B,C,D,F,G], rather than along any other path through this network, and that each hop shown has a cost of 1. Using traditional network configuration and destination-based routing:

- Router B must be configured to examine traffic for any packets sourced from Server A and destined to Server H, and redirect such traffic toward Router C, rather than along the shortest path through Router E.

- Router C must be configured to examine traffic for any packets sourced from Server A and destined to Server H, and redirect such traffic toward Router D, rather than along the shortest path through Router E.

- Router D must be configured to examine traffic for any packets sourced from Server A and destined to Server H, and redirect such traffic toward Router F, rather than along the shortest path through Router E.

Each of these configurations represents policy that is *dispersed*, either manually or through some automation system, through the network. The policy is, in effect, in the "control plane in the mind of the network operator," rather than in the actual programmable control plane used to manage the network. In a programmable network, this information would be captured in the actual control plane of the network, increasing the amount of state being carried through the network.

State is not the only complexity measure impacted, though. Once this policy is captured in the control plane through a programmatic interface, it will be changeable more often than through manual configuration. Thus, the drive toward programmable networks also increases the speed at which information must be disseminated through the control plane (in reaction to changes in policy).

> **Note**
>
> The policy implemented in this example to carry traffic along a less than optimal (metric wise) path through the network could be implemented in any number of ways, including ingressing the traffic into a tunnel or LSP.

Finally, the programmable interface is an increase in the breadth and depth of the interaction surfaces between various devices in the network; this is covered in the section "Surface and the Programmable Network," that follows.

Policy Consistency

One of the problems with distributing policy throughout a network is the large number of control and management interfaces used by the wide array of forwarding devices. A device or service that specialized in stateful packet filtering will have far different configuration options and capabilities than a device that is primarily designed to forward packets. A programmable interface would allow an intelligent controller to query each device in the network and determine where and how to apply any given policy in an optimal way without regard to the user interface provided at each device. Even if the programming API is inconsistent across devices, producing translators for a machine readable interface is much different than creating "screen scrapers" to discover and manage state.

Programmability can also resolve a second source of complexity by converting many complex policies directly into control plane state at the controller, rather than through the local interface of each device. Returning to Figure 10.2, assume:

- Router B is a device manufactured by one vendor, and uses *Policy-Based Routing* to implement the policy discussed. This entails configuring a set of policies, wrapping those policies in a set of forwarding rules, and then applying the policies to the relevant interfaces on the device.

- Router C is a device manufactured by a second vendor, and uses *Filter-Based Forwarding* to implement the policy discussed. This entails configuring a set of policies, wrapping those policies in a set of forwarding rules, and then applying the policies to the relevant interfaces on the device.

- Router D is a switch that must be configured to examine the Layer 3 information, rather than Layer 2 information, carried in the packet to perform the operations required.

- Router E is actually a stateful packet filter; source-based rules for this device must be configured through security policies.

Each of these devices requires a different interface (and set of logical constructs) to achieve the desired outcome. If each them had a programmable interface, however, a single piece of software, running on one or more controllers, could distill the policy into local forwarding rules for each device, and install the forwarding rules required on each one. This, in effect, centralizes the logic of the policy while distributing the result of the policy by using forwarding plane proxies in place of the policy itself on each device in the path. Each of the policies involved interacts in one place—on the controller—rather than among devices.

Once again, this type of operation places more state into the control plane. The policy that was once configured locally on each device is now captured within the control plane, albeit in a simplified form. This also increases the speed at which the control plane must disperse information among device, as the operator is interfacing directly with the forwarding tables in each device, rather than with the slower management oriented human readable user interface on each device.

This example also shows an increase in the interaction surface; each device must now interact with a controller that provides a version of the policy distilled for use in the various forwarding tables, rather than acting independently based on local configuration. At the same time, however, this interaction surface moves from "the mind of the network operator" into the controller, making it more manageable.

Policy Complexity

In the field of economics, there is a concept called *moral hazard*, which is defined as:

In economics, moral hazard occurs when one person takes more risks because someone else bears the burden of those risks.... Moral hazard occurs under a type of information asymmetry where the risk-taking party to a transaction knows more about its intentions than the party paying the consequences of the risk.[2]

---

2. "Moral Hazard," Reference, *Wikipedia*, n.p., last modified June 6, 2015, accessed June 20, 2015, https://en.wikipedia.org/wiki/Moral_hazard.

A similar hazard exists when abstracting or simplifying complexity in the realm of network policy. Once policy is centralized into a single set of code, there's no specific reason to maintain discipline in building the forwarding plane policy, or to consider alternatives to installing new per hop behaviors to solve any problem at hand. As an example, consider the case of early EIGRP deployments. Because many engineers believed EIGRP could handle any network topology, they designed EIGRP networks with no aggregation and no failure domains. Much the same happens in some large-scale BGP deployments; the protocol appears robust enough to handle anything, so why bother with failure domains?

Centralized policy, particularly in the form of the programmable network, can result in the same sort of sloppiness; human nature hasn't changed much since EIGRP was invented and first deployed, after all. When the easiest tool to use is the hammer, every problem quickly becomes a nail.

Surface and the Programmable Network

The preceding sections focused primarily on state and speed in the programmable network, but what about surface? Figure 10.3 will be used to examine this piece of the complexity puzzle.

When using a distributed control plane and a management system:

- Surface 1, between the originating host and the first hop router, is primarily a function of any information Host A places in the packet. For instance, the source address, the destination address, the type of service, and other factors actually carry information between the host and the router, implying an interaction between these devices, and therefore a surface. This interaction surface, however, can be said to be rather shallow, as it contains

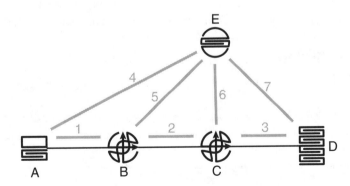

Figure 10.3 *Surface in the Programmable Network*

minimal information, and neither the host nor the router have any information about the internal state of the other device.

- Surface 2, between the two routers, is actually two surfaces. The first is the information carried inside the packets being forwarded along the path, and it has the same characteristics as the surface between Host A and Router B. The second is the routing protocol (or other distributed mechanism designed to carry reachability and topology information through the network). This second surface between Routers B and C has more depth, as each device is actually trading some level of information about internal state, and more breadth, as this surface actually reaches across every forwarding device participating in the control plane within the failure domain.

- Surface 3, between Router C and Server D, is similar to Surface 1.

- Surfaces 4 and 7 don't (normally) exist in a network primarily dependent on a distributed control plane.

- Surfaces 5 and 6, in a network with a primarily distributed control plane, represent a management interface. While this surface is both deep, because it carries internal device state, and broad, because the management device typically interacts with most or all of the devices connected to the network, this surface doesn't reach directly into the forwarding information in any meaningful way. From the forwarding perspective, this surface is actually shallow. This surface is actually shallow enough that it can often not be monitored with little impact on actual network operation (although this wouldn't be recommended!).

When considering a programmable network, however:

- Surfaces 1 and 3 remain the same.

- Surface 2 can either remain the same or have a reduction in complexity. If the control plane is completely centralized, rather than running in a hybrid mode (the distributed control plane operates alongside a centralized system that modifies forwarding information based on policy requirement), the only surface interaction between Routers B and C would be at the packet level, much like Surface 1.

- Surfaces 4 and 7 may contain a good deal of state in near real time, such as how much information the application needs to transfer, quality of service requirements, how fast the application should transfer information based on the network's state, etc. These two surfaces, then, can become much deeper and broader.

- Surfaces 5 and 6 now contain actual forwarding state, both as it exists and how it should be, being carried between the controller and the forwarding devices. These two surfaces will become much deeper, as the internal forwarding state of each device is exposed and modified by the controller.

- If the controller is deployed in a hybrid mode, where a distributed control plane discovers reachability and topology in near real time, and a centralized system overlays the control plane to implement policy, there is also a new interaction surface between the two control planes. The centralized control plane must be notified of changes in reachability or topology in near real time, and then calculate and implement policy changes as needed to preserve the policies imposed on the network. This interaction surface is both deep and broad.

An interesting problem in the surface states is the newly minted feedback loops, for instance along surfaces 3, 6, and 7. The network has always been capable of impacting application state. Once the application is capable of impacting network state, however, a feedback loop forms. While such feedback loops can have a strong positive impact, particularly in the form of injecting applications requirements into the control plane's operation in near real time, and in allowing applications to "see" network conditions in near real time, such feedback loops can be dangerous as well. This is an area the network designer deploying programmable networks must pay careful attention to if stability is a goal.

> **Note**
> Chapter 8, "How Complex Systems Fail," discussed the various failure modes of such feedback loops.

Impact on Failure Domains

Failure domain separation through loose coupling of different systems (and multiple pieces within these systems) is a foundational concept in large-scale network design. Does the programmable network have an impact in this area? Figure 10.4 illustrates failure domains and programmable networks.

> **Note**
> Controller B actually has a connection with each of the switches shown in the spine and leaf fabric; for clarity, these are shown as a group, rather than individual connections.

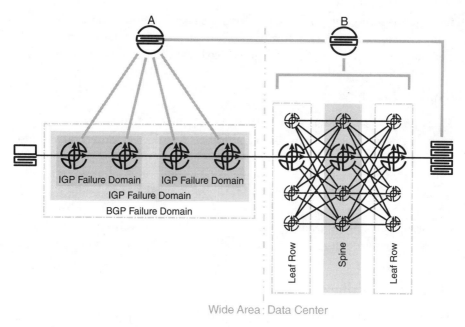

Figure 10.4 *Failure Domains and Programmable Networks*

Four specific instances of failure domain impact need to be examined here.

Wide Area Failure Domains

In the distributed design on the left side of the diagram, *internal* reachability and topology information is carried by an IGP underlay, while *external (or edge)* reachability is carried in BGP as an overlay. This separates edge (or external) reachability from internal reachability, providing two different failure domains with fairly loose coupling between the two. The IGP can further be broken up into multiple failure domains along topological boundaries by hiding reachability, topology information, or configuring other forms of information hiding.

When a controller is deployed to either replace or augment the distributed control plane, these various failure domains are replaced with a single failure domain. Whether this is a positive development or not depends on the ability of the controller to handle faults, the amount of policy being managed, and other factors—but the reduction in the number of failure domains goes against the best common practice of years of experience with network design, and needs to be seriously considered as a tradeoff.

What if there are two controllers, rather than one? Two controllers managing the same set of devices must be synchronized in terms of state through some mechanism—hence they will actually form a single failure domain in response to many common errors. For instance, if a malformed packet carrying control information causes the first controller to fail, it will likely cause the second to fail, as well.

> **Note**
>
> It is possible to have a more federated controller design, where each controller can send instructions to several forwarding devices, and some mechanism is used on each device to determine which controller's input should be accepted. This type of mechanism would represent another form of information hiding, as the decision of which state to accept, and which policies should be accepted from each controller, is a distributed form of state. This state must, of course, still be configured or managed in some way—the complexity doesn't "go away," it just moves from one area of the network to another.

Data Center Failure Domains

The distributed protocol design as presented in the illustration has each leaf row and the spine row shown as a separate BGP autonomous system—a fairly common design in very large-scale data centers (especially supporting commercial cloud-based workloads). Because network devices within any given row (either leaf or spine) are not interconnected, each BGP speaker only maintains eBGP connections. Failure domains must be seen in two ways in this type of design:

- eBGP is known for its loose coupling and is often used to connect two different failure domains. In this design, then, each router is effectively a separate "failure domain" from a control plane perspective, as counter-intuitive as that might seem.
- The entire BGP routing system is, however, a single failure domain.

An alternative might be a simple IP or IP/MPLS underlay with a separate BGP, VXLAN, or other overlay. Replacing either of these with a single controller, or a set of redundant controllers, once again turns what is originally a set of loosely coupled systems into one system, reducing the number of failure domains.

> **Note**
>
> Use of BGP for Routing in Large-scale Data Centers (draft-ietf-rtgwg-bgp-routing-large-dc) describes using BGP as a standalone protocol in large-scale data center fabrics in detail.

One option here is to use one controller for the underlay, and another for the overlay, breaking them into separate failure domains, to recover some of the separation in the original design.

Application to Control Plane Failure Domain

In a network that is not programmable, there is little interaction between applications running on the network and the control plane—hence the application and the control plane represent either completely decoupled or loosely coupled failure domains (with the primary coupling being in the area of packet headers carrying information between the application and the network devices). Putting an interaction surface between these two systems actually creates a larger failure domain, as there are failure modes that can reach across the controller/application divide.

Further, presumably most of the applications running on the network will have such an interface, providing yet another channel through which many complex systems can interact in unforeseen ways—hence the applications themselves can be unintentionally coupled into a single failure domain through the controller. As an example, two different applications might "fight" over the quality of service settings for a particular set of links, eventually causing a chain of events that causes one of the two applications (or both) to fail.

Controller to Controller Failure Domain

The connection between controllers A and B must be watched carefully to ensure loose coupling is maintained between them. If these two controllers unintentionally form a tightly coupled pair, the entire network becomes a single failure domain—contrary to all good design principles.

Final Thoughts on Failure Domains

A final area to be careful of is in band signaling, which tightly couples access to the forwarding devices to the state of the forwarding devices themselves. Consider out of band control channels to create a truly stable network if building for centralized control—and remember to consider the complexities of building and maintaining the out of band network itself.

In short, it's important to consider the tradeoffs involved in enlarging failure domains through more centralized control of the network. Take care to examine each interaction surface carefully, particularly looking for potential instances of tight coupling, and think through ways of enforcing loose coupling in these areas. One good way, if the entire distributed control plane is being replaced, is to run multiple controllers, each one providing reachability for either one specific topo-logical area of the network or one virtual topology. Connect the controllers with the loosest coupling possible—traditional BGP could be a good choice.

A Final Thought

Programmable networks are surely in the future of every network engineer—the complexity and management of distributing policy to thousands of devices is quickly unmanageable in any large-scale environment. The rush to centralize, though, needs to be balanced with serious consideration around the complexity tradeoffs.

There is no silver bullet for complexity.

Traditional network design holds a lot of lessons for the new world of pro-grammable networks, from separating failure domains to thinking through how and where to distribute policy to potential feedback loops. One useful way to think through these problems is to consider a layered model for the control plane, as illustrated in Figure 10.5.

In this model, there are four essential tasks a control plane handles:

- Discovering the topology and reachability
- Determining the shortest path between every pair of reachable nodes attached to the network
- Hiding information or building failure domains
- Traffic engineering

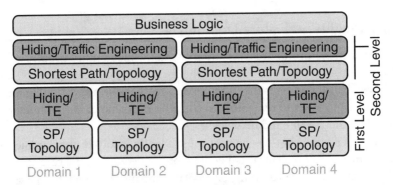

Figure 10.5 *A Layered Model for Managing the Control Plane*

Each of these four functions is repeated at each "layer" of the network. As a simple example, consider an underlay/overlay:

- There will be the shortest path and topology discovery in the underlay protocol.

- Information hiding and traffic engineering will be implemented in the underlay, as well, through aggregation, flooding domain boundaries, (potentially) fast reroute, and other mechanisms.

- There will be the shortest path and topology discovery in the overlay control plane that is separate from the underlay.

- Information hiding and traffic engineering will also be implemented in the overlay—service chaining, examined in the next chapter, might be one example.

By breaking the control plane out into functions rather than protocols, engineers can get a better feel for what each protocol in a network control plane should do and build layers of functionality that will provide an optimal balance between functionality and complexity. This is similar to the way network engineers have built layers into protocol stacks and applications to manage complexity and scale problems.

Chapter 11

Service Virtualization and Service Chaining

In the early days of network engineering, two words could be used to describe the applications running over the network: *simple* and *few*. There were several different ways to transfer files, a few ways to talk to someone else (such as email and message boards), and perhaps a few other applications of note. In these ideal times, the end-to-end principle reigned supreme, with hosts only talking to other hosts (or bigger hosts called servers) and the occasional mainframe or mini (remember those?).

This has changed over the years; each new generation of users and businesses have added new ideas about what networks need to support and laid requirements on the network itself.

First, there were firewalls, which protect data and systems from attackers. Then the network monitoring tools, and the deep packet inspectors in the form of intrusion detection systems. To save ongoing operational expenses on long haul links, wide area accelerators were added to the path. A single server couldn't handle the load thrown at it, so load balancers were inserted. Over time, to account for the increasing scarcity of IPv4 address space, network address translators were pushed into the path. Appliances running a set of services were installed throughout the network, effectively moving intelligence out of the end hosts and into the network itself—bumps in the wire the host didn't know about now manipulate, fold, and spindle almost every packet transmitted anywhere beyond a single hop. Applications now run "on" the network, in the sense that the APIs that connect the different pieces of the network together are actually resolved across the network itself. Three different things cause this model of adding appliances to add services to break down:

- The added complexity of policy distribution throughout the network. Chapter 4, "Operational Complexity," has a more lengthy discussion on policy dispersion versus complexity, but essentially policy spread throughout the network is much more difficult to manage than policy concentrated in a few processes or places.

- The added cost of installing and managing appliances. Each appliance not only represents a cost, but also represents power, space, cabling, and an entire lifecycle that must be managed. Each of these things adds operational and/or capital costs.

- The virtualization of the network. Supporting multiple tenants, deeper segmentation for security, and more efficient use of the network requires virtualization. Pushing virtualized circuits through an appliance, rather than physical ones, is much more difficult to deploy and manage for several reasons. For instance, a virtual topology can be moved almost anywhere in the network without regard to topology (in fact, in spite of topology). Moving an appliance-based service from one location to another, or even just the state contained in the appliance from one location to another, is problematic (if not impossible).

So why not virtualize the services as well? This is where Network Function Virtualization (NFV) enters the picture. This chapter will discuss several aspects of service virtualization, including examining some of the specific cases where services are being virtualized, and the concept of service chaining, which is required to move traffic to these virtualized services (where they were placed into the packet stream before). The topic of complexity isn't addressed directly here; rather it is reserved for the next chapter, which explicitly deals with the tradeoffs in complexity around the virtualization of services.

Network Function Virtualization

In 1994, a group of engineers formed the company *Network Translation* and designed the first PIX firewall. The security features were evident from the start, but considered secondary—the PIX was first developed to do Network Address Translation (NAT). In the face of discussions around Address Allocation for Private Internets[1] and Traditional IP Network Address Translator,[2] the IPv4 address

---

1. Y. Rekhter et al., "Address Allocation for Private Internets" (IETF, February 1996), accessed September 24, 2015, https://datatracker.ietf.org/doc/rfc1918/.

2. P. Srisuresh and K. Egevang, "Traditional IP Network Address Translator" (IETF, n.d.), accessed September 24, 2015, https://www.rfc-editor.org/rfc/rfc3022.txt.

space was showing the first signs of running out. Cisco acquired the PIX in late 1995, shipping and maintaining the product with new revisions until 2008.

Engineers in the Cisco Technical Assistance Center, being curious folks (as most engineers are), quickly pulled the cover off the first few PIX devices shipped to their local labs, and discovered an Intel processor (for most models) and standard Ethernet chipsets.

Note

The PIX was constructed using Intel-based/Intel-compatible motherboards; the PIX 501 used an AMD 5×86 processor, and all other standalone models used Intel 80486 through Pentium III processors. Nearly all PIXes used Ethernet NICs with Intel 82557, 82558, and 82559 network controllers, but some older models are occasionally found with 3COM 3c590 and 3c595 Ethernet cards, Olicom-based Token-Ring cards, and Interphase-based Fiber Distributed Data Interface (FDDI) cards.[3]

There was also a single piece of custom silicon, the PIX-PL in the original models and the PIX-PL2 in later models. The PIX-PL accelerated encryption because the Intel processors used for general processing couldn't switch packets fast enough. These PIX-PL chips [and other hardware acceleration Application Specific Integrated Circuit (ASICs)] are, in a sense, at the heart of the NFV narrative. As with the first two generations of PIX, the most convincing reason to deploy an appliance in the middle of a traffic flow (as a middle box) is for the custom ASICs designed into the box.

Note

A number of vendors sell appliances rather than installable software services for reasons other than the included custom ASICs, such as controlling the performance of the service, to provide for simple licensing, the inclusion of some higher end processor than is available on the equipment normally available in a network for functions such as cryptography, or simply to increase incremental revenue.

The question is: When can the general purpose processor already included in the appliance take over all the packet processing duties, and hence when can the appliance be replaced by a more generic/general purpose device? This point was reached

---

3. "Cisco PIX—Wikipedia, the Free Encyclopedia," n.p., accessed April 30, 2015, https://en.wikipedia.org/wiki/Cisco_PIX.

sometime after 2008, but before 2015 (the year of this writing)—though there's no "generally agreed on date" for the transition, for most network applications.

> **Note**
>
> The crucial words in the statement above are *for most network applications.* Networks are, in a sense, simply a "concession to human impatience." There are only a few things that can be done by a high-speed link running across an ocean that can't (in theory) be done using a standard carrier's overnight box holding a large number of solid-state drives. But humans are infinitely impatient, so there will always be some things for which the speed of a general purpose processor won't be fast enough, so appliances and custom ASICs most likely have a long life ahead of them. The more likely result is that the number of such devices will remain fairly steady over time, but as networks increase in size and scope, the percentage of custom silicon switching hardware will decrease as a percentage of hardware sold and deployed. This is all a matter of tradeoffs—you've either missed something crucial about the environment, the problem, or the solution. If you take only one thing away from this book, it should be this: there are always tradeoffs. If you don't see any tradeoffs, then you're not looking hard enough.

Once this trend of fast general purpose processors meets the virtualization of networks and applications, a question becomes obvious: *Why should these applications run on appliances?* In fact, running deep packet inspection, stateful filtering, load balancing, and all other services that live within the network can run on "fast enough" general purpose processors, and therefore be run on the general purpose compute and storage resources already residing in the network.

NFV, then, solves two sets of problems—or rather, is at the confluence of two different trends:

- The explosion of virtualization in the network, and the desire to provide "in the network" services to the resulting virtual networks.
- Replacing expensive physical appliances containing custom packet switching hardware with less expensive (and better understood) general purpose computing resources.

NFV: A Use Case

To make all this a little more clear, it's useful to work through a use case showing how these two trends merge into a single concept; the network illustrated in Figure 11.1 will be used as an example.

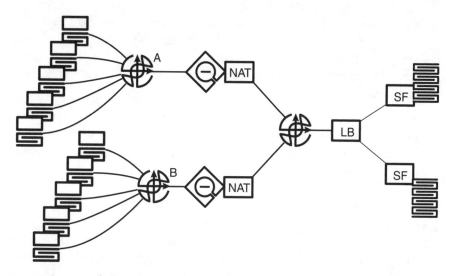

Figure 11.1 *Pre-NFV Network and Services Design*

Figure 11.1 shows the network connectivity and services commonly required to provide email services to a large number of hosts. The path of traffic through the network can be traced as:

1. A host attached to either Router A or B sends an email packet toward one of the two servers, shown on the right side of the illustration

2. First, the traffic must pass through one of the routers, to be ingressed into the network, have any QoS markings imposed, terminate any tunnels (such as an IPsec SA or an MPLS VRF), and any basic filtering performed (such as source-based spoofing filters).

3. Then the traffic is passed to a firewall appliance, where several actions may be taken. For instance, passing the flow through a stateful packet filter that validates each packet against an existing stream, or performing deep packet inspection to check for the presence of an attack or malware in the flow's contents. A common operation, at least with IPv4, is NAT (or, more likely Port Address Translation).

4. Once the traffic is through the first appliance, it is passed to a router, which then directs the traffic into the part of the provider network where the email servers are located. The next hop shown in the diagram is a load balancer.

5. In this particular situation, a single server cannot support the load of all the clients, so the network operator has configured a number of servers, each with access to the same database backend. Each of the mail servers is,

then, operationally identical, with access to the same set of mail stores. The load balancer, another appliance, determines which server has the least amount of load, and hence should handle any new incoming requests. This service requires the load balancer to maintain state about each connection and each server.

6. The traffic is passed from the load balancer to the mail server, but along the way must pass through a Spam Filter (marked with SF in the diagram). This might be an appliance, or it might be a process or application running on the mail server itself.

In each case, the service is actually an application running on an appliance; the appliance must be placed in the path of the traffic as it moves between the host and the server, or between the two endpoints in the network. Putting an appliance into the network, and wiring the network such that traffic of a certain type must pass through it, can be called *manual service insertion*. A useful way to think about this type of service insertion in the network design is *bringing the service to the traffic flow*.

What if these services could be virtualized, and run in fairly standard compute and storage resources? One option would be to place standard compute and storage resources throughout the network, and create instances where needed to intercept traffic flows as they pass through the network. The primary operational expense this would save is in the cost of the appliances themselves—perhaps there is some savings here, but this model still largely depends on a *scale up*, rather than a *scale out*, model of providing services.

Scale Up versus Scale Out

One of the crucial distinctions application developers make is between *scale up* and *scale out*. Scale up is what most engineers are accustomed to designing around; a single server is scaled, in terms of amount of memory, storage, and processing power it has to fit the task at hand. In network hardware terms, this is much like purchasing a single large multicard chassis-based system that with plenty of slots, power, and processing power, and increasing the number of ports by installing new line cards over time as the network grows. In the application world, a database server might have additional discs added over time, or more memory, as different parts of the system near their maximum utilization. There are three problems with the scale up model.

First, scale up assumes there is something more that can be added to the system, and that such incremental improvements add incremental costs. In the real world, however, going from a 1TB disc array to a 2TB disc array might, or might not, be a matter of adding additional physical discs. The next increment might actually mean upgrading to a larger box all the way around, which means forklifting the old box out of place, moving all the data, and installing a new one. This can be expensive.

Second, scaling a platform or component up can cost more than simply adding incremental capacity. To return the drive space example, a 500GB drive might be similar in cost to a 1TB drive. Moving to a 2TB drive might, however, more than double the cost of the component or the platform. Purchasing four times the capacity, especially at the higher end, may well mean paying much more than four times the cost.

Third, scale up often means purchasing more than you need when the system is installed, and trying to anticipate the growth of the system over time. This leads to a rather suboptimal investment model, such as the one shown in Figure 11.2.

In Figure 11.2, any time the gray dashed *capacity* line is above the darker dashed *demand* line, the business is paying for capacity it isn't using. This would be true, for instance, in the case of a large chassis system that only has a couple of slots used—the additional slots, power, processing, and space are all paid for, but not in use. On the other hand, when the darker *business* line is above the lighter gray *capacity* line, the business is not operating at capacity—growth may actually be stunted, or the business might be forced to replace network capacity with employee time to fulfill customer demands. This will virtually always result in lost opportunity costs.

How does scale out deal with these two situations? While scale up builds single systems that can be upgraded to increase their capacity, scale out builds smaller systems that can split the load of a single task effectively. For instance, rather than using a pair of chassis switches to provide the core of a data center, a set of smaller switches connected through a fabric that spreads the load through equal cost load sharing over a higher number of paths are used. In the application world, scale out normally involves breaking any given application up into its component parts, and then allowing as many instances of each component part (a thread or process) to be created on an as-needed basis.

Instead of using a scale up model, inserting these services onto generic hardware scattered throughout the network, why not move to a scale out model? This is precisely the idea behind NFV; Figure 11.3 illustrates virtualizing functions in the network.

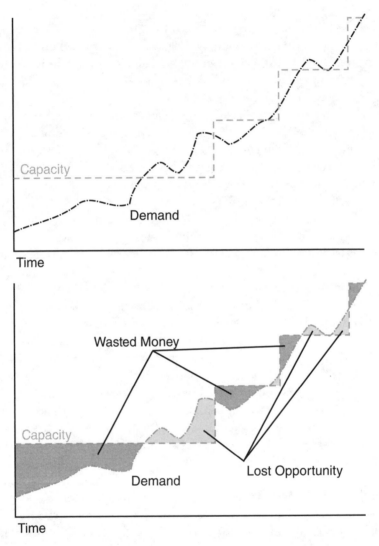

Figure 11.2 *Growth versus Capacity over Time*

In Figure 11.3, each of the component services normally performed in an appliance has been made into a separate process, and is being run on generic compute and storage attached to the data center fabric. Rather than having appliances configured inline that perform stateful packet inspection, for instance, a pool of processing elements that perform the same function are simply attached to the data center fabric. In the same way NAT, SES, and the mail

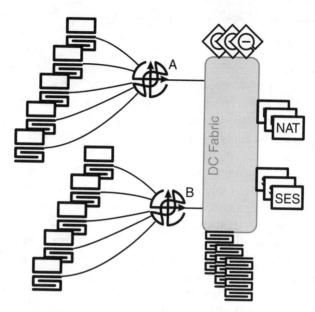

Figure 11.3 *Virtualizing Functions in the Network*

servers themselves are all converted to processes running on generic compute and storage resources attached to the data center fabric.

The range of services that can be virtualized and placed on the data center fabric, or "in the cloud," in more common parlance, is wide. For instance:

- The termination of services for mobile devices, including tunnels, operational and business services, billing, and the full range of support for these devices can be virtualized into a data center fabric.

- Content replication and duplication can often be more efficiently handled in virtualized scale out processes, rather than in customized appliances.

The problem with scaling out network services in this way should be obvious at this point. With the scale up model, the network engineer could place appliances into the path of the traffic as it passed from host to server, or from host to host. In the scale out NFV model, traffic somehow still needs to pass through these same services, but there's no obvious way to enforce this sort of traffic flow through a packet-based network with simple destination-based forwarding.

Service chaining provides a solution to this problem.

Service Chaining

Service chaining relies on modifying the path of a flow through a network overlay—or along a tunneled path in a virtual topology—to channel traffic through the set of services required to ensure the network operator's policies are enforced. Figure 11.4 returns to the previous example, showing how a service chain can be used to push the traffic along a path required to ensure traffic passes through all the correct services in the right order.

In this case, traffic arriving from the host is passed through Router A, and placed in some sort of tunnel with an endpoint so it arrives at one of the packet inspection processes within that pool. Once each packet has been processed, it is encapsulated in a way that causes the traffic to be carried to a NAT process and then on to a process that does spam filtering, and finally to the mail server itself. At each of these steps, the packet is not forwarded based on the destination address—which would take the packet directly through the fabric to the mail server, its final destination—but rather to the next service in the chain.

How is this accomplished? There are three basic models that can be used to form a service chain:

- The initial service can be imposed by the ingress device on the chain, which is Router A in this case. Once the packet arrives at the first service in the

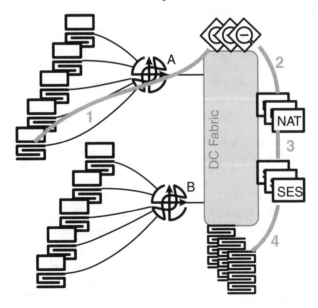

Figure 11.4 *Chaining Traffic through the Services*

chain, the first service (or the local hypervisor virtual switch) imposes the correct encapsulation onto the packet to carry it to the next service. The next service to impose on the chain is determined by some local policy within the service itself. Once the final service has handled the packet, it simply forwards each packet based on the destination address.

- The initial service, and all subsequent services, can be imposed by the switching devices within the fabric. This is similar to the first option, above, but each segment in the chain is imposed by devices in the network (Top-of-Rack switches, for instance), rather than by the service processes themselves.

- The initial service, and all subsequent services, can be imposed by the first device the packet encounters—the Data Center (DC) edge switch in the case of a cloud deployment, for instance. In this case, the edge switch is given information about every service through which packets destined to any particular service must pass, and some way to build a chain of headers that can be "stacked" onto the packet that will carry each packet through this chain of services.

Examples of each of these types of deployments follow.

Service Function Chaining

The IETF chartered the Service Function Chaining (SFC) working group in late 2013 to —:

> ... document a new approach to service delivery and operation. It will produce an architecture for service function chaining that includes the necessary protocols or protocol extensions to convey the Service Function Chain and Service Function Path information to nodes that are involved in the implementation of service functions and Service Function Chains, as well as mechanisms for steering traffic through service functions.[4]

The SFC working group does not define encapsulations in the traditional sense—the SFC header does not contain any information about the source or destination of a packet, so it cannot be used for forwarding. Rather the SFC header contains a chain of services that can be acted on by either the services within the chain or by devices along the path that know how to unpack and interpret this header.

---

4. "Service Function Chaining Charter," n.p., accessed May 9, 2015, https://datatracker.ietf.org/wg/sfc/charter/.

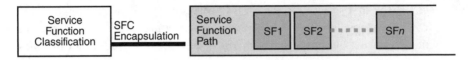

Figure 11.5 *Service Function Chaining Architecture*

Figure 11.5 illustrates the architecture of SFC.

The SFC specifications do not assume any underlying tunnel mechanism, but the work has largely taken place with the base assumption that either VXLAN (documented in A Reference Path and Measurement Points for Large-Scale Measurement of Broadband Performance[5]) or NVGRE [documented in Network Virtualization using Generic Routing Encapsulation Extensions (draft-sridharan-virtualization-nvgre)] will be the "common base," or perhaps default tunneling protocol, in use. Figure 11.6 illustrates what is considered a normal process for chaining packets through a SFC enabled overlay using one of these tunneling protocols.

In this illustration:

1. A packet is received from some host by the DC edge router. This device examines the packet, and determining it is part of a flow destined to a mail server connected to the fabric, imposes a service chain header with the correct set of services through which this packet must be routed before it can be delivered to the mail server itself. Once the service chain is imposed, the DC edge router encapsulates the packet into a VXLAN, NVGRE, or

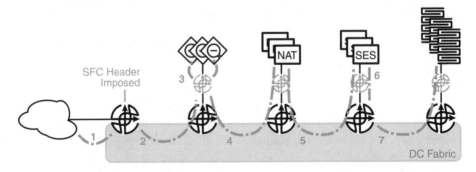

Figure 11.6 *Service Function Chaining Example*

---

5. M. Bagnulo et al., "A Reference Path and Measurement Points for Large-Scale Measurement of Broadband Performance" (IETF, February 2015), accessed September 24, 2015, https://www.rfc-editor.org/rfc/rfc7398.txt.

other tunnel, and forwards the packet toward the first hop inside the fabric, the stateful packet inspection service.

2. The packet is received by the virtual switch (VSwitch) running in the hypervisor of the blade server on which the packet inspection service processes or containers are configured. The network administrator has configured the service chain to terminate in the VSwitch rather than the stateful packet inspection processes themselves because these processes are not SFC aware— so the VSwitch is acting as a "proxy" for these services along the service chain.

3. The VSwitch de-encapsulates the packet, presenting it to one of the stateful packet inspection processes in a format the process will understand. Once the packet has been processed, the packet is switched toward the mail server, which directs it back through the VSwitch.

4. The VSwitch will now reimpose the correct SFC header, place the packet into the correct tunnel to reach the next service in the chain (in the case, a NAT service) and forward the packet back out over the DC fabric.

5. The NAT service, being SFC capable, receives the packet and processes it as needed. The NAT service uses local routing information to build the correct tunnel encapsulation to carry the packet to the next service along the chain. In this case, the next service is the email filtering service, which also happens to be SFC aware.

6. The SES service, having processed the packet, notes that the service chain has ended, and the packet may be forwarded on to its final destination—the mail server itself. The SES service removes the SFC headers and forwards the remaining IP packet through the VSwitch toward the ToR switch it is physically connected to.

7. The ToR receives the packet, examines its local routing information, and forwards the packet over the DC fabric to the mail server.

SFC is, then, primarily an example of the first (and potentially the second) kind of service chaining outlined above—the services, themselves, control the forwarding of the packet through the data center (or cloud) fabric by taking advantage of tunneling mechanisms that already exist within the overlay (or virtual) network.

Segment Routing

Segment routing is a product of the Source Packet Routing in the Network (SPRING) working group of the IETF. The basic concept is the same as SFC, but

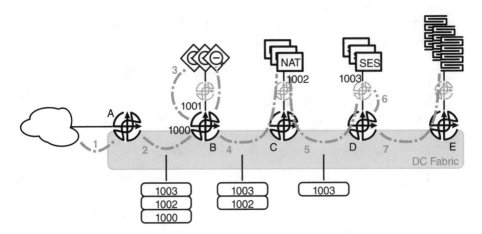

Figure 11.7 *A Segment Routing Example*

rather than assuming the processes along the path will manage the service chain, SPRING assumes the routing control plane will actually manage the path of flows through a network. SPRING can use one of two modes of operation, as illustrated in Figure 11.7.

To understand the flow of traffic in this illustration, it's important to start with one basic definition. A *segment* actually represents a network segment (like an Ethernet segment, however, it might not actually be Ethernet) or an adjacency between two devices. In practice, a segment is normally assigned to a routed interface much like a destination IP address, or perhaps the inbound interface to the device that knows how to reach the service or the segment where the service lives. This might seem a little confusing, but the point is to get the traffic to the service (or collection of services) that lives on a specific segment. While SFC routes to specific *services*, SPRING routes to specific *segments*. This makes sense from the perspective of segment routing, as it is control plane focused, rather than specifically service focused. In the real world, there might not be much of a difference between the concept of a *service* and a *segment*, but understanding the terminology is important when trying to understand the technology.

In Figure 11.7:

> ### Note
>
> This description focuses on using MPLS to transport a packet along a segment route through a network. SPRING actually defaults to using a loose source route header option in IPv6, but it's simpler to illustrate using an MPLS label stack, so that's what is used here.

1. Traffic is received by the ingress router. The destination address is examined, or some form of packet inspection takes place to determine the type of information the packet is carrying (such as HTTPS SSH), and thus into which service chain the packet needs to be inserted. Once this is determined, an MPLS label stack is imposed onto the packet, called the SR Tunnel. This stack encodes the list of segments that the packet must visit before being released from the tunnel at the tail end.

2. The packet is forwarded based on the outer MPLS label; the packet is forwarded along the LSP for MPLS tag 1000, where it reaches the first router in the chain. Router B has been configured to swap label 1000 for 1001, and forward the packet along to one of the packet inspection processes in the pool. This is called a *continue* in segment routing; the current outer label is replaced, rather than popped, before the packet is forwarded.

3. Router B forwards the packet based on the new outer MPLS label, this time to one of the packet inspection processes. Just like SFC, a segment can actually be an anycast destination in SPRING. This allows the packet to be forwarded to one of a set of segments, each of which has (at least) one instance of a particular service attached to it. The packet inspection service finishes processing the packet, and forwards it back to Router B.

4. Router B now pops the outer label, as this segment has been completed. This exposes second MPLS label in the stack as the new outer label. Router B forwards the packet, based on this new outer label, through the LSP indicated by the label value, 1002.

5. The MPLS label 1002 happens to indicate an adjacency between a virtual switch connected to Router C and a NAT service. The NAT service is directly participating in the service chain, so it processes the packet and pops the outer label, exposing the next label in the stack, with a value of 1003. The NAT process forwards the packet out through Router C, which simply switches it based on the outer label toward the SES service next in the chain.

6. The SES service receives the packet, processes it, and pops the final label in the stack, exposing the IP header. At this point, the service forwards the packet toward the hypervisor to forwarding based on the original layer 3 forwarding information.

7. The hypervisor uses the IP destination address to forward the packet toward the final mail server, completing the journey of the packet through the service chain.

As segment routing can use MPLS LSPs as its underlying transport, it's possible for the path of a flow through the network to be defined using something other than simply the list of services or segments packets in the flow must visit. It is possible, for instance, to use a centralized controller computing a path through the network constrained by available bandwidth, latency, or other factors, and then signal the path using PCEP.

Segment routing, then, provides a lot of flexibility to the network operator in defining a set of services or segments through which a particular flow must pass on its way through the network.

A Final Thought

NFV, combined with some form of service chaining (whether SFC, SPRING, or some other option), provides a powerful set of tools for operators to organize their networks around services, rather than around traffic flows. Essentially, rather than bringing services to the traffic flow, these technologies allow the operator to bring the traffic to the services. This has always been possible with policy-based routing, hacks with source- or policy-based routing, various forms of tunneling, and other options—but none of these are as architecturally clean as the options presented in this chapter.

With this background in place, however, it's important to return to the concept of complexity. What are the complexity tradeoffs involved in these forms of "extreme traffic engineering"? The next chapter addresses this question.

Chapter 12

Virtualization and Complexity

Network services, such as stateful packet filtering, network address translation, and billing per unit of data transmitted, have traditionally been associated with appliances. If you wanted to block access to a particular application or part of the network, you would purchase an appliance called a firewall, mount it in a rack, and cable the network so traffic passing into the network would pass through the appliance. But why should packet inspection, for instance—ideally positioned as a software service to support rapid deployment of new features—be tied to an appliance, and hence to a specific physical location in the network? And why should a specific set of services, no matter how logically grouped, be associated with one specific physical appliance? Instead of a bundle of related services tied to a physical appliance mounted in a rack, it should be possible to run individual software-based services (perhaps even microservices) on generic hardware located anywhere in the network. This would allow the operator to scale services out as needed, and manage the lifecycle of services from a software, rather than hardware, point of view.

Virtualizing services in this way, however, presents a secondary problem. If the service is virtualized, and can therefore be placed anywhere in the network, how can traffic be directed through it? When connecting physical appliances, traffic is directed through the service by cabling the appliance into the network. Obviously some sort of "virtual cabling" is needed. Tunneling and policy-based routing (or filter-based forwarding) are the obvious solutions to this sort of problem, but they add a lot of complex configurations that need to be managed. As services are brought online, or as policies change dynamically, the entire infrastructure of tunnels and/or policy needs to be tuned—a difficult, if not impossible, task.

Service chaining, a technique allowing the network operator to treat each service (or microservice) as a sort of building block within a larger service, can resolve these problems. Deploying a technology such as service chaining allows the architect to design the network around optimal usage of resources, rather than around the services through which traffic must flow while passing through the network.

Virtualizing services into generic hardware running anywhere on the network, and using service chaining to build a larger, customized application out of the virtualized services, seems like a win/win situation. By allowing the operator to disconnect the physical and logical locations of a service from the physical topology, service chaining and virtualized services allow a great deal of flexibility in building applications on top of the network, in scaling the network and services, and in disconnecting hardware lifecycles from service lifecycles. This appearance should immediately raise a red flag. *If you haven't found a tradeoff, then you haven't looked hard enough.*

This chapter is focused on exploring the tradeoffs in service virtualization. The first section considers the concept of policy dispersion and network virtualization, along with the direct relationship between policy and complexity in managing a large-scale system. The second section considers other complexity factors when deploying service virtualization, including failure domains (tight coupling) and troubleshooting (MTTR)—with a slight detour through some coding history as it relates to maintainability in the real world.

The third section considers the orchestration effect—how service virtualization allows the operator to treat the network as a set of services and processes, rather than as a topology and devices. This abstraction brings a great deal of power to the table, in terms of connecting to business drivers, but it also brings its own level of complexity into the design space. The fourth section of this chapter considers some practical advice on managing the complexity service virtualization and chaining introduce into network designs. The final section provides some final thoughts on service virtualization.

Policy Dispersion and Network Virtualization

Chapter 4, "Operational Complexity," touched on policy dispersion a bit. Figure 12.1 provides an example as a refresher on the concept, and to continue discussion around policy dispersion and service virtualization.

In this small network, there is a single policy—each packet must pass through a stateful packet inspection while passing between the originating host (on the left side of the diagram) and the destination server (on the right side of the diagram).

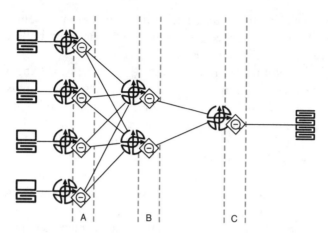

Figure 12.1 *Policy Dispersion*

Assuming that the stateful packet inspection service can be virtualized, or somehow placed anywhere in the network topology, where should it be inserted and configured? At point A, point B, or point C in the topology?

If the policy is configured at point A, it must be configured and managed on four different devices. Any change in the policy must be distributed to each of these four devices in a way that produces roughly equivalent service for each of the users impacted. Somehow this policy must not only be distributed consistently, but also within a short time period. Remember the CAP theorem from Chapter 1, "Defining Complexity?" Keeping the configurations of a large number of devices scattered throughout a network is a direct application of this theorem—consistent, accessible, and partitionable, choose two. As the configuration is spread out over multiple devices, partitionable is chosen by default, so either accessible or consistent must suffer. Most often, consistent is the element of the triad that suffers; network operators often "give up" on managing the configuration of every device in the network in real time.

While configuring the policy at point A has the downside of increasing management strain, and the certain result that not every device is going to be configured the same in near real time, it has a compensating positive feature. Any packets that would otherwise be discarded because they fall outside the policies configured on the stateful packet filtering devices will be discarded early, which means network resources will not be wasted carrying packets that will ultimately be dropped to the filtering device. It also exposes a large part of the network to unfiltered traffic—there is some remote chance an attacker could use this "unfiltered space" through the network as an attack surface.

What about placing the stateful packet filtering at point C? This does reduce the number of devices that need to be managed to one—but it allows unfiltered traffic to pass through the network.

Placing the stateful packet filter at point C doesn't just use the network less efficiently; however, it also means the device placed at point C must be able to support the same load and traffic flow that devices placed at point A would. In other words, the single device at point C must be able to scale to four times the size of the same devices positioned at point A in the network.

There are two problems with the current service model, then. *First*, the service must be brought to the traffic flow. While some degree of traffic engineering can be admitted, in the end all traffic must flow through some appliance or device that instantiates the service in order for the policy to be applied. *Second*, the service must be scaled in a way that accommodates its placement in the network, rather than in a way that accommodates its usage. Neither of these are ideal from an operational or business perspective.

What if instead of bringing the service to the traffic—placing the stateful packet filters in the network where the traffic will necessarily pass through them—the traffic is brought to the service? This would disconnect the location of the service in the network from the implementation of the policies the service represents, and it would allow the service to be scaled out, rather than up.

This is precisely what service chaining allows the operator to do. Service chaining lets you bring the traffic to the policy, so you can implement the policy in a fewer number of places, across a smaller set of devices, preferably virtualized on a standard set of hardware. Figure 12.2 illustrates the same network after gathering the stateful packet inspection services into a single, scalable service running in one location in the network, with chaining used to pull packets through the server to the final destination.

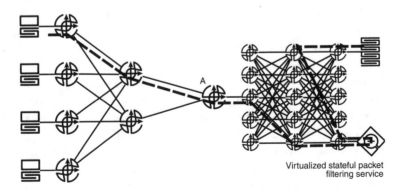

Virtualized stateful packet
filtering service

Figure 12.2 *Appliances Replaced with a Virtualized Service*

Examining a few different points along the state/speed/surface model will help to bring the various complexity tradeoffs into sharper focus.

State and Service Chaining

The primary driver behind virtualizing the services is the reduction in the amount of policy dispersed throughout the network. Done correctly, service virtualization can move policy from a large number of devices (hundreds to hundreds of thousands—in the case of virtualizing the network edge for mobile devices, such as cell phones) into a single data center fabric. Once these services are moved, the policy that goes with them can be centrally managed through an automation system. This is a huge gain for the operator, because both across the board and individualized policies can be efficiently managed, lowering cost and complexity from a policy perspective.

From the perspective of the control plane, however, the amount of state in the network increases.

First, there must be some form of tunneling and the associated control plane in place to carry traffic that is transmitted to one destination through a chain of services instead (as described in Chapter 11, "Service Virtualization and Service Chaining"). Assuming that the virtualized services will reside in a data center, tunneling and the associated control plane information isn't going to add a lot of additional complexity. Most data center networks are already built with an underlay that provides some form of simple switching through the fabric (often IP or IP/MPLS only), and then an overlay that provides a richer control plane for virtualized connectivity, the necessary tunneling mechanisms will likely already be in place.

Second, the service chain must be imposed someplace—there must be some device that creates a tunnel header with information about each service, and any packet within a chained flow must be passed into the tunnel (or have the service chain header written into the packet) in some way. To accomplish this, the service chain itself must be carried through a control plane or management system to the edge of the data center network (generally the inbound fabric edge or gateway). This service chain information represents an additional state carried through the control plane—hence an increase in the amount of control plane state, and an increase in the complexity of the control plane.

In the area of state, then, virtualization offers a mixed bag. It reduces policy dispersion and decreases state from a policy perspective, but it increases state in the control plane, and increases network stretch. As with all things in network design, no single answer is the "right" answer for every network. Most networks will probably see their complexity decrease in aggregate complexity through the virtualization of services, while a smaller percentage might see an increase in aggregate complexity.

State and Optimization

Carrying a flow through a service chain will almost certainly increase network stretch. Comparing Figures 12.1 and 12.2 amply illustrates the increasing stretch as the service moves from residing on an inline appliance to an offline service along the path to, finally, a virtualized service connected to a data center fabric. While the data center fabric is (or should be) optimized for very low latency, low packet loss levels, low jitter, and all the "rest of the best" in quality of service, there are still several additional hops through the network. The flow must move through the data center edge (gateway), three (or more, depending on the network topology) hops through the fabric to the Top-of-Rack (ToR) switch, to where the virtualized stateful packet filtering service is located, through the hypervisor and virtual switch on the compute side of the ToR, back through the hypervisor and virtual switch, through three more hops through the fabric, and finally to the server. Increasing the stretch in this way will increase the complexity of the data plane through which the flow must travel. There are several additional queues, several additional points where packets must be de-encapsulated and then encapsulated, etc.

Increasing the stretch in this way also reduces the efficiency of the network in terms of pure utilization of resources. The efficiency of the network overall might increase through virtualization, but the amount of bandwidth required to handle one flow will increase in aggregate as the stretch of the path through the network increases. The optimization of the network therefore suffers, at least in terms of efficiency of bandwidth utilization, through virtualization.

Comparing Figure 12.1 with Figure 12.2 exposes the amount of time a packet must spend passing through the network before being filtered, illustrating the optimization tradeoff in service chaining. In most service chaining solutions, traffic is tunneled through the network, reducing the security exposure risk to some degree (tunneling is not a strong security mechanism in general, but it at least prevents internal device interfaces from being exposed to external traffic). Unfiltered traffic is still carried through the network only to be dropped at the filter, wasting bandwidth, power, and other resources.

> **Note**
>
> This illustration covers traffic passing into and out of the data center fabric, and, as such, illustrates the worst case to examine the tradeoff engineers' need to look for when considering service chaining. For east/west traffic within a data center or cloud fabric, these tradeoffs may run in the other direction—service chaining might actually provide better optimization in terms of network utilization. Engineers need to be aware of both situations, and carefully consider where complexity is being added, and how optimization is impacted.

Surface and Policy Interaction

Returning to Figure 12.2, how does the DC edge router, marked Router A in the diagram, know what service chain to impose on the packets in the inbound flow? This information must be carried in the control plane in some way—a point noted in the previous section on state—but how is it communicated to the control plane to be carried to the edge router? There must be some connection between the control plane and an outside system that provides this information. What must this system do?

- Determine what the correct policies are.
- Determine which flows map each to which policy must be applied.
- Determine where the virtual services are in the network that can supply those services.
- Determine the correct service chain to push packets through that set of services.
- Communicate this service chain to the control plane.

Ignoring the added complexity of this external system—what might be called orchestration, as it orchestrates which flows map to which service locations—the interaction between the control plane and this system is another surface that must be accounted for. Adding a new interaction surface to allow these tasks to be completed will clearly increase the complexity of the network as a complete system.

Surface and Policy Proxies

Another interaction surface to consider is the connection between packet level policy and forwarding policy. When traffic enters the DC fabric at Router A, there must be some form of classifier that recognizes that this packet belongs to a specific flow onto which a specific service chain must be imposed. This classification mechanism essentially serves as a proxy for the services through which any given packet or flow must be chained. The process of centralizing one policy has effectively dispersed another sort of policy to the edge of the network in its stead.

There are a lot of differences between these two sets of policies, of course:

- Packet inspection policy has a (potentially) deep set of filter/pass policies that must examine an array of fields. The information examined includes information about the flow that spans packets, such as the state of the flow, the type of information being transferred, and valid and invalid encodings.

- Packet classification is generally designed to operate on the minimum amount of information possible, such as a destination address or a five tuple (the source and destination addresses, the source and destination ports, and the protocol).
- Packet inspection normally stands alone in the network; packet inspection might be combined with other services on a single appliance, but conceptually you wouldn't mix packet inspection with load balancing, for instance.
- Packet classification is normally performed across all packets to support a wide array of services. Packets can be classified and chained at a network edge for packet inspection, load sharing, and a number of other services.

A broader way to state is that by replacing the actual packet inspection policy at the network edge with a packet classifier that directs traffic into a service chain, you are replacing a specialized service with a more generic one. While this doesn't eliminate policy dispersion, it allows multiple services to share the same channel and implementations along the network edge. Hence, complexity is not *eliminated* from the edge through service chaining, but the *weight of complexity* can be moved from the edge toward the centralized services.

Using forwarding policy as a proxy for a more complex policy deeper in the network has another side effect worth considering—the interaction surface between the control and forwarding planes actually becomes deeper, not just broader. Carrying policy in the control plane means the control plane is not only responsible for determining reachability, but also for carrying policy that must be applied to packets as they pass through the network. There must be hooks or interaction points between the control and forwarding planes on each edge device to ensure that the policy information carried in the control plane is interpreted, installed, and otherwise managed correctly.

Other Design Considerations

Several complexity tradeoffs don't fit neatly into the state/speed/surface model; these will be covered in this section. Three specific areas should be of concern to the more traditional network designer:

- The size of failure domains.
- The relationship between abstraction (hiding state) and the MTTR.
- Network operation predictability.

Coupling and Failure Domains

One of the first lessons network engineers learned (the hard way) was that fail-ure domains are an important part of the design. Two tightly coupled systems can form a single failure domain; a failure in one will "leak" into the second, causing a failure from the first to spread to the second. An example of this is in route redistribution as illustrated using the network shown in Figure 12.3.

In this illustration, Routers A is sending some large number of routes to Router B through eBGP. To make the scenario realistic, assume that this is a full default free Internet routing table, so more than a half a million routes (at press-time, but it's bound to grow over time). Router B is configured as a route reflec-tor client of Router E, so it is passing this full table on within the AS. Router B is also, however, configured to redistribute a small number of the routes learned through eBGP, from Router A, into a local OSPF process. While such redistribu-tion between protocols is uncommon, there are real-world situations where it is useful.

If such redistribution is configured, it's common for the redistribution to fail in some way. Either an operator misconfigures a filter (perhaps the filters are based on a community someone disables because they don't know what it's being used for) or the redistribution code has a defect (both, again, are real-world situations). The result of the failure is all the BGP routes being redistrib-uted into OSPF, and the failure of OSPF to converge. OSPF's failure then causes BGP, which relies on underlying IP connectivity to operate correctly, to fail as well, so the entire network crashes.

OSPF and BGP are tightly coupled in this situation—not only through redis-tribution, but also through BGP's reliance on OSPF to provide the underlying

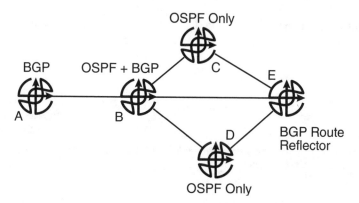

Figure 12.3 *Coupling and Failure Domains*

reachability it needs to operate. Still, this type of situation often surprises network engineers, who assume that the filters on redistribution, or the process of redistributing routes between two control planes, separate the failure domains by removing or reducing coupling.

Rather than crashing the network, it's also possible for traffic forwarded to destinations behind Router A to be black holed at either Router C or D. Assume that a packet is forwarded to Router C by Router E with a destination somewhere beyond Router A. As Router C is not running BGP, it must rely on routes learned through OSPF to build the forwarding table entries on which this packet will be switched. If BGP is not being redistributed into OSPF at Router B, how will Router C know about the destination? It won't—hence, it will drop the traffic. In this case, both control planes (BGP and OSPF) can be operating properly, but combined they cause a network failure. Again, the two systems, in this network configuration, must be tightly coupled for proper network operation.

In terms of surface in the complexity model used throughout this book, there are two interaction surfaces involved.

- Redistribution, which is controlled for breadth by redistributing at a small, well-defined number of points in the network. The depth of this interaction surface is controlled through redistribution filters—so although it is a deep interaction, it is limited in scope to the minimum possible.

- The interaction between reachability provided by one system and the operation of the other system is not very deep, but it is very broad. The failure of the depth control in the first point of contact between these two protocols causes a failure in the second—a classic cascading failure case across multiple interaction surfaces between two systems.

Software design has long worked around the same fundamental concepts. For instance:

> **Note**
>
> When services are loosely coupled, a change to one service should not require a change to another. The whole point of a microservice is being able to make a change to one service and deploy it, without needing to change any other part of the system. This is really quite important.[1]

---

1. Sam Newman, *Building Microservices*, First Edition (O'Reilly Media, 2015), 30.

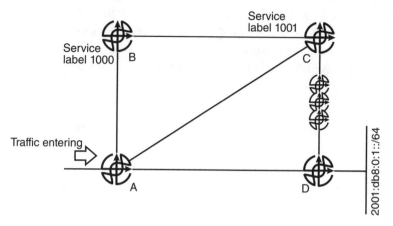

Figure 12.4 *Tightly Coupled Failure Domains in a Service Chain*

Imposing a service chain carried by the control plane at the edge of the network creates just this sort of coupling between systems. Using service chains binds the control plane to the services architecture, and the services architecture to the data plane, or the forwarding state. This sort of coupling essentially combines the services, any orchestration service that ties services and service chains together, and the control plane into a single large failure domain. Figure 12.4 illustrates one case where a failure in one system can impact the other systems in a catastrophic way.

In Figure 12.4:

- A packet enters at Router A with a destination prefix of 2001:db8:0:1::/64.
- Router A has some policy that imposes a service chain on this packet to pass through the service labeled 1000, then 1001, and then to be released for normal forwarding.
- The packet follows the service chain to Router B, which removes the first label and then forwards it to Router C.
- The packet follows the service chain to Router C, which processes the packet, removes the service chain, and forwards along the shortest path to 2001:db8:0:1::/64.
- The shortest path from Router C to 2001:db8:0:1::/64 is through Router A.
- The packet is forwarded to Router A, which has some policy that imposes a service on this packet to pass through the service labeled 1000, then 1001, and then to be released for normal shortest path forwarding through the network.

The problem should be obvious. If the flow toward 2001:db8:0:1::/64 is large enough, it's possible to move from a simple failure of the service chain to a cascading failure—the looping traffic can easily overwhelm one of the three links over which it is passing, causing the distributed routing protocol to fail, as well.

Troubleshooting

The effective troubleshooting of a network is heavily dependent on a few underlying processes, such as half splitting—the process of:

1. Finding the path of the signal or information through the system.

2. Finding a "half way" point in this path.

3. Measuring the signal at the halfway point to determine if it is correct (as expected) or not.

4. If it is as expected, find the point halfway between the current measurement point and the end of the signal path and repeat.

5. If it is not as expected, find the point halfway between the current measurement point and the beginning of the signal path and repeat.

The ability to troubleshoot a network (or any system) depends on the ability of an engineer to understand the path of the signal, or the flow of information, through the system. Edsgar Dijkstra described this situation in more eloquent terms in his paper on *goto* statements in programming languages:

> **Note**
>
> My first remark is that, although the programmer's activity ends when he has constructed a correct program, the process taking place under control of his program is the true subject matter of his activity, for it is this process that has to accomplish the desired effect; it is this process that in its dynamic behavior has to satisfy the desired specifications. Yet, once the program has been made, the "making" of the corresponding process is delegated to the machine. The unbridled use of the go to statement has an immediate consequence that it becomes terribly hard to find a meaningful set of coordinates in which to describe the process progress.[2]

---

2. Edsgar Dijsktra, "Go To Statement Considered Harmful," *University of Arizona*, n.p., last modified 1968, accessed June 5, 2015, http://www.u.arizona.edu/~rubinson/copyright_violations/Go_To_Considered_Harmful.html.

Dijkstra—the inventor of the most widely used SPF algorithm used in link state protocols—is essentially saying here that *goto* statements make it much harder to connect the flow of the information with the flow of the code. Instead of simply reading the code, someone trying to troubleshoot and fix a problem must "break context" by following *goto* statements wherever they lead, trying to put the entire flow back together in their heads. Turning to Dijkstra's argument again:

> ### Note
>
> My second remark is that our intellectual powers are rather geared to master static relations and that our powers to visualize processes evolving in time are relatively poorly developed. For that reason we should do (as wise programmers aware of our limitations) our utmost to shorten the conceptual gap between the static program and the dynamic process, to make the correspondence between the program (spread out in text space) and the process (spread out in time) as trivial as possible.[3]

Transferring this to the networking world, and service chaining in particular, is simple: *a service chain is the software equivalent of a goto statement in code.*

Coders now use *goto* widely—there are over 100,000 *goto* statements in the Linux kernel code[4]—but they do so within patterns (or models) that make it easy to understand what the *goto* is being used for and how to trace information flowing through the process. Multiple *goto* statements being used instead of an *if/else* construction is considered bad form, but using *goto* to break out of a loop when an error has been encountered is considered okay. A *goto* leading to another *goto* is considered particularly a bad form, as this often leads to *spaghetti code.*

In the networking world, creating a spaghetti flow with service chaining can be just as easy (and just as bad) as creating spaghetti code using *goto* statements in a program. The result is a disconnect between the flow of the information through the system and the service chain itself, causing major headaches in troubleshooting, high MTTR, and high Mean Time Between Maintenance.

As a practical illustration, consider the network engineer who is trying to resolve a problem with jitter through a particular network. The engineer begins at the network edge, examining the table entries that will be used to forward packets in flows of a specific type through the network. Examining the forwarding table on the inbound device, the engineer finds a set of flow labels.

---

3. Ibid.

4. "Goto," *Wikipedia*, accessed June 5, 2015, https://en.wikipedia.org/wiki/Goto#Criticism_and_decline.

Now what? What precisely does this set of flow labels mean? Which network segment will this packet flow over? That information is abstracted out; the engineer must connect the label with a forwarding path by stepping deeper into the forwarding table. The path itself is disconnected from the topology, as well.

Each of these disconnects reduces the ability of the engineer to quickly grasp and troubleshoot the problem at hand—making troubleshooting network level problems a complex problem, indeed.

Network Operation Predictability

One often unstated network design principle is predictability. Two specific considerations drive the desire for predictability in a network design:

- It's difficult to measure things that are constantly changing in any way that actually provides a meaningful baseline. If the state of the network is constantly changing, including the path of particular flows or application traffic, it's difficult to get a feel for what "normal" looks like. This inability to determine what "normal" looks like directly impacts the ability of the network engineer to predict future requirements, and to repair problems once they appear. It's hard to know what is broken if you don't know what "working" looks like.

- It's hard to know what the state of the network will be after any specific failure occurs. If a link fails, where will the traffic move, and what will the impact be on the links it moves to?

Network engineers can get into something of a panic if they can't answer these kinds of questions—they're fundamental to the ability to predict how much additional bandwidth is needed, where quality of service needs to be applied, controlling delay and jitter, and many other things.

It makes more sense to try and get a handle on a bigger picture—to mine the network for information, rather than to try and make per link predictions. Not everything can be defined in the design or deployment phase of network engineering; sometimes it must be discovered, instead.

The Orchestration Effect

Rising above the wire, however, service chaining and function virtualization can improve the ease of which you can understand and manage the flow of information through the network in two ways.

First, service chaining abstracts out the topology—much like a link state flooding domain boundary—leaving just information about what services a particular flow must pass through, and how those services modify the flow. This abstraction relieves the orchestration system, which is spinning up services and matching flows to services as needed, from dealing with more fine grained details, such as how traffic will actually flow through the network. In the same way, this abstraction allows those who are more business minded to focus on the flow of information without getting involved in how the network actually works. This can improve the connection between business drivers and network engineering (in design, implementation, and operations), providing a pathway between the two worlds.

This effectively separates topology from policy, layering the control plane. Each resulting layer deals with one type of information well, and interacts with the other layer through a well-defined and constrained surface. This follows the *cohesion principle:* gathering related behavior together, and pushing unrelated behavior into other components. This also helps implement the *single responsibility principle:* focusing each particular service or component on doing one good job well.

Second, virtualizing functionality allows services to be broken into smaller pieces that can be scaled out, rather than maintained as larger monolithic units that must be scaled up. Each service then becomes a fairly standard "thing" that can be managed separately, including being placed where there are resources on the network rather than where the traffic is already flowing. Virtualization, combined with service chaining, allows services to be managed as low-touch services, rather than as high-touch appliances, or unique, custom engineered solutions (also known as "special snowflakes").

Scale Up versus Scale Out

Scale up and scale out are commonly used terms in application development—but they aren't terms network engineers already run in to. What do they mean? The difference between the two can be likened to creating multiple parallel resources versus creating one single larger resource. Figure 12.5 illustrates the two concepts.

If Process 1, for instance, becomes overloaded in the scale up solution, the entire compute container must be made larger. The application is simpler, in some ways, to develop, as interprocess calls are "local" within the application, and mechanisms such as shared memory can be used to simplify passing arguments and implementing features. In the scale out solution, each process must be

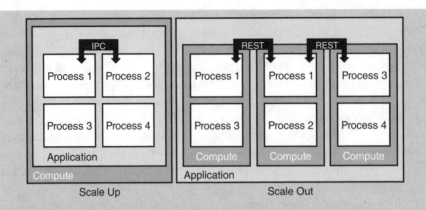

Figure 12.5 *Scale Up versus Scale Out*

made to be self-contained, and the application must be broken up into smaller services or microservices. Each of these services runs on (potentially) different compute platforms, possibly even using different languages and environments, and communicates across the network through some communications interface such as REST. However, once the application has been broken up into pieces, each process can be scaled, replaced, and managed independently.

Once the application is broken up into processes, each process can actually represent a service, and the services can be chained together using service chaining. You saw that one coming, didn't you?

An analogous situation in network engineering is the difference between higher speed links and parallel links of a slower speed. When traffic overruns a single link, there are two options: upgrade the link to a higher speed (scale up), or add more parallel links (scale out). Each has advantages and disadvantages, of course.

Managing Complexity

It's important to go back to the beginning of this book and consider the role complexity plays in the network. It's impossible to *resolve* complexity; rather, complex solutions are required to solve hard problems. The most network engineers, designers, architects, and all the other people working in and around networking technologies can do is to *manage* complexity. Don't be afraid of complexity, but don't allow complexity to build where it doesn't add any value. In the spirit of this line of thinking, how can network engineers manage complexity when service virtualization and chaining come into play?

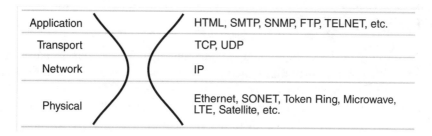

Figure 12.6 *The Hourglass Model of Reducing Complexity*

First, return to the basics. Remember the hourglass, illustrated in Figure 12.6?

Strive to build an hourglass in the network, as this facilitates loose coupling across domains and allows you to separate complexity from complexity. While you might not have multiple physical layer protocols, you might face the temptation to deploy a dozen different control planes, and a matching number of transport overlay mechanisms, onto a single fabric. After all, what does it hurt if you run VXLAN, NVGRE, MPLS, and MPLSoGRE on the same IP infrastructure? What does it matter if there are multiple SDN controllers, BGP, and some other mechanisms all tangled up as overlapping control planes?

The difference it makes can be seen by returning to the model of complexity built earlier around state, speed, surface, and optimization. Each additional control plane adds another layer of state; each additional transport system adds another interaction surface. A rule of thumb here might be: since you can't control complexity in some areas of the network, for instance the way applications run across the network and the path traffic takes through the network, keep a tight lid on the complexity you can control. This will encourage the hourglass model, ultimately making the complexity manageable.

Second, remember the lesson of *goto*. Once you start using *goto*, it can be addictive. "Why not just place this part of the service over here in this data center, and that part over there in another one? Why can't we service chain between various databases on the backend, and between services on the front end, and between business logic in the middle?"

The answer is *because you're going to end up with spaghetti code*. Just as spaghetti code is unmaintainable within an application, it's also unmaintainable between the services that result from breaking an application up. Build a framework around what is, and isn't, allowed with the *goto* statement of service chaining. One suggested rule, for instance, might be "no traffic, once it passed through a service, should pass through the same service again." This would be the equivalent of not having *goto's* chained through a number of modules, making it impossible to mentally connect the traffic flow with the logic (or services) flow.

A Final Thought

Given the complexity of building and managing virtualized services and service chaining, why are so many large network operators moving in this direction? The primary reason is actually that the business logic and development folks are(for once) throwing complexity back over the cubicle wall. Whether the complexity belongs in the network, or in the application and business logic, is ultimately a business decision. Often, though, a few factors dictate that pushing this complexity into the network makes sense. For instance:

- Making the application development process match the flow and pace of business operations allows IT to drive more value. This, in turn, makes IT a more integrated part of the business—a good thing.

- Breaking monolithic applications into individual services allows the business to compose applications on the fly. This means new services can be developed and offered without building them entirely from scratch; reuse of existing services is easier than reuse of existing monolithic applications.

- Breaking monolithic applications into individual services allows the development teams to build and manage applications in a way that prevents a number of traditional problems—such as the huge, large-scale application that runs on a server sitting in the corner that everyone is afraid to touch, but is crucial to the business' operation.

Given the cost–benefit tradeoffs, service virtualization is normally actually a good tradeoff, rather than a bad one. This is why the concept is becoming so popular, particularly in large-scale service provider networks.

Chapter 13

Complexity and the Cloud

Cloud computing is one of the big movements in the networking and information technology worlds right now. Mostly everyone wants to either build a cloud, or use one. In response, the industry has built a set of definitions, practices, and concepts around cloud computing that almost everyone knows—and almost no one really understands.

The promise of cloud, of course, is that by putting your stuff in the cloud you're outsourcing all the infrastructure and management to someone else—someone who, in theory, can manage the infrastructure cheaper than you can, and can provide you with on-demand services as you need them. Moving to the cloud should save you lots of money and time. At least that's the theory.

This chapter will consider complexity and the cloud. Does moving to the cloud really solve all the complexity problems you face on the networking, compute, and storage infrastructure front? Or does it just move the complexity someplace else? Does cloud provide "the" silver bullet for complexity, by throwing all the complexity into someone else's lap, or is it really just another set of options and tradeoffs engineers need to consider carefully?

Given everything discussed about complexity in this book, the answer should be one you know well already—cloud isn't the ultimate solution to all your network complexity problems. You can move complexity around, but you can't get rid of it or solve it.

This chapter will approach cloud from three perspectives. The first is a model around complexity and the cloud, the second is an alternative model useful for breaking down the types of services being supported. The final section will discuss some more specific complications and complexities when considering cloud as a solution.

Where Does the Complexity Live?

Given you've read to this point, you already know that you can't eliminate complexity. In fact, you can't really toss it over the cubicle wall very effectively all the time; sometimes the result of splitting the problem in the wrong place, and trying to offload the wrong parts, is more complexity than what you started with. To avoid these results, it's often useful to model the problem space in some way, so you can think through the complexity tradeoffs in terms of state, speed, and surface. Figure 13.1 illustrates one model you can use to break the tradeoffs down into manageable pieces.

This figure illustrates three distinct types of deployment for any particular application or system. There are, in the real world, any number of varying degrees between these three (for instance, hybrid cloud), focusing on these three points along the continuum is useful for understanding some of the basic issues in play.

In every case, you must manage the business logic, application development, making decisions about what to store where, process management, and anything else related to the actual building and running of an application to meet a specific set of business needs. As you move from right to left, however, different pieces of complexity trade off against one another.

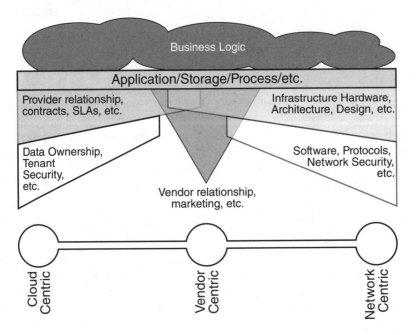

Figure 13.1 *Where Complexity Lives*

Cloud Centric

Starting at the far left, a cloud centric deployment is to move (or create) all processing and data storage into a cloud provider's service. This can be very attractive, as it allows the business to focus on the actual information processing aspects of the problems at hand, removing entirely any interaction with infrastructure hardware, architecture, network or compute and storage design, infrastructure tools and software, control plane protocols, and all the other pieces that relate to running a network. These pieces can be a huge administrative load, particularly for businesses whose main focus is on a product or service, rather than on technology.

On the other side of the tradeoff, though, are a bundle of added business and technical complexities. On the business side is the reliance on a provider for your business, including responsiveness and trust. It's important to note that most providers have their own business plans (big surprise, right?), and the alignment of their business plan and your business plan isn't always completely overlapping. In other words, the provider can be concerned about the state of your business to grow theirs—but this doesn't always work out the way you think it might.

But we're not a technology company . . .

One of the most difficult confrontations between a technologist and a business person comes down to the words, "we're not a technology company." I can well remember the first time I encountered the words; when discussing a new project with a high level manager at a large manufacturer, the executive said: "This is all neat stuff, but we're not a technology company. We build widgets, and that's all we're really interested in." Focusing on a core competency is a major part of what any business person learns early on—and it's a valid and important skill. Even for engineers, focusing on a core competency is a major point in determining career choices, training consumed, and so on. However, there is another side to this problem—it doesn't matter what you build, make, or learn, you're always in the information business, whether you like it or not.

One of the most tempting things about moving processes and information to the cloud is that it (apparently) takes the business out of the IT world. The reality is, however, that no matter how far you move out of the *technology* world, you're still in the *information business* alongside whatever your core competency is. When you outsource your technology, you need to be careful about outsourcing your information as well. The belief that you can take a business "out of the IT world" is dangerous from a business perspective.

Outsourcing information and/or the technology needed to deal with the information might, or might not, be acceptable in different situations—but either way, it needs to be considered for what it actually is, rather than as a simple solution to a set of complex problems. In outsourcing information, you might end up being better able to focus on a set of core competencies. Or you might end up being unable to manage the information you need in a way that gives you a strategic advantage. Each case needs to be approached with an open mind and independent thinking, along with real thought about when information, itself, is part of the core competency, and when it's not.

Vendor Centric

The vendor centric model is the one most of the networking world tends to live under. For any given project, a set of requirements are set out, and then a set of vendors are examined to see what products they might have, or are planning to have, that will meet those requirements. Engineers don't tend to think of this type of model as a form of outsourcing—but it is. What's being outsourced is some basic (or high-level) design work, management of the network software process (including protocols), and the designing and building of the hardware components.

There are many positive attributes to this type of outsourcing. It places the company in the position of having a vendor partner who is doing much of the fundamental research needed to keep up with technical trends, and "one number to call" when things go wrong. This solution can be much like using plastic building blocks to build a castle—the options are limited, yes, but they are often limited to things someone with more expertise and experience knows should work. This can take a lot of engineering load off the company while allowing semicustomized solutions that can keep the business ahead of the game, while retaining ownership of the data within the business itself.

The business still needs to interface with the business logic, applications, and information handling pieces of the puzzle, but doesn't need to think as hard about network design and architecture, equipment life cycles, and other related matters. The other side of this tradeoff is the business must now manage a set of

WHERE DOES THE COMPLEXITY LIVE? **271**

vendor relationships, including finding people who are qualified in that specific vendor's equipment and vendor lock-in through training, legacy gear, mindset, and many other potential factors. While this is the choice most companies make, it can actually be the worst of both worlds—vendor relationships can be as difficult to navigate as provider relationships, design constraints can stunt business growth by limiting opportunities for strategic advantage, and the business ends up being bound to the vendor's growth plan through upgrades and new product rollouts.

Network Centric

The network centric vision might best be described as aligning with the white box trend in networking technology. In this area, the infrastructure hardware and software might be outsourced to different companies or vendors, untying the two, and the IT staff takes on more of the integration work to put all the pieces together into a single unified whole.

Moving down this path requires a large, competent IT staff, so it's not for the faint of heart in terms of raw complexity. The engineers involved in these sorts of projects must be technology focused, rather than vendor or offering focused, and know how to integrate and manage the different pieces to make a unified whole. In the real world, of course, more complex vendor focused deployments and network centric deployments may be very similar in complexity levels from an engineering perspective, as virtually no vendor-based solution actually covers all the requirements for any given project or business plan.

The tradeoff in complexity from an engineering perspective is untying the business from a vendor's upgrade path, being able to right size the network to the job at hand, and being able to quickly take advantage of new ideas in design and architecture to reap competitive advantage.

Is There a "Right Way?"

It's tempting to choose one path among these three and declare it "the right way." In reality, however, many different ways might be best for any particular application or business. For instance, outsourcing sales tracking might be a good idea, while at the same time building custom software on a network centric data center for manufacturing processes unique to the company. The point here is to find a set of models that help the architect think through the complexity and business tradeoffs, rather than providing a pat answer.

Centralize What?

While the first model of cloud services can be helpful in understanding the trade-offs in using a cloud service, the second model covered here can be more effective in understanding the range and scope of cloud offerings. There are, in any specific application or technology system, only a few real moving parts:

- **Storage**—where the information is stored when it's not being actively used for something
- **Infrastructure, or plumbing**—the parts of the system that move information around between the other system components
- **Compute**—the computing power used to actually do the processing required
- **Software Environment**—the set of software and services on which the application is developed and deployed, including an operating system, database system, and other components
- **Intelligence/Analytics**—the logic used to process the information, and the code that implements this logic

While each of these components can be very complicated in themselves, these are the only four real components of any information technology system. Everything else either builds, manages, or somehow interacts with one of these four things. Cloud services, then, can be broken down by what they centralize, virtualize, or outsource as outlined in the list that follows:

- **Storage as a Service**: A number of services effectively offer centralized storage and synchronization with minimal processing and/or applications APIs to lay on top of the service. This correlates to simply outsourcing storage. Some services in this space, at the time of this writing, include DropBox, Google Drive, SpiderOak, Azure Storage, and Amazon S3.
- **Infrastructure as a Service (IaaS)**: A number of cloud services provide storage, network connectivity, processing power, and other tools within a hypervisor framework. Users must install their own operating system within the virtual machines spun within the service, build any connectivity, and build other services as needed. The service will always include some form of storage system—so IaaS always includes storage as a service, even if storage isn't the primary focus. This is a form of centralizing storage, infrastructure, and processing, but without the intelligence and/or analytics.

- **Platform as a Service (PaaS)**: It implements storage, infrastructure, and processing services, like IaaS (above), but includes the software environment, as well. Generally the intelligence is in the form of operating systems installed on the virtual machines, some form of database backend, and other services.

- **Software as a Service (SaaS)**: Implements the centralization of all the components of an application, including storage, infrastructure, processing, a software environment, and intelligence, up to and including business logic. SaaS can actually be implemented under many rubrics, including Software Defined Wide Area Network.

Asking "what is being centralized," or even better, "what is being outsourced," allows you to clearly think about what interface between the business and the technology is being deployed to solve the business problem.

As an example, consider Desktop Virtualization (DV, or thin client). This is an interesting case because it clearly centralizes and outsources storage, infrastructure, processing, and the software environment. But does it centralize intelligence and/or analytics as well? This would depend on what the DV service offers in the way of applications that are preinstalled on the virtual desktops. Generally speaking, however, DV is only going to include minimal services that might be considered at the intelligence level in the model. This means the primary security concerns are going to be around the storage of files being worked on in the DV environment, rather than the actual implementation of business logic in applications deployed on a PaaS cloud, for instance.

Cloudy Complications

With these models in the background, it's a bit easier to consider the actual complexity tradeoffs involved in moving services into the cloud, and to determine which type of service might fit better in a public, private, or hybrid cloud—or whether some services should just be deployed in a more traditional manner. This section explores several specific areas of complexity that need to be managed when pushing applications or data to a cloud service.

Security

Security is, by far, the most commonly cited reason for businesses not to place their data in the cloud. This is well covered territory, but it's worthwhile to consider some of the forms of attack possible against a cloud-based service, the countermeasures, and the attendant complexity issues.

Centralized data is a bigger target. In the early 1960s, a gang took the money bags from a Royal Mail train travelling between Glasgow and London. They raided the train on a tip that it would be carrying the excess cash from dozens of banks between the two cities, being carried into London for storage over a bank holiday weekend. The take was the largest in British history to that time, and most of the money was never recovered. The lesson is that while the excess holdings of any specific bank wasn't large enough to merit such a carefully orchestrated plan, the total of their holdings, gathered in a single place, were well worth spending the time and effort to take.

In the same way, the total holdings of a service provider's cloud offerings may offer enough rewards to attract well designed plans to "take the entire haul." Each business user of such a service might believe their information is not worth attacking, because the value of the data would not cover the costs of taking it— but the aggregate of information might present a far different picture.

> **Note**
>
> At presstime, several very large breaches in cloud-based systems have been in the news. Some of these breaches have resulted in the loss of millions of records containing personal information that could well be used for nefarious purposes, such as identity theft or even extortion. These types of breaches should make businesses think seriously about the security of the information they're storing in cloud-based environments, and to be very serious about security audits and breach procedures. You can outsource your data, but you can't outsource the responsibility of cleaning up the mess if your data is breached.

The complexity added here is two-fold. The users of the cloud service must audit the cloud provider to ensure security, and track all breaches into the provider's service, rather than just the ones impacting the data the customer cares about. Any breach could be just the visible top of a much larger breach. The users of the cloud service may also need to take more steps to protect their data given it is being stored off site, or rather outside the physical bounds of their network's operational space.

The counter to this concern is that professional cloud providers can often afford to build security systems that are far beyond the ability of just about any of their customers—so while centralized data is a bigger target, it is also easier to defend.

The tradeoffs might very well break even, but the user of a cloud service needs to be aware of the additional complexity involved in managing security from a

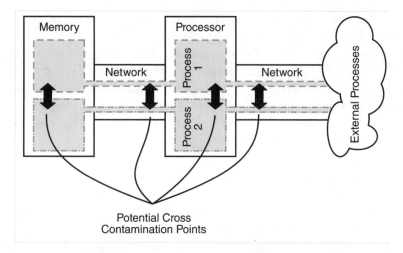

Figure 13.2 *Possible Cross Contamination Points in a Virtualized System*

"one off" position—without direct access to the infrastructure, policies, or control mechanisms that protect the information stored in the service directly.

Cross customer contamination. A cloud environment represents a set of virtual machines, interconnections (networks), database tables, and storage spaces located on a set of physical resources. Any time there are multiple processes running on a single processor, some form of cross contamination is always possible—a type of security threat where one process' data can be read or modified by another process running on the same hardware. Figure 13.2 illustrates possible cross contamination points in a virtualized system.

This is often blocked by the virtualization software, but users on a shared system still need to check for such corruptions and data breaches, if possible, adding complexity to the applications deployed onto these shared infrastructures.

Physical Media Management. In 1981, a major (class 5) hurricane came up the Gulf Coast of the United States, flooding New Orleans and necessitating the evacuation of the city. During the disaster itself, and in the cleanup following, many buildings were destroyed, or gutted and essentially rebuilt. This brings up a perhaps odd, but still important, question—what happens to the hard drives that hold all your corporate data in such a situation? If a tornado strikes the data center in which a cloud service you rely on resides, scattering hardware, will your data still be secure?

Users of cloud services need to verity the status of their data in the case of physical disasters, the disposal of hard drives and other equipment, and even the loss of single hard drives to rouge employees or inside threats. Often there is little the cloud user can do other than simply trust the provider's processes and controls, but some types of information might need to be encrypted, or require special handling for applications deployed in a cloud environment.

Who controls the crypto? Finally, most cloud providers encrypt data at rest (on a hard drive or other storage device) so that users cannot see one another's data. However, if the provider is providing the encryption, then the provider must have the key used to encrypt the data. This means at least one person working for the provider has access to the keys, and hence can read the data itself.

The user of the cloud service has at least three options:

- The first is to encrypt any information stored in the cloud service within the processes using the data, so it's secured by some encryption coded into the applications running in the cloud environment as well as the provider's encryption. This option can add a good bit of overhead to the development and processing requirements for any application within the cloud environment, and it's not always a practical solution.

- The second is to trust (and potentially audit) the controls the cloud provider uses to manage access to the information stored in the cloud environment.

- The third is to regularly audit the security systems in place, actively checking for security breaches—or perhaps to hire a third party auditor to take on this role.

Data Portability

A second area of concern in the complexity space for information and applications stored in a cloud environment is data portability. Particularly in the case of centralized intelligence (largely SaaS deployments), the applications developed and maintained by the cloud provider may be stored in a very specific format. If the business decides to switch providers or applications, retrieving any information from the service can range from easy to impossible. In PaaS, this may be less of a concern, as the business is actually developing applications to run on the cloud provider's service, and hence controls the formatting and storage of information.

While this might seem like a rather obvious, or even mundane, problem, the cost of moving data out of the cloud environment is rarely considered in any analysis of the advantages and disadvantages of moving applications or storage into a cloud environment. Moving data between formats can add a great deal of complexity in the deployment of a new process or application. This is something businesses considering outsourcing to cloud-based services need to specifically ask about at the beginning of the process—rather than waiting until the end.

A Final Thought

This chapter has strayed from the state/speed/surface model of complexity used in the rest of this book—but complexity, for the network engineer or architect, doesn't just come from protocols or topologies. The complexity tradeoff in cloud computing can be seen as falling into one of two broad categories—the complexity of the business process versus the infrastructure complexity, and the complexity of managing a relationship versus the complexity of managing a network infrastructure. There is a continuum from totally outsourced/centralized to totally insourced/managed the architect can follow, and a variety of useful models for organizing the decisions and tradeoffs involved.

Even in places where you might think you're safe to "offload" complexity by "throwing it over the cubicle wall," you need to look hard for the complexity tradeoffs, because there is always a complexity tradeoff involved someplace.

Chapter 14

A Simple Ending

This book has covered a lot of heavy, theoretical materials. It began with a general overview of complexity, and moved through various networking technologies to illustrate the complexity found in a wide array of networking technologies. What do you do with this information? There are, of course, direct applications within these pages; this chapter attempts to bring all the lessons learned in the examination of each of these areas into focus.

The chapter begins with a short review of complexity as a theory, and then reviews the three-part model used here to describe complexity. The final section develops a number of practical steps you can take on a day-to-day basis to manage complexity. The goal is not to provide the answers, but rather to provide the questions and framework that will help you find the answers for any given situation. The end goal is a set of tools, and a new way of looking at old tools, that will help you manage complexity in every area of network design and operation.

Defining Complexity

Complexity is difficult to define, at least partly, because different engineers find different things complex—and some researchers even argue that complexity is just an "observer problem." Rather than providing a precise definition, it's better to consider two specific components that always appear to be related to perceived complexity. It might not be possible to define complexity down to a single statement, but it's possible to describe complexity in a way that makes it recognizable.

Difficult to Understand

Anything that is difficult to understand is often perceived as being complex, whether or not it really is. What often makes complexity difficult to define is that things that appear to be complex to one person are seen as simple by another—or things that appear to be complex by an observer missing key facts, pieces of information, or training. Any definition of complexity needs to reach beyond this observational problem, however, and find some way to say, "this is complex," regardless of whether any particular observer believes that it is complex. In fact, one of the most difficult problems to solve in the world of design is the belief that complex things are simple, leading to an insufficient level of attention being paid to the complexity that is really there.

Rather than arguing that the appearance of complexity should define complexity, it is better to find some more objective measure—and perhaps that objective measure can be found in the idea that complexity involves attempting to solve for sets of items that are actually mutually exclusive. Things that are complex, then, involve solutions to paradoxes, or the attempt to come as close to resolving a set of problems for which there is no ultimate solution. The closer the solution tries to come to solving an ultimately unsolvable problem set, the more complex the solution must become.

Unintended Consequences

This second description of complexity is actually related to the first. When faced with a problem that cannot be solved the natural tendency of an engineer is to go ahead and try to solve it. The result of this exercise is an increasing array of unintended consequences—latent problems that don't appear in the original design, but show up later in unanticipated states or situations. Of course, unintended consequences might also just be a symptom of poor system design, or a system design that has been pushed far outside its original operating envelope. But even in well-designed systems, there will be unintended consequences.

Large Numbers of Interacting Parts

Finally, complex systems tend to have a large number of interacting parts. Just how these parts interact and the relationship between those interactions and complexity are details left to a section just ahead in this chapter.

What Makes Something "Too Complex"?

While it is certainly true that complexity is a necessary result of any response to a hard problem, it is always possible to have a poorly implemented solution that is too complex—what might be called inelegant, unsustainable, or, even, "it won't scale." While it's easy enough to recognize such situations in the extreme cases, or cartoon depictions of strange machines that provide simple services through long and unrepeatable chains of events, what measure can be used to find such systems in the real world? Several measures suggest themselves. A system that solves the problem is more than likely too complex, but:

- The cost of maintaining the system overwhelms the cost of simply dealing with the problem in the first place.

- The complexity of the resulting system is worse than the complexity of simply working around the problem.

- The mean time to failure and/or the mean time to repair are so great that the users of the system end up having no way to address the problem that's supposed to be solved for long stretches of time (the availability is too low to allow the system to meet business needs).

- The insertion of repairs or changes causes a large number of unintended consequences, each of which is difficult to understand and trace to a root cause, and many or some of which are repaired without any understanding of how the implemented fix actually solved the problem.

In the first chapter, "Defining Complexity," the chart in Figure 14.1 was used to illustrate the relationship between robustness and complexity. As the complexity of the problem increases, the complexity of the solution must also increase. At some point, increasing complexity in the solution stops increasing robustness. Instead, further increases in the complexity of the solution actually begin to decrease the system's robustness. This can be considered the point where the solution becomes *too complex*.

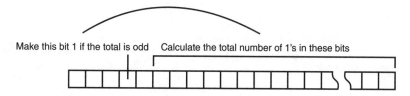

Make this bit 1 if the total is odd   Calculate the total number of 1's in these bits

Figure 14.1 *Complexity versus Robustness*

It's important to remember that systems aren't necessarily created too complex, but rather move from some simpler state to a more complex one over time. It's useful to think of the process of increasing complexity as *ossification*; much like bones or other organic materials are hardened into stone over time, a flexible and robust design can be hardened through the replacement and addition of different pieces over time. These replacements are seen as hardening the system—and, in fact, they do harden the system. However, as the system is hardened, it also becomes brittle. The result is a system that is hard to break, but once it's broken, it shatters, rather than degrading gracefully.

Complexity Is a Tradeoff

Why not just "solve" complexity? Why not find some way to build a system with a perfect fit to the problem that simply isn't complex? The simple answer to this is *the world just isn't built that way*. While there may be some philosophical or "deep math" reason why this simply isn't possible, the why doesn't matter—what does matter is that complexity is a tradeoff. For any given set of three interrelated pieces of a problem, you can choose two. Figure 14.2 illustrates this concept.

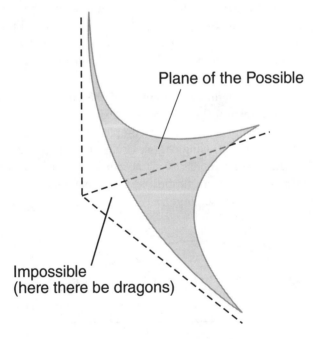

Figure 14.2 *The Three Pronged Tradeoff Complexity Problem*

There are a number of examples of this three-sided complexity problem, including:

- **The CAP Theorem.** There are three desirable traits for any given database: *consistency, accessibility, and partitionability.* Consistency refers to the results of any given operation by any given pair of users at any given point in time. If a database system is consistent, any two (or more) users accessing the same database at the same time will retrieve the same information—or rather, every user of the database has the same view of the data, no matter when it is checked. Accessibility means just what it sounds like, the ability of any user to access the information in the database at any time. Partitionability refers to the ability of the database to be partitioned, or split-up, onto multiple hosting systems. It is impossible for a database to have all three of these attributes to the maximum possible level at the same time.

- **Quick, Cheap, High Quality.** It's a well-worn maxim in just about every area that you can choose to build something that's cheap and of high quality, but it will take a long time; you can build something quickly that's of high quality, but it will cost a lot; or you can build something quickly that's cheap, but quality is going to suffer. This applies for everything from software to nuts and bolts.

- **Fast Convergence, Stability, Simple Control Plane.** In network architecture, decreasing the convergence time will always either cause the complexity of the control plane to increase, or it will cause the network to lose stability so it is more likely to fail.

There is probably a virtually infinite number of these "three sets" in every area of engineering (and life at large). That they exist in many different areas and realms should cause us to be alert to their existence and involvement in every engineering problem we work on—and not only the obvious ones, but also the "deeper" ones. For instance, the last example in the above list is not one many network engineers tend to think about when they're tuning a network for high-speed convergence, but it's just as real as the first two in the list [in fact, it's a result of, or corollary to, the first point, the consistency, accessibility, and partitionability (CAP) theorem].

Complexity, then, will always be a tradeoff in the real world. The key point to remember is to assume that anything you're working on will involve a complexity tradeoff.

Modeling Complexity

This book has used a single model to explain, examine, and comprehend complexity: state, speed, and surface. Each of these three is interrelated to the other in every system you work on, so a solid understanding of these three aspects of complexity can be very helpful in managing complexity in the real world.

- **State:** The amount of information carried, held, or otherwise managed within a single component or system. Within this book, the state has primarily related to the amount of information carried in the control plane, but it could relate to just about any type of information, including things like the state of the window in TCP, or the neighbor list used in a routing protocol to ensure two-way connectivity before bringing up a peering session.

- **Speed:** The rate at which the state being carried in the control plane changes. Throughout this book this has been related to the rate at which the topology changes, driving changes in the reachability information carried by the control plane. There are many other examples, however, such as the rate at which the data being carried through a network changes, or the rate at which security credentials time out and must be replaced.

- **Surface:** The surface can be described as the depth and width of the interface between any two subsystems of a system (or any two interacting systems). The more two systems share state, or one system relies on a deep understanding of the state contained in another system, the deeper the interaction between the two systems. The more points at which two systems touch, or interact, the broader the interaction surface between the two systems. Broader and deeper interaction surfaces cause the state in one system to be more closely (tightly) tied to the state in another system, thus increasing the likelihood of unintended consequences in one system based on a state change in another. As the interaction surface increases in depth and breadth, the more difficult it becomes to understand and account for every possible consequence of any given state change. This is simply a factorial or array multiplication problem. Increasing the elements increases the number of possible combinations, and hence the number of possible final states. At some point, it's impossible to know or test for every combination. Further, if each system or subsystem uses some form of abstraction to hide its internal actions in relation to a specific piece of information, the problem becomes almost infinitely complex.

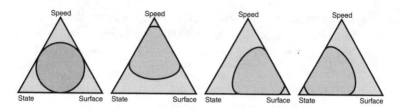

Figure 14.3 *Speed, State, and Surface as a Three-Sided Problem*

While the model of state, speed, surface, and complexity doesn't entirely fit into the triplet model shown in Figure 14.3, it does provide a solid way of approaching the complexity problem in network design, from protocols to policy.

Engineers can either optimize for speed, state, or surface. Consider network convergence speed as an example:

- **Optimize for Speed:** The network can be optimized for speed of convergence by increasing the state in the control plane—for instance, by calculating and carrying remote LFAs in the control plane, the network can converge almost instantly to any topology change. The calculation and carrying of remote LFAs, however, represents an increase in the state carried through the network. Another option to increase the speed of convergence might be to build a tighter link between the layer 2 (or physical) state of any given link in the network and the layer 3 (or logical) state of that same link. This, however, will necessarily increase the interaction surface between these two layers of the network, and thus increase complexity.

- **Optimize for State:** The network can be optimized so the control plane carries the minimal state possible. For instance, the control plane can be configured to discover and cache reachability only when it's needed, rather than when the topology changes (in near real time). However, this will ultimately reduce the speed at which the network converges by disconnecting the control plane's view of the topology from the real state of the topology (in CAP theorem terms, trading consistency for accessibility), thus slowing the network's convergence down. The interaction surface between the control plane and the physical layer (the actual topology of the network) also becomes more intertwined when the control plane is optimized to minimize state.

- **Optimize for Surface:** It's possible to build a network in strict layers, where no layer interacts with any other layer except in very minimal ways. For instance, a logical layer riding on top of a physical layer can be designed to completely ignore any errors reported by the physical layer, thus reducing the interaction surface between the two layers to nothing more than encapsulation (and perhaps address mapping). However, this will slow down the speed of convergence, resulting in potentially suboptimal network operation, and increase the amount of state the overlying logical layer needs to carry to properly operate.

Even within the state/speed/surface model, then, there is a three-sided problem that needs to be managed and considered when designing a network.

Managing Complexity in the Real World

Network engineers are in a complex situation—it's impossible to resolve hard problems without dealing with complex solutions, and yet complexity, itself, is an unsolvable problem. Is managing complexity simply "tilting at windmills" (or perhaps "tilting at perfect security")? No. Rather than abandon the field, or simply ignore complexity, network engineers need to learn to manage complexity in every day design work. This final section of this final chapter provides some thoughts and tips toward this end.

Don't Ignore Complexity

You can't run, and you can't hide; there's no point in even trying. You're going to encounter complexity; ignoring it doesn't make the problem go away, it just allows the problem to fester under some rug in some corner of your network. The complexity problems you create today will come back to haunt you in just a few years. To quote someone who's spent years looking at complexity:

> *Trying to make a network proof against predictable problems tends to make it fragile in dealing with unpredictable problems (through an ossification effect as you mentioned). Giving the same network the strongest possible ability to defend itself against unpredictable problems, it necessarily follows, means that it MUST NOT be too terribly robust against predictable problems (not being too robust against predictable problems is necessary to avoid the ossification issue, but not necessarily sufficient to provide for a robust ability to handle unpredictable network problems.*
> —Tony Przygienda

That call at 2AM might not be pleasant, but solving it the wrong way might cause a much worse call at 2AM sometime down the road. Hardening the network against all failures eventually means to make it fail spectacularly when a failure is hit that you didn't predict—there's just no way around this reality.

When dealing with engineering problems, then, a little humility around what can, and cannot, be solved is in order. Don't ignore complexity, but don't think you can solve it, either. Instead, remember to treat every situation as a set of tradeoffs—and if you don't see the tradeoffs, you're not looking hard enough.

Find a Model to Contain the Complexity

Many of the models used by network engineers are really just ways to contain complexity. For instance, there is nothing that actually constrains network designs into a hierarchical pattern (in fact, there are a number of other patterns out there to draw from in the area of design). So why do engineers use the hierarchical model so consistently? Because it provides a container around the complexity involved in designing a large-scale system with so many moving parts. Like the engineer who only wears black and gray, or the person who wears a "self-imposed uniform," premaking some decisions aids in making other decisions more quickly.

So the first action you should take when dealing with complexity is to find a model that can contain the complexity. Whether it's a layering model, a traffic flow model, a modularization model, or some other model, finding a model to contain the complexity will help you to abstract out specific components, and start to understand the system as a whole.

A word of caution, however—don't stop at the first model you find. Instead, seek out and use as many models as you can to describe any specific system. Each model you use is actually an abstraction of the problem—and abstractions are leaky by their very nature. Each model—each abstraction—will be leaky, but it will be leaky in its own way. While you can never completely describe any complex system using a single model, nor even a collection of models, the more models you interact with in relation to a system the more you will understand the system and its behavior as a whole.

Some possible models might be:

- **A Packet Flow Model**. Network engineers normally think in terms of control plane state, rather than packet flows. It's often useful to turn this line of thinking on its head—starting with any particular device, work through what links would be used, what queues would be passed through, and what middle boxes would be encountered when sending traffic to any other device. This is particularly useful when services are virtualized throughout the network.

- **A State-Focused Model**. Ask how each piece of information is carried through the network, what state is necessary to carry the information, where each piece of state originates, and how it reaches the point where it is used. For instance, to switch a specific packet, a router must have some reachability information, some information about which next hop it needs to use to reach the destination, and some information on how to encapsulate the packet. It might also need information on how to queue the data while it's in transit through the router, and possibly special handling instructions of some type. Where does all this information come from? What process provides the information within the router, where does that process get this information, where does this information originate, how often does it change, etc.?

- **An API-Focused Model.** Lay out the various components of the system, and then describe the interaction surface between each of these pairs of components. This will give you a good idea of the depth and breadth of the interaction surface between each pair of components. After you're done with the pairs, think through any three-way interaction surfaces, etc.

- **A Policy-Focused Model.** The hierarchical network design model is, in reality, a policy-focused model (given aggregation is a form of policy applied to control plane state). Where is policy applied, and why? What impact does the application of this policy have on the traffic flowing through the network? Does it make the traffic flow more optimally, or less? What are the tradeoffs for each policy, and each point within the network where that policy can be applied?

Thinking through models that answer each of these questions will help you wrap your head around the complexity you face in real systems.

A Final Thought

If you've reached this section, you've read through a lot of very difficult to understand text that's very focused on theory (if you've skipped ahead, shame on you—go back and do your reading like a real engineer!). It might, at times, seem difficult to see how to apply the theoretical side of network engineering to the real world—but the connection is definitely there. Learning the theory will enable you to see problems more quickly, ask better questions, know what to look for (and how to look), pick up new technologies more quickly, and know how to evaluate technologies.

There are, in the real world of engineering, no unicorns standing under rainbows to be found. There are only tradeoffs—tradeoffs in complexity that you now know how to navigate more successfully.

Index

REGISTER YOUR PRODUCT at informit.com/register
Access Additional Benefits and SAVE 35% on Your Next Purchase

- Download available product updates.

- Access bonus material when applicable.

- Receive exclusive offers on new editions and related products.
  (Just check the box to hear from us when setting up your account.)

- Get a coupon for 35% for your next purchase, valid for 30 days. Your code will be available in your InformIT cart. (You will also find it in the Manage Codes section of your account page.)

Registration benefits vary by product. Benefits will be listed on your account page under Registered Products.

InformIT.com–The Trusted Technology Learning Source
InformIT is the online home of information technology brands at Pearson, the world's foremost education company. At InformIT.com you can
- Shop our books, eBooks, software, and video training.
- Take advantage of our special offers and promotions (informit.com/promotions).
- Sign up for special offers and content newsletters (informit.com/newsletters).
- Read free articles and blogs by information technology experts.
- Access thousands of free chapters and video lessons.

Connect with InformIT–Visit informit.com/community
Learn about InformIT community events and programs.

informIT.com
the trusted technology learning source

Addison-Wesley • Cisco Press • IBM Press • Microsoft Press • Pearson IT Certification • Prentice Hall • Que • Sams • VMware Press

ALWAYS LEARNING   PEARS

CISCO.

ciscopress.com: Your Cisco Certification and Networking Learning Resource